PRAISE FOR *101 SKILLS YOU NEED TO SURVIVE IN THE WOODS*

"I have a whole shelf of books on survival, tracking, bushcraft and booby traps, some military field manuals from my time in the SEAL teams, some written by former operators and some from the civilian sector. What is lacking in most of them, however, is what I would consider the most important aspect of all, the underlying foundation of these skill sets, the 'make-or-break' quality, if you will. That elusive elixir is *mind-set*, and Kevin's book (as well as Kevin himself) has that in spades."

-JOEL LAMBERT, former Navy SEAL and Discovery Channel host

"Kevin Estela has written the new quintessential guide to emergency survival. This practical manual will give you the confidence and knowledge to successfully thrive in the woods."

-DR. NICOLE APELIAN, survival skills instructor

"The amount of useful information and how easy it is to understand raises the standard with regard to handbooks on survival skills and their execution."

-MIKE DOUGLAS, founder of Maine Primitive Skills School

"This book is the bible of everything survival. It's not a onetime read, but a lifetime reference that can be read over and over. Kevin practices survival like most people breathe—in a natural, no-nonsense approach from years of teaching and using his survival skills in practical ways."

-GARY HUMPHREY, UK Special Forces survival instructor and Discovery Channel presenter

"Kevin Estela's no-nonsense approach mixed with positive attitude and humor will prepare you and build a quiet confidence in your skills. This book will lead you down the path of survival skills and keep you on solid ground during your adventures!"

-BEN PIERSMA, owner of Ben's Backwoods, authority on bushcraft and survival tools

"With an extensive background in wilderness living and experiential teaching, Kevin Estela delivers a rare blend of field-tested skills that can save your life while boosting your confidence in the backcountry."

-TONY NESTER, director of Ancient Pathways Survival School

"It's great to see a comprehensive publication from an accomplished outdoorsman, writer and instructor. This is a must-have for your survival library!"

-JASON GUSTAFSON, owner of Lester River Bushcraft

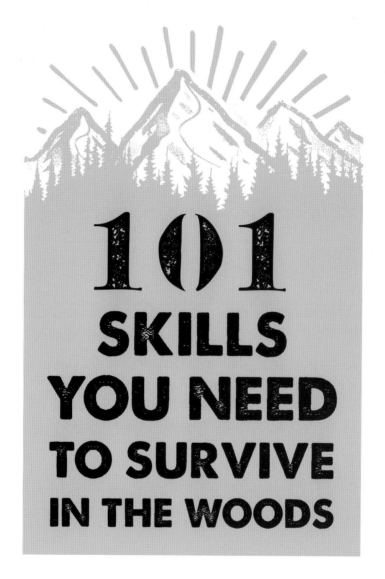

101 SKILLS YOU NEED TO SURVIVE IN THE WOODS

The Most Effective Wilderness Know-How on Fire-Making, Knife Work, Navigation, Shelter, Food and More

KEVIN ESTELA
Founder of Estela Wilderness Education

PAGE STREET
PUBLISHING CO.

PAGE STREET
PUBLISHING CO.

First published in 2019 by
Page Street Publishing Co.
27 Congress Street, Suite 105
Salem, MA 01970
www.pagestreetpublishing.com

Distributed by Macmillan, sales in Canada by The Canadian Manda Group.

23 22 21 20 19 1 2 3 4 5

ISBN-13: 978-1-62414-742-5
ISBN-10: 1-62414-742-9

Library of Congress Control Number: 2018961820

Cover and book design by Sara Pollard for Page Street Publishing Co.
Photography by Kevin Estela, Mike Travis, Dwayne Unger, Mike Lychock, Amanda Czaplicki and Price Brothers Outdoors

Illustrations by Lauren Harton

Printed and bound in China

A portion of the proceeds from the sale of this book will be donated to the Estela Wilderness Education Fund.

DEDICATED TO

My father, Jose Estela, MD, my greatest inspiration;
my wilderness-survival mentor Marty Simon from the Wilderness
Learning Center, who honed my skills and became one of the greatest
friends of my life; and Pamana Tuhon Christopher Sayoc Sr., who gave me
an invaluable mind-set and training, welcoming me into the Sayoc Kali
tribe. The knowledge, skill sets and direction you three have given me
are the stars I continue to follow and value so greatly.

CONTENTS

AUTHOR'S FOREWORD

A quick drive to the store can turn into a survival situation. At any time, you can find yourself in a life-threatening emergency that will have one of two outcomes. You will either address the problem in front of you and survive, or you will fail and die.

For some, the idea of the wilderness represents a welcome escape from their reality, and yet others view the wilderness as dangerous and unknown. What tempers your perspective of the wilderness is knowledge. The great Japanese swordsman Miyamoto Musashi stated, "The purpose of today's training is to defeat yesterday's understanding." The knowledge found in this book is meant to empower you and provide you with the hard skills you need to survive.

Skills inspire confidence. A strong swimmer would not hesitate to consider diving into the water when their pleasure boat takes on too much water. The "life of the party" endowed with the gift of gab would gladly take the microphone and deliver an impromptu speech at a wedding. A skilled grappler would have no issue escorting the drunk uncle out of the backyard at the family barbecue. All of these scenarios would be very different if the protagonists were not skilled. Many survival resources provide excellent theoretical knowledge but are light on practical skills. Some survival schools want their students to adopt their spirituality and become clones of the school's founder. I want the readers of this book to become both knowledgeable and skilled. Religion and spirituality are deeply personal and not the focus of this work. As for becoming like me, adopt a similar mind-set, skill set and physicality, but don't worry about dressing or talking like I do.

I place great value on learning, and I have dedicated my life to educating. This book is filled with information, and there are additional great print and online resources you can use to supplement your education; however, I recommend you seek out a qualified instructor and training group that will take your skills development as seriously as you do. Find a school or training program that fits your style, and don't change yourself to fit theirs. Do not let this book, as proud as I am of it, be your sole teacher. Books do not replace human interaction and instruction.

Keep in mind as you read this book that there were plenty of people who died for these skills. Many emergency and survival lessons have been paid for in blood, frostbitten fingers, broken bones, exposure and death. We must learn from the mistakes made, make adjustments and keep history from repeating itself in our life's timeline. As you read about the various skills in the following chapters, think about those who made the ultimate sacrifices and those who survived and carried these skills with them to pass on to the next generation. I did not invent these skills, but I have adopted them and love passing them on to others. I encourage you to find at least one skill you are proficient in and share it with someone you care about. Keep these skills alive by teaching them. Perhaps that deed will repay you by keeping you alive at some point in your travels.

SURVIVAL MIND-SET AND READINESS

NATURAL FEARS AND HOW TO MITIGATE THEM

You don't need to be a psychologist to understand humans have natural fears. Simply observe enough novices spending the night in the woods for the first time, and you'll see plenty of fears come to the surface. Fear is an emotional response, and it can have a paralyzing effect on us. While a little fear can motivate us and help trigger the fight instinct, too much fear can signal our brains for flight or freeze. In a survival situation, when your mind is left to wander to dark places, it's natural for the emotional roller coaster to take your thoughts for a wild ride. Your desire to survive may be overpowered by the fear of your situation. When you don't have to worry about the day-to-day normal routine of your life and you're presented with new stressors, the pressure and reality of your abnormal survival situation can wreak havoc on your emotional well-being.

Since these fears impact the outcome of our survival, how do we manage them and keep a level head? We must understand our emotions are powerful and seek out logical thinking instead. Logic requires no emotional input; there is no place for it. We need to think about why we fear what we fear. If we think about our fears this way, we can create a plan to deal with them. Logical thinking is the enemy of emotional responses to stress like fear. Rather than wait for an emergency to put us through stress, we can make our training simulate what we may encounter. We don't have to wait for something to happen to us to experience it for the first time. Even if we can experience something in our minds, the mental repetition of visualizing preframes our minds for action. We can embrace strength and power by facing our fears and coming closer to them with each day. We can harness our fears and turn them into something else.

POSITIVE MENTAL ATTITUDE (PMA)

My father knew the power of optimism and humor, and he instilled both of them in me at a young age. He taught me to laugh off hardship and setbacks and to keep driving forward. Self-deprecation is a great coping mechanism, and being able to smile through hardship has tempered my resolve. It has been an integral part of the hard-fought success I've experienced in life.

The opposite of positivity is negativity, and those who would rather focus on the negative invite toxicity into their minds. Positive thinking, on the other hand, is what it takes to fight off the gravity of your emergency or survival situation. Positive mental attitude (PMA) was referenced in many survival manuals I read as a teenager, and it is just as relevant today as it has been over the years.

Positive mental attitude isn't easily maintained when the world seems to be working against you. When nothing seems to be going your way, think of what you still have control over. In a survival situation, you win little victories by proving you can gather firewood, collect wild edibles you can identify, make tools out of natural objects and use your mind and your resources. As you accomplish tasks, think about how these little victories prove you are not helpless. You prove to yourself you have control over something when you may otherwise believe you have no control over anything. If you can accomplish something, you can accomplish something else. Even when you face a setback, like losing a fish, reframe the experience: be proud you hooked it, and tell yourself you'll catch another. As you build little victories, you also build an optimistic perspective. Our mental state can be very fragile in stressful times, and we must constantly win these little victories if we wish to win the fight for our life.

TRUST YOUR TRAINING

If and when a survival situation happens, we can fall back on our training and go to work. In Sayoc Kali, the Filipino martial art created by the late Pamana Tuhon Chris Sayoc, we use the expression "trust your training" to reinforce its value and remind us of the correct course of action. We believe that if your training is sound, then when you call upon it in an emergency, your outcome should be favorable. In the same way combative training should be realistic, your wilderness and survival training should reflect reality, too. The more you incorporate training modifiers, the better you will be at adapting to adversity.

Throughout this book, you will read about ways you can modify the skills presented to increase the difficulty level. Sometimes this means putting completion of a task against a time restriction; other times it means performing a task with one hand instead of two. Still other times, your training can be made more difficult by using lesser quality equipment or smaller equipment. At all times, you should mentally catalog the repetitions you complete while learning from your experiences.

I believe in the idea of training hard and fighting easy. Ideally, your training should push you to the far limits of your comfort level. When the suck factor of an emergency or survival situation starts to weigh on you, remember how much harder you trained leading up to that moment. Remember how you rose to the occasion before and how you can again. It's very rare to hear of someone who performs at a level higher than their training when the situation is real. Invest in your safety by taking your training to new levels under conditions you have control over now, rather than when it is too late.

THE FEEDER MIND-SET

One of the first lessons taught to me by my Sayoc Kali instructor, Manong Rich, was the idea of feeder mind-set. In blade training, the feeder is the person in control of the situation. This could be the person with the blade or the person on the defensive from the blade who has the upper hand. In a much broader sense, feeder mind-set means someone who is proactive rather than reactive. The feeder is an optimist who can reframe any situation as a learning experience instead of being a victim or someone who dwells on negativity. The feeder is capable of logical thought and sideways thinking when all options seem to invoke emotional responses and dead ends. In Sayoc, being the feeder is the goal. The opposite of feeder is the receiver. Receivers let situations happen to them, and they lack control of their thoughts and actions. Receiver mind-set is a formula for failure. It's always better to be the feeder.

Sayoc Kali prepares its practitioners to deal with physical encounters, and the lessons learned on the mat become teaching metaphors to deal with emotional, financial, spiritual and interpersonal issues off the mat. Since starting my training in Sayoc, and especially since earning Associate-Instructor ranking, I have found Sayoc teaching methodology to pour over into how I teach bushcraft and survival skills. Sayoc practitioners who have attended my classes have tracked how I teach wilderness skills and they easily recognize how the material is taught as Sayoc inspired.

As you read through this book, you should detect a no-nonsense approach to skills. Each of these skills is designed to keep you safe and make you more ready to deal with emergencies in the field. Each of these skills is feeder-based. Each of these skills and how it is presented is the result of Sayoc Kali training. It is what separates my teaching style from others in the wilderness skills instructor circles. I owe so much to Pamana Tuhon Chris Sayoc, the Council of Tuhons, full instructors, associate instructors, apprentices and practitioners and must recognize their contributions to this collection of skills. They have made me a better feeder. A firm understanding and ownership of these skills will develop the feeder in you.

ASSESS READINESS

Ready is a state of being, not a rhetorical question. What we consider "ready" may not actually be ready. Through studying Filipino martial arts, I have been exposed to the Sayoc Readiness Formula. This three-part equation is comprised of awareness, preparedness and willingness. Awareness is understanding your surroundings, knowing your capability, and the location of the gear you have at your disposal, where ingress and egress points are, possible threats and other factors that orient you to your environment. Preparedness is the gear you have on hand, your experience and training and the ability to be resourceful. Willingness is what you are committed to doing leading up to, during and after an emergency/survival situation.

All three of these requirements—awareness, preparedness and willingness—must be present if you want to be truly "ready." You can be a combination of two and not be ready. For example, you can be aware of wilderness survival situations and be willing to spend time and money to train and purchase gear, but if that training and gear are not appropriate, your preparedness will be lacking. If you say you are aware and prepared but lack willingness, you probably are not willing to do what it takes—like using your gear to test

The Sayoc Kali readiness formula comprises awareness, preparedness, and willingness. All attributes must be present to be considered "ready."

its strengths and weaknesses or testing yourself to see your capability. You can also be prepared with physical fitness and willing to give 110 percent of your being, but if you are thrust into a situation without knowing which threats can impact you, you are not ready. You need to know what you're getting into, determine how you can equip yourself with what you need and have the desire to win.

My goal is to make you ready for safe wilderness travel and problem solving in emergency and survival situations. Readiness is what I strive for in my life, and I have made it my business to help others, like you, determine readiness and how to become more so with thoughts, words and deeds.

BE BETTER EVERY DAY

With each day that passes, we should seek to become stronger than the last. We owe it to those who came before us and those who were taken too soon to be better versions of ourselves each day. We need to recognize that our goals fall on a timeline somewhere in the future, and we should be realistic with our training and the returns on our investment in time and effort. We can't assume we will reach our goals overnight, but rather get a little closer with each day. As you learn new skills and improve your performance in other skills, you improve your survivability one day at a time. Being a student for life is accomplished one day at a time.

What you consider a better version of yourself is up to you. I learned the importance of continual study and have made it a point to become a "white belt" in something new when I wanted a challenge. With any activity I deliberately put

myself into, I set realistic goals for improvement. It is easy to become frustrated with slow progress, but even if you don't advance or succeed, you always learn. One of the most important skills of the student is knowing how to ask questions. One of the most important jobs of the teacher is knowing how to elicit those questions from students.

EMBRACE STRENGTH

Our thoughts become our words and our words become our actions. In other words, when we feel down and negative, we have a tendency to speak about our feelings. When we speak about our feelings, they manifest in our actions. You can imagine how this downward cycle can lead to weakness and failure. We should embrace power and think positively, as it is one way to grow stronger. In Sayoc Kali, we don't use the term "weak hand" to describe our nondominant hand. By referring to one of our hands as "weak," we assign a negative word to describe the power we possess. In a survival situation, you need to believe you are capable, and this starts with embracing strength. In Sayoc Kali, we don't have a "weak hand" but rather our nondominant hand is considered an "other strong hand."

LIVE AND DIE WELL

The purpose of learning survival skills is to ensure your life doesn't end before it must. If you care about your family, your livelihood and your goals, you owe it to yourself to train and familiarize yourself with ways to meet your basic survival needs. Something I've heard that comes up frequently in discussions with people who don't train is some form of criticism along the lines of "What are you paranoid about?" Training to survive an emergency isn't paranoia as long as that emergency is realistic. Cars crash off roads, hikers get injured, power outages and natural disasters happen. All the skills contained in this book help you become more ready to deal with them. I don't train because I'm paranoid; I train because I love my life and want to live well.

At the Wilderness Learning Center, our motto is "Always prepared, prepared all-ways." As you learn to build fires, construct shelters, access and treat water and so on, you'll find the process of becoming a better survivor, something that inspires confidence and builds training you can fall back on regardless of what life throws at you. You can't predict and you can't custom order what your survival situation will look like, but the more you train and incorporate modifiers, the more you'll realize you are ready for anything you have to deal with. My goal in writing this book is to empower you, my readers, with the knowledge and skill set that can be applied in your outdoor travels. If reading this book and owning the skills contained in it can mitigate your fears, lower your stress and make you less uncomfortable, I did my job as a writer and an instructor.

Something not mentioned in many survival discussions is the concept of dying well. You may be wondering how this concept relates to a manual designed to keep you alive. Dying is a natural part of living. We're born, we age, we die. Death is usually associated with weakness, but it doesn't have to be. We can be powerful even in death as long as we leave a legacy that lives on long after we're gone. We can choose to make our final actions brave and respectable. Dying well is dying on our

terms in a way others will honor afterward. Never quitting, never submitting, never turning negative, fighting for our lives until our fight ends: that is dying well. When my grandfather protected his family in the Philippines during World War II, the family motto became, "To the last drop." In other words, no one stops fighting until the last drop of blood drains from your body. This explains how and why I embrace strength and work to become stronger with each day.

At some point in your training, you will recognize the benefit of becoming more ready. When your deliberate training is difficult, you'll find an extra workload in your profession doesn't seem unbearable. When you face true hardship, your responsibilities in your career don't feel like work at all. Nature has the power to change your perspective, and as you master the skills presented in this book, you'll find yourself longing for your next trip away from civilization where you can truly relax and live well.

THE TEACHING METHODOLOGY USED IN THIS BOOK

The material found in this book and how it is presented is the culmination of a lifetime of study under incredible mentors. The skills presented are not my own but belong to the countless outdoorsmen who came before me. How the material is presented in courses, clinics and articles is what has set me apart in the survival community as a trainer/instructor. Over the years, I've worked as a tutor, a coach, a teacher and an instructor. I've been formally trained in lesson development and implementation and as a professional educator. I've also learned how to fine-tune what works and how to adjust what doesn't. It is my goal to provide information that will keep you safe in the great outdoors and make your skills-based performance better. I don't want you to simply accomplish a skill; I want you to get better with each attempt and understand how to analyze your performance. The process is just as important as the product. As you read through this book, you'll notice how the information starts with a basic understanding of what you need to know; the further you delve into each section, the more you'll see skills-based self-assessments you can try. With each of these, you'll be provided tips and tricks to make accomplishing these tasks easier and your performance better.

EMERGENCY VS. SURVIVAL VS. BUSHCRAFT

Throughout this book, I will address essential survival skills that overarch into emergency situations as well as bushcraft living. Prior to reading through these skills, you should understand what I mean by "survival" more specifically.

Emergencies are immediate concerns, and they must be dealt with quickly. Emergencies can be minor, but they can aggravate the sum total of your circumstances. Emergencies can be addressed and resolved, or they can become survival situations. Emergencies are urgent and happen unexpectedly. Emergencies require immediate attention, and unfortunately for us, they probably will happen when we are not ideally ready for them. Both the response to an emergency and the resolve are time sensitive.

Once an emergency situation extends past an immediate response or past the window where

the best solution is available, the emergency becomes more of a survival situation. When an emergency becomes a survival situation, the original problem may become the least of your concerns. Survival situations are complex emergency situations. Survival needs include staying warm, providing shelter, staying hydrated, signaling for help and tending to first-aid and traumatic injuries. In an emergency, one of these may be the start of your problems. In a survival situation, all of them are your concerns.

The lines separating emergency and survival situations are somewhat clear. The line separating bushcraft from emergency and survival skills is more vague. Bushcraft skills are traditional skills used to live with the land. Bushcraft skills include utilizing natural resources and knowing how to craft what is needed from the landscape. Emergency and survival gear can run out, become lost or break, but if you have a firm understanding of bushcraft, you can be resourceful and possibly find a solution from the land. Friction fire skills, natural cordage and debris shelters all fall under bushcraft skills. Many of these skills can be called upon in a survival situation, or they can be leisurely practiced on a weekend trip. Many of my trips to the outdoors are bushcraft themed, and I prefer knowing I can rely on the land the way I was taught. I still pack modern gear just in case my vacation turns sour.

Bushcrafters have evolved over time with advancements in equipment, but the skills have remained the same. Some gear like wooden knife handles and cast-iron pans may appeal to the nostalgia of the bushcrafter but may not be the best option for survival. Gear should be selected to best accomplish a mission. While flint and steel are a fun novelty fire starter I enjoy playing with, if given the choice in a torrential downpour, a box of road flares and a case of artificial fireplace logs would be my choice time and time again. In a survival situation, you don't have time to play.

Blending bushcraft, survival and emergency skills will give you the best of all worlds. You will find these skills complement one another, and the strengths of one will compensate for the weaknesses of the other. You will ultimately decide how much emphasis to place on each while becoming a more ready version of yourself.

CARRY THE RIGHT GEAR

Your job in a survival situation in the great outdoors is to stay alive, and the right tools make that job easier. You need to carry good multipurpose equipment that will help you work through the problems you'll encounter. As you consider what you should carry, what you would like to carry and what is simply nice to carry, don't forget to be practical and logical with your decision making. For example, you should daily carry some sort of knife for its utility. You may want to carry a large fixed blade on your belt, and you may find it nice to have multiple blades on your person, but ultimately you should have something you can carry in a practical manner, such as the humble Swiss Army Knife, in your pocket rather than no knife at all.

Your pocket is where your physical preparedness starts, and it is considered your first line, level one, or "Every Day Carry" (EDC) gear. EDC gear is your first line in the concentric layers of preparedness. Pocket carry items are generally items used frequently in daily tasks. Some sort of

lighter, handkerchief or bandana, folding knife, flashlight, wallet, mobile phone and keys have made up my EDC items for the majority of my adult life. Depending on where you live and the possibility of threats around you, you may want to pack a small pistol, spare magazine and tourniquet as well. Pocket carry items aren't items that would be your first choice for long-term survival, but they will get you through many of life's little emergencies.

Working outward from the pocket, the next line of gear, level two, is that found on the belt and fanny pack/satchel. While this equipment is more robust for harder use, it's also bulkier, which means it's best carried outside of the pockets of your clothing. This equipment includes a sturdy belt knife (my personal preference is a fixed blade just under 4 inches [10 cm] long with a handle 4¼ to 4½ inches [10.8 to 11.5 cm] long), a canteen with cup and spoon and a carrying pouch that holds additional emergency gear. I also carry a dedicated baseplate compass, additional cordage, a small tarp, folding saw, compact hatchet/tomahawk or light machete, larger fire starter, fishing/trapping gear, headlamp, whistle, mirror, small boo-boo kit, a hat and gloves. This larger kit is what I usually consider my bare minimum kit I will reach for when going for a hike in the woods. It is also the kit I use the most frequently, so I make it a point to check the status and condition of my gear for wear and replacement.

The next lineup of gear you have is your extended camp gear. This is the equipment you will have for the purpose of extending the duration of your trip into multiple days and nights. While you can survive the night with your level two gear, level three gear adds a significant amount of comfort to your outdoor experience. This gear includes a more dedicated shelter like a backpacking tent or an enclosed hammock, a sleeping bag or quilt, sleeping pad, a mess kit with a larger pot for treating large quantities of water, camp ax and bow saw, area tarp, canister-fuel stove, freeze-dried foods and so on. While this equipment is nice to have, it is not always necessary for survival, and if an emergency happens when you're on a single-day hike, you probably won't have any of it on you.

Further layers can be found in your vehicle as it takes you to and from your area of operation and in your home. Additionally, you can stock your workplace with items, but the more we focus on gear, the more we generally rely on these resources instead of resourcefulness. Focus on carrying multipurpose items and seek to address the needs of the outdoorsman. The ten essentials should be viewed as needs instead of ten individual items.

If you view them as a list of ten items, you may fail to pack all the gear necessary to address the need. Instead, think of the practical gear you can carry to satisfy each of these needs. Examples are provided below.

TEN ESSENTIAL NEEDS

1. Cutting needs (pocket knife, folding saw, belt knife, chopping tool)
2. Fire-starting needs (ferro rod, lighters, homemade tinder)
3. Hydration needs (canteen, cup, purification tabs/drops)
4. Shelter needs (clothing, tarp, sleeping bag, ground pad)
5. Signaling needs (phone, mirror, whistle, EPRB)
6. Trauma/first-aid needs (individual first aid kit [IFAK], boo-boo kit, tourniquet)
7. Cordage/binding needs (duct tape, paracord, jute twine)
8. Navigation needs (map, compass)
9. Illumination needs (headlamp, flashlight, glow sticks)
10. Food/food-gathering needs (fishing kit, trapping kit, .22 firearm)

BEYOND THE BASICS

1. Sleep (when you can get it, including naps)
2. Diet additives (seasoning, fats, comfort foods)
3. Morale boosters (photos, tokens, keepsakes)
4. Company (many hands make light work)

FIRE SKILLS

"What's your fire?" —*Pamana Tuhon Chris Sayoc*

One of the earliest memories I have of learning the importance of fire came from my father while hiking the trails at the Barnes Nature Center in Bristol, Connecticut. While the trails were not far from civilization, my father stressed the importance of carrying matches and knowing how to build a fire. He would ask me questions that tested my understanding of the importance of having a kit and knowing how to use it. He told me he was prepared to light a forest on fire if it meant getting rescued in an emergency, and I believed him. I would take books of matches from above my parents' fireplace, run to the backyard and build little twig fires. I practiced making fires and became very proficient at making them. I learned how to build fires in all different types of weather, and I started carrying a lighter of some sort on me even though I wasn't a smoker. To this day, I don't leave my house without a Swiss Army Knife and a lighter in my right front pocket.

Fire starting is a primal skill. If you don't think fire matters when you are all alone in the woods, try spending a night there without one. It is absolutely a psychological companion. There is a sense of power transferred from the heat of the flame to you when you are able to warm yourself, cook your food, boil water for a hot drink and dry out your clothes. Eat a meal cold or drink only semi-frozen water, and you'll welcome the first warmth that touches your lips. Fire can help you signal for help, cut down trees, illuminate your way, heat your shelter and so much more. Firemaking is a skill you can never practice enough and one you will draw upon frequently with each trip you take into the woods.

All fires have three basic requirements: heat, fuel and oxygen. You can look at any attempted fire and determine why it is smoking or otherwise not lit by troubleshooting those three basic needs. Smokey fires could be the result of wet wood or not enough oxygen getting to the fuel. There could be plenty of fuel and oxygen in a wood pile but without enough heat, that wood pile will not ignite. If you have enough oxygen and heat but not enough fuel, your fire will burn out. Troubleshooting fire this way is often all it takes to give a novice fire starter some success. Also, the novice should never forget to supply an abundance of fuel, heat and oxygen throughout the entire development of his fire.

Fire should be thought of in stages, and no fire should be built that can't be put out. Fire

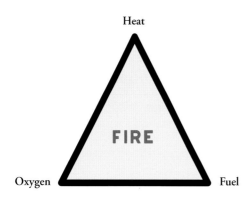

A fire has three components: heat, fuel and oxygen.

craft is the art of fire preparation, fire starting, fire maintenance and fire extinguishing. Fire preparation is the act of clearing a location of easily flammable materials, building a rock ring if desired, collecting fuel of various sizes and ensuring you have all requirements prior to making a fire to limit the number of trips you need to make once the fire starts. You may have to build a platform to lift the fire from the cold and damp earth, build a log windbreak for the flames or dig a pit to keep all the heat and coals centralized in one spot. Fire starting is the act of igniting fire with friction, spark, flame or chemicals. Fire starting is a stage you may need to only visit once in the life of a fire. Or you may need to revisit it if you run out of fuel or your smaller fuel doesn't catch the next-size-up fuel. Fire maintenance is tending to a fire. This may require moving large logs to maximize air-flow, slowing the fire by spreading it out, banking the fire to slow the burn even further or stoking the fire to get it rip-roaring. The final stage in the life of a fire is the extinguishing of it. You must ensure you put it out and no hot spots remain. This is not accomplished by simply burying a fire but by dowsing it completely with water. There should be no smoke rising from the ash pile when you're done, and it should be cold. Always be prepared to arrest a fire if it starts to spread, and take precautions long before you light your fire.

I mentioned earlier how you should have various types of fuel ready before you light your fire. Fuel is broken down into tinder, kindling, small, medium and large fuel. Tinder is easily turned into an orange glowing coal with little more than a spark. Tinder extends that spark and coal with friction fire building, and it can be blown into a flame, usually short-lasting, if the tinder bundle is large enough. Tinder can also take a flame and light that way as well. Kindling is the next stage in fuel. Kindling will likely not take a spark, but it will still burn readily with a small single flame. The small twigs found on the underside of evergreen trees are a prime example of these. Kindling is small in diameter—spaghetti-noodle width, ideally. As you progress to small, medium and large fuel, you want to only double in thickness each size you move up. From those spaghetti-noodle-sized twigs, jump to pencil lead, jump to finger thickness and so on. As you start to notice your fire burning wood more efficiently with more heat coming from the base, add wrist-sized fuel and larger fuel following that doubling rule each time. Jumping to a fuel too large for a fire will reduce the chances of it catching, lower the output of light as well as heat and possibly smother it if not enough air gets in. Be patient with your fire building and build your fire right the first time every time.

SKILL #1
RECOGNIZE GOOD TINDER

When they demonstrate proficiency with man-made premade tinder, my students graduate to using less optimal prepared tinder like the unraveled fibers of jute twine. Again, once they demonstrate the ability to start fires with different tinders, they graduate and continue the progression of learning to build fires with other types of tinder. At some point, I have students take a walk with me, and we look for tinder off the land. Even after the most torrential downpours of rain, my students and I are able to find something in the area we can get to take a spark. At first, the idea of finding something dry and tinder-worthy seems difficult, but when you think about what is needed for a spark to turn into a flame, the requirements are pretty simple.

As I take my students on walks through the woods for tinder, I constantly stress "light, fluffy/flaky and dry." By "light" I am referring to little to no water weight, which also means seasoned and ready. "Fluffy and flaky" relate to texture as some of the best tinders feel this way. Consider how cattail fluff resembles and feels like cotton and how yellow birch bark flakes off easily. "Dry" is very self-explanatory, but I stress it in my requirements, because even though the tinder you have could be light and fluffy/flaky, you can dry it out next to your body or in a pocket of a warm jacket. Your body can dry out tinder to some extent as can dry air flow. Ideally, you should have premade tinder on you, but when you can, learn to use the tinder from off the land

and preserve the best tinder for when the stress level is high and firemaking is critical.

The king of all naturally found tinder is birch bark. Gray, yellow and white birches all have bark with a heavy oil content. With a strong and deep scrape of your ferro rod, a longer-lasting spark will catch in your birch bark tinder and ignite it. Taking birch bark from a tree will not kill it as long as you don't crown or girdle the tree. That is, don't strip birch bark around the entire circumference of a tree past the inner bark. Birch bark holds its oil content for years, and even the bark found on fallen and rotten birches will work as tinder.

As mentioned, cattail fluff also makes a good tinder. You must realize the fluff from the seed pods does not have a long-lasting fuel source like petroleum and cotton balls, and thus burns for a short while. The same is true of milkweed pods. The seed fluff found inside milkweed pods will take a spark, but it won't burn for long. You can always use the fluff with a fuel source like rendered animal fat or salvaged oil to burn longer. This same fluff can warm you two ways. You can burn it or you can stuff your clothes with it as insulation.

Another excellent tinder is found in the bark of cedar trees. Using the back of your knife or the edge of a sharp rock, you can scrape the bark with one hand and collect the dust and fibers with the other. This tinder is extremely fine and will blow away if you are not careful. When I use cedar bark as tinder, I try to place it in a flammable container or within a depression I make in a larger tinder bundle.

Thick grapevines are also good places to look for tinder. Since the grapevine grows vertically, it is found up off the ground and away from the moisture. The outermost bark of the grapevine peels off easily and can form a sizeable birds' nest with little effort. The bark can be twisted and rolled between the palms of your hands and made more fine to take a spark.

Some of the best tinder you'll find in the woods is ready to light with little to no preparation necessary. In the winter, for instance, you'll find there are leaves still attached to the trees that didn't fall during the autumn. These leaves are marcescent, and they are ready to accept a spark from your ferro rod. Depending on where you are, the type of tree you'll find with marcescent leaves will vary. Sometimes you'll find oaks, sometimes you'll find beech, sometimes the leaves will be found on a branch that snapped off and both branch and leaves were left to dry in the wind. Just make sure your leaves crunch when rolled around in your hand. Leaves don't have the same pedigree as birch bark, but they work well.

Leaves found on the ground will also serve you well in your fire starting. The leaves that have been on the ground for a year or two will work best, and these are identified by their almost gauze-like appearance. Just as you did with the leaves found on the trees, roll the leaves you find between your fingers and listen for that crunch noise. Listen for the unmistakable dry noise and use the leaves that feel and sound the driest.

Your average ⅜-inch (1-cm) ferro rod will last you thousands of strikes. Experiment with what you find in the woods to start small fires you can make quickly and extinguish thoroughly with minimal effort.

Both cedar bark fibers (top) and birch bark strips (bottom) make excellent tinder.

SKILL #2
FERRO ROD TECHNIQUES

In my opinion, the ferro rod is the ultimate fire starter that combines multiuse capability with durability, lifespan, convenient sizing, water resistance and ease of use. There are better fire starters available if you are willing to sacrifice one of these attributes. A road flare produces a hot flame, but it is single use, larger and requires a specialized scraper to ignite it. The combination of ferro rod, scraper and prepackaged tinder is my top recommendation for fire starting. The ferro rod helps me inspire students of all ages and types and convinces them they have the power to change their circumstances.

The first method of ferro rod fire starting you need to learn is also the most common of those using two hands. Holding the ferro rod steady and moving the scraper at a 45-degree angle from the rod, sparks are created if you push hard and swiftly. The harder you push, the more ferro rod you will scrape off and more substantial the sparks will be. The back of your knife, a dedicated scraper, a carbide sharpener or even a piece of glass can be used as a scraper to generate sparks. You can also hold the scraper steady in place and drag the ferro rod backwards. In both of these methods, you want to pin your ferro rod to the material you wish to ignite. If there is no risk of knocking over your fire set up, pushing the scraper forward makes sense. If there is a risk, or if you find yourself striking your knuckles on rocks inside the fire ring, you will likely prefer to draw your ferro rod backwards. You should recognize that effectiveness with the ferro rod can be attributed to isolating the motion in one component and moving the other.

The ferro rod is a great tool to use with two hands, but in an emergency situation, you may find yourself limited to using one of your hands. Accidents happen, many by mechanical injury, and there is a possibility you will brace your fall or arrest your movement by extending an arm, forearm or hand that can get broken in the attempt. When my students find success with two-hand ferro rod starting, I have them build multiple fires and become comfortable without any additional modifiers. Owning a skill doesn't come with a few fires built just as much as a marksman doesn't consider taking three shots at a target a thorough range session. When my students have built multiple fires, I put them on the task of building more but limited to one hand only. They are allowed good tinder and can use as many petroleum cotton balls (PCBs) as necessary since the real skill I want them to focus in on is scraping the ferro rod and generating sparks with only one hand.

As you recall, the ferro rod works best when you isolate movement with one hand and move the other. You can perform a one-hand fire by using the other parts of your body. You can step on your ferro rod handle and lanyard holding it in place. With a PCB at the end of the rod, you can scrape horizontally to create a spark and ignite the tinder. You can also position your ferro rod vertically and hold it in place with the bottom of your foot as you scrape downwards. Another option that works well is to stick your knife into a log, tap the butt of the handle with a wooden log (be careful if your handle is made from softer

A ferro rod creates sparks that easily ignite birch bark.

material and not a strong modern synthetic) to drive it in deeper. The ferro rod can be scraped on the spine of the knife and the PCB can be placed along the tang. When it is lit, the burning tinder can be picked up by pinching it between two twigs and it can be transferred into your fire setup.

With these methods, you can build a fire easily. Train each hand equally, not just your dominant hand, until you don't stress making a fire using a ferro rod. When you graduate to a level of competence and you feel comfortable, start to handicap yourself and add training modifiers by doing the exact same scraping methods with harvested tinder instead. Own this skill set and you'll be well prepared to get a fire going in the great outdoors on demand.

The author's ½ x 4" (1.3 x 10–cm) Solkoa ferro rod can easily fit in a pocket.

SKILL #3
FIRE MULTIPLE WAYS

Fire starting follows a progression. The spark or flame you light ignites tinder; tinder ignites small fuel and eventually larger fuel. It makes sense that your fire will grow from small to large, but how you organize your fire lay, that is, the way you position logs, will dictate what type of fire your end product will look like. Piling branches and logs haphazardly with no rhyme or reason doesn't take into account air flow, burn time, fuel availability and fire output. An essential skill to master is learning how to construct a fire lay to meet your needs—whether that is maximum heat and light, cooking, long burning or warmth while sleeping.

TIPI
Of all the ways you can build a fire, the tipi is perhaps the most commonly known and most widely celebrated style in and out of survival communities. The tipi fire has the same pyramid profile as the shelters used by some First Nations tribes, and it is a classic way of building a fire. The tipi fire has strengths and a handful of shortcomings to its design.

I make tipi fires when I want a tall fire for maximum light or one that will burn quickly. I've used tipi fires for boiling water, for rewarming myself after emerging from a winter shelter and when building bonfires for celebrations. When done correctly, the tipi fire should collapse on itself even if it is built tall, keeping the footprint it creates relatively small. The tipi fire can be used in conjunction with other fire lays (described later) and constructing one is simple. If you have an

The tipi is a classic way of building a tall fire and will burn quickly.

abundance of softwood pencil-lead-thick twigs, you can use a bouquet-sized quantity inverted to create the base of your tipi. Otherwise, you can drive a single forked stick into the ground to angle additional sticks on and around, forming your tipi structure. You may not be able to drive a stick into the ground but rather balance sticks in tipi form. That is one of the potential drawbacks to this fire lay: it can be difficult to set up.

At the center of your tipi should be your best tinder, and as you build your structure up and out, you can add additional fast-burning material intermixed with larger fuel. When you build your tipi, take into consideration where the wind is blowing from and create a "doorway" to the center of your fire facing it. That will help your fire build and burn on its own. When built correctly, the larger fuel on the outside acts like a chimney, sending the flames straight up from the center.

LOG CABIN

The basic log cabin or "criss cross" is built by placing two logs parallel to one another and then two more parallel to each other and perpendicular to the first two logs, forming a square with this pattern repeated over and over. If you're from the hashtag generation, the log cabin can be called the hashtag fire as the structure looks like the "#" sign from above. I've built and used the log-cabin fire while demonstrating smoke generators, for cooking and boiling water and for building up a large supply of coals for use in woodcraft projects. The log cabin is a great fire to build when you need steady heat, flame and a consistent burn.

The log-cabin fire resembles the classic toy Lincoln Logs.

You should always build your log cabin on a flat surface, and if you have logs or branches with forks at their ends, you'll find the construction becomes even more stable as the forks serve as kickstands and prevent the logs from rolling off one another. Forked sticks aren't necessary to provide stability as slight curves in wood give similar results. Since the branches and logs alternate, they create gaps for air all around. This fire can be modified for cooking by building a smaller fire, like a tipi fire first, then laying green wood around it and a platform of green branches at the very top. Green wood will prevent the structure from burning as quickly. Extremely flammable tinder and kindling are placed "inside the box" you build, and when a signal is needed, the box is lit and green vegetation is placed on top of the structure.

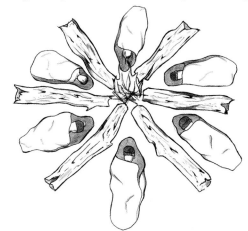

A group star fire warms all.

STAR FIRE

The star fire resembles the spokes on a wheel with the fire placed at the hub. The star fire can be made with long logs and it can be used with a large group with each member sleeping between the spokes. This placement makes it easy for anyone in the middle of the night to push a log near them into the center of the fire. It isn't the most practical fire for a single person to build, but in a group it makes sense.

You can build a log cabin with whole logs, halves or quarters. You'll find it is an effective way to pile on wood for an overnight fire, and it burns consistently from end to end. It is longer lasting than a tipi fire made from the same size and amount of wood, but the flame will not be as high.

When you build a star fire, it isn't a bad idea to slightly lift the end of each log to make the hub slightly higher than the far end and keep the flame centralized. Don't lift it too much or build your fire in a way where the log or any burning bits could roll down from the center onto you. Also, if you find the spoke burning too fast, you can roll the log back and forth in the dirt and it should snuff out the flame while allowing the end in the center to burn.

LONG FIRE

The long fire extends the length of your body and is used as a "blanket" of warmth as you sleep. A shallow trench is dug with dirt piled up on each side where a fire will be built. The long fire can have one or two sides with the head and toes area kept open. Generally, you want to build your fire in a way where it will continue to burn through the night, and this usually means incorporating larger logs. If you don't have an ax or saw to cut large logs, don't worry. Many times, you'll be able to find dead and downed trees or dead standing trees that can be knocked over or broken in half between two trees.

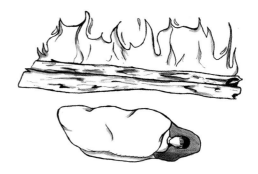

The long fire provides maximum heat while sleeping.

The long fire can also be used in conjunction with a lean-to shelter made from natural materials or a space blanket. Since the smoke from the fire can enter your shelter, you might want to sleep with a long hooked staff to poke, prod and pull your fire lay, so you don't have to leave your shelter in the middle of the night. On the coldest of nights, make sure you gather enough wood before you retire for the night.

The firebed variation of the long fire with buried coals is one commonly used when the ground is cold but dry. It will turn damp dirt into mud if you're not careful, which is why the standard long fire is preferred for northern forests and wet environments.

SKILL #4
THE COVERED FIRE

We can plan for every contingency, but something we have no control over is the weather. Rain is the form of precipitation that has the most power to zap morale, and when it starts to come down, we need to adjust our plans accordingly. Even though our skin is waterproof, our clothing may not be, and when you are cold and wet, you run the risk of losing critical body heat quickly. Cold alone can be dealt with, and being wet can be addressed if you only have to worry about drying off. The combination of cold and wet is extremely dangerous and should give you concern. Luckily, a fire can be used to dry clothes and that same fire can warm your body. There's a problem though: you need to build your fire in a torrential downpour.

If you recall, all fires require heat, oxygen and fuel. If your fire is hot enough, it will dry out the wet wood and burn regardless of what is coming down overhead. In a torrential downpour, just getting your fire started is usually the toughest part of the fire process. You may find your frustration level to be at an all-time high as matches get snuffed out, lighters won't ignite and even petroleum-soaked cotton balls don't want to catch wet kindling on fire. Your frustration will continue to build as your efforts seem to have no effect on your fire situation. This is when you need to take a step back, slow your haste to build a fire and run a mental checklist of how you prepared your fire. Sometimes the culprit to building a fire in the pouring rain is not building a base to get your fire up and off

Broad-leafed plants can protect your fire from the rain.

of the wet ground. Other times, your culprit is not having enough tinder that will dry out your kindling. Other times, you may not have built a sufficient structure to shield your fire from the rain above. A simple "umbrella" can usually be built with peeling bark, broad-leafed plants or even if you cut a flap of soil or moss, lift it and build the fire underneath it. If you are wearing a rain jacket, you may have to kneel down, open up your jacket and make a small fire under the protection of your body and garment.

You can also build a tipi-shaped fire with large fuel stacked up as the exterior of your tipi. Instead of building your tipi from small fuel outward, when it rains, you need to go big early and start with the exterior structure. When the exterior is built, you can build your fire underneath it like you normally would. Make sure you double up on the amount of tinder you use with this type of fire setup. The extra heat the tinder

A large fire requires a tall canopy.

SKILL #5
DAKOTA FIRE AND *H* FIRE

There is an allure to stealth camping, that is, camping in a manner when and where people don't know you are in their area. If done incorrectly, you can get spotted, chased and possibly caught and arrested. When done correctly, you can spend a peaceful night outdoors, and no one knows the better. Something I bring up in my courses is the idea of light signature at night. A small- to medium-sized fire can be seen in the open, but in the dark woods, you can wander only 100 feet (30 m) or so to visit the little boys' or girls' room, turn around, and you won't be able to locate your camp. At night, a fire's light is a dead giveaway to your location, and in a survival situation, you want to be seen. Then again, some survival situations may call for reducing your light signature. In times like these, you can utilize the Dakota firepit to your advantage.

The Dakota firepit is a fire setup that incorporates two holes that are dug into the ground and connected. Ideally, one hole runs horizontally and the other runs vertically. If possible, the hole that runs horizontally is positioned in a manner where the prevailing wind will feed it. A fire is built in the horizontal hole and the heat is pushed up and out of the vertical hole. One of the two holes can be dug downwards and the other diagonally, with both connected in the middle. When constructing the two holes, you want to leave enough earth to support the walls surrounding the tunnel. Usually 6 to 10 inches (15 to 25 cm) of earth will do, and the hole you

will give off will offset some of the dampness in your kindling. Keep feeding more and more tinder underneath your tipi structure, and don't stop until you notice the smaller fuel catching. Even then, it doesn't hurt to fuel the fire with more tinder and nurse it until the next size fuel catches. Make sure not to exhaust all of your tinder, since you may need to grab a handful to get your fire going again if your structure collapses, a gust of wind blows out the growing fire or if it gets too wet in the process.

If you know rain is coming and if you have some time to prep for it, you can build a jungle fire with a canopy over your pit. The height of the canopy over the fire depends on how large the fire needs to be. A small fire won't throw as much heat as a large fire, and therefore the canopy need not be built too high off the ground. One important consideration is that vegetation can burn. The longer your fire burns underneath your canopy, the drier your canopy will become. At some point, when your canopy dries out enough and the temperature hits the flashpoint, your canopy will catch fire from the bottom side on up.

dig doesn't need to exceed 12 inches (30 cm) in diameter.

The Dakota firepit is useful for cooking and also very practical when it is windy out. If you try cooking with a fire on a windy day, you'll find the heat from the fire is often pushed away from underneath your cooking pot. Sometimes it is easier to put your cooking pot next to the fire instead of resting or suspending it on top of a fire. The wind will push the flame into the side of the pot and you just need to be mindful to rotate it to prevent your meal from burning or getting hot on only one side. When you use a Dakota firepit, the wind helps to turn your pit into a furnace, and you can get strong and consistent heat out of the chimney hole of your pit. If you line the top of the pit with at least three large stones, you will have enough airflow under your pot and be able to keep it just above the opening to not snuff it out.

You'll notice your Dakota firepit can withstand high winds and rain, and it will dry out wet wood quickly. Ideally, you want to use the driest wood possible to reduce the smoke signature just as much as you have reduced the light signature. It is a great skill to learn and can be applied in exceptional circumstances.

Another version of a fire meant for discreet use is the *H* fire. This fire is built by cutting two flaps into the ground that resemble the capital letter *H*. The flaps are opened from the center outward and left attached at their ends. A fire is built in the depression made, and the flaps serve as both shades to conceal the light signature and wind breaks on two sides. The *H* fire can be smothered quickly (most fires should be entirely put out with complete soaking, but some fires

A Dakota firepit is the answer when wind and rain make it difficult to cook over an open fire.

in certain situations may require less effort) by dropping the *H* flaps back down and the ground can be tamped on to make it look like no one was even there. This fire set up can be essential if you don't have rocks to build a fire ring and want to keep your fire contained to a depression in the ground. If you cut your flaps from a section of grass, the grass around the firepit can dry out and burn very quickly. For smaller fires, this setup works great, and as long as you have a spare water bottle you can put out your cooking fire with, this fire setup will quickly become one of your favorites.

SKILL #6
ONE-MATCH FIRE

The one-match fire is a great way of getting a small fire going with nothing more than a single match and properly assembled resources. This skill teaches you how to conserve your resources and use minimal paper or wooden matches or the shortest burn of a lighter. A standard book of paper matches gives you twenty chances to light a fire unless you split your matches and if that is your course of action, you must make sure your fire prep is exceptionally good. One-match fires can be assembled with materials broken off and collected with only your hands. The one-match fire also reinforces the idea that you don't need a cutting tool to build a fire.

Your best option for a one-match fire is to look for softwoods like balsam fir, hemlock and pine. The twigs from these trees ignite easily and if you look under the low-hanging branches, you'll find plenty of pencil-lead-thick twigs that are dried and crack when broken off. You want to collect enough small twigs that you have trouble holding the twig bundle together with both hands. As you collect the twigs, you'll notice the bundle will be narrow where you hold it together and flared out like a bouquet of flowers at the top. When you eventually light your fire, you will turn this bundle upside down and it will stand like a tipi fire. Like all other fires, you don't want to stop at the pencil-lead thickness; you'll want to progress to larger fuel. The same branches from which you snapped twigs can also be used in your fire. Dead pine trees have branches that grow in a spoke-like pattern. Many times, these

The one-match fire is a classic fire challenge with or without a knife.

branches make the best quick fire fuel, as the base of the branches that connect to the trunk of the tree have resin built up that burns very hot.

One final word on making fires with matches. Always ignite your match near the base of your fire or where you plan on lighting your fire. The hottest your match will ever be is when it is reacting. Always support the head of your match with your fingertip, and after you strike your match, have it nearby your tinder or twig bundle to take advantage of the chemical reaction. Hold your match upright and it will burn as expected, horizontally and it will burn faster, and if you invert your match, it will burn the fastest. Don't forget the hottest part of the lit match is the tip of the flame. If you only have one match, make sure to use it right.

SKILL #7
COOK WITH FIRE

Always rest your cooking pot on a good base.

Boiling water is an essential skill, and I prioritize it over cooking food with fire. Following the rule of threes, your body will need water long before it needs food. Boiling water is my preferred method of treating bad water over filters and additive pills or drops. It sounds simple enough. Boil water by using a metal container and apply enough heat until you see large bubbles rise from the bottom of the pot to the surface.

In the process of boiling water, there are some problems that may affect your success. Your water can spill into your fire because of an unstable base. Your water can fail to reach boiling point, because the wind is pushing the heat sideways instead of upwards. You can even burn your pot if you try to melt snow without starting with a little water in your pot from the start. Luckily, these problems have simple remedies. A good base can be constructed with three rocks positioned in an equilateral triangle or you can use the log-cabin fire with sturdy green wood as a temporary base. You can also just put your pot directly on the coals in your firepit. When the wind is blowing strong, you can either build a wall to shield your flame or place your pot on the far side of the fire and have the wind push your flame into the side of your container. As far as boiling water from snow, you can melt some snow easily by building a snowball on a stick and propping it up next to a fire where the snowball can drip into your pot until you have enough water to boil.

Log-cabin fire lays and three-rock methods for boiling water will also apply to cooking stews and soups. Soups are less likely to burn to the bottom of your pot than stews, and if you can keep flames from hitting the bottom of the pot you're using, you drastically decrease the chances of burning your pot or your food.

When the time comes to cook meat over a fire, remember how the pros do it, and you'll avoid some of the most common mistakes. Avoid cooking with the flames from your fire touching your food as it will char the outside and leave the inside uncooked. Also, make sure any fat that drips from your meat doesn't ignite and create an oil fire that will blacken your food and char it. Your best option for grilling cuts of meat, sausages and bone-in meat is to build a fire, establish a bed of coals and cook over the heat.

If you have the resources, another method of cooking with fire is accomplished with hot flat rocks. This method works best with thin cuts of meat that would cook quickly on a hot grill pan at home. Using a flat rock collected from an area where water doesn't pool to avoid explosions, build a fire over the rock and sustain it for 30 minutes to an hour or longer. Keep your fire burning long enough to cover the rock with hot coals. Right before you are ready to cook, use an evergreen bough or green leafy branch to brush away the coals, exposing a bare rock surface. Place the meat you want to cook directly on the rock and use it like a hot frying pan. If you have animal fat, you can even "grease" your rock by rendering it down on the hot rock before you start cooking. This will keep your food from sticking if it has a tendency to.

You should cook with hot coals as much as possible and use a *T* fire. Much like the long fire, you create a fire lay to burn logs horizontally. Think of this lay as the horizontal part of the letter *T*. From this fire lay, you pull out coals perpendicular to the fire, forming the vertical part of that *T*. This lets you burn a fire and cook over coals simultaneously. Your fire doesn't need to be underneath your food; only your coals do. As more coals are needed, they are pulled from one part of the *T* to the other.

SKILL #8
CARRY FIRE

You should never put out a fire you can't restart. You can be short on resources, you could have lost your fire starter, you could be injured and have limited physical ability—the need to maintain your fire is very real. You may find yourself in a situation where you need to carry your fire with you and keep it burning throughout your travels. You may also find learning how to keep an ember glowing that can later be turned into a flame is a good skill to master.

Carrying a flame from one campsite to another is a common skill I assess in my students during courses. Students are given the opportunity to assemble a fire bundle, and they take time wrapping tinder with strips of bark, dried grasses, leaves and any other material they feel will smoulder like a burning cigarette. The success rate, at first, is not very high. Common issues students have is either snuffing the burning ember out by covering it or letting the burning ember burst into flames that burn too quickly. Other times, students will find they cannot hold on to the fire bundle, as it becomes too warm for their exposed hands.

To successfully carry a fire from one campsite to another, you must remember the basics of building a fire. When done correctly, a good fire bundle requires little to no tweaking. You will want to take into account how far you need to travel and how large your fire bundle needs to be. Too small of a bundle, and you'll end up handling it like a lit match about to burn out. The components of the fire bundle should be flammable

The author carrying a fire bundle during a winter class.

SKILL #9
BANK A FIRE

There are times when you need to slow down the rate at which your fire is consuming your supply of fuel. Perhaps you are facing limited good firewood or maybe venturing out to get more wood is a bad decision. You may find the idea of burning a fire overnight wasteful if the weather is warm enough, you have enough insulation and don't need the warmth from a fire. There are other times when you may have to leave your fire ring while you are out fishing, hunting, gathering or collecting more wood and would rather not have your fire burn out, requiring you to restart it. In times like these and many other scenarios, you will be well served by banking your fire.

By banking a fire, you save your resources to tap into them at a later time. By eliminating one of the three requirements needed for wood to burn, you can slow the rate you burn through your firewood. This is done by smothering burning logs with ash, not coals. You need to practice with this skill and you'll find mixed results as you tinker with covering the brightest burning embers of a log after rotating them to the 12 o'clock, 9 o'clock, 3 o'clock and 6 o'clock positions. I prefer placing the hottest embers on a log sideways. As long as I completely cover the log, I know the weight of the log won't smother the embers against the bottom of the firepit, and when I place an evergreen bough over the top, it will prevent the ashes from blowing away in a stiff wind. You may discover a different method that is equally effective. My way is not the only way, and there are many ways to bank a fire correctly.

and should be constructed in a way that it will burn like a lit cigarette or cigar. If your bundle only burns from the inside, the outer wrapping will prevent the air from getting to the burning coal. If your outer wrap burns faster than the inner core/contents, you'll end up dropping it as you won't have a place to hold onto it. My most successful students have used peeled, thin layers of birch bark and moss to wet the outer layers and suppress it from flaming up.

One solution to the challenge of carrying fire is found in the form of powdered charcoal from your last fire. The charcoals you have in your firepit, as long as they are dry, will burn slowly as embers, and additional charcoal pieces can be added to your bundle before the others burn out. This will require you to carry one container of dry charcoal and another with lit coals.

Banking embers with ashes slows the burn rate.

SKILL #10
EXTINGUISH A FIRE

Before you bank your fire, consider what resources you will need to get your fire going when you return to it. It is a good idea to keep a supply of tinder nearby that will catch a flame when put into contact with burning embers and coaxed with some gentle breaths. Even though your tinder may catch the larger fuel on fire, as it will increase the heat in your firepit, it is prudent to have some larger fuel to begin the fire-starting process over until you are certain the larger fuel has caught again. Something that makes blowing your glowing embers back into flame is a strong breath concentrated through a tube. You can use a tent pole, a hollowed out section of bamboo, Japanese knotweed shoots or any other hollow tube.

Survival means being resourceful. This means finding uses for resources and using your resources carefully. Just as you would not want to waste energy by walking aimlessly, you also don't want to waste your energy cutting more firewood than you actually need. You don't want to have to replace wood, thereby burning calories, by cutting more if you don't have to. I consider banking a fire an essential skill, especially when you need to conserve your energy in a long-term situation. If you're not properly fed, you will grow weaker with time. Banking a fire will help you avoid wasting energy.

If you have to move your location and abandon a firepit, you want to make sure that firepit is completely extinguished. Stamping out a match thrown on the ground or putting out a cigar butt that way will work because of the small scale, but you shouldn't employ the same methods for extinguishing fires that are much larger. If you have been using a firepit for a considerable amount of time and there has been a significant amount of wood (even a weekend's worth of firewood) burning, there is likely a strong bed of coals and ash. The ground around your firepit may be extremely dry, and you never know if there is an ember that will jump from the firepit to a dry patch of leaves or nearby tinder supply. Leaving a fire to burn is a recipe for disaster, but you can take precautions to ensure it is out. You also don't want to simply bury your fire under dirt. While dirt will cover the fire and prevent oxygen from getting to the fuel, there is a high amount of heat left behind that could continue cooking and warming up flammable materials in the pit to the point of ignition.

Whenever I start the process of extinguishing my campfires, I always remove any large fuel from the center of the pit and arrange it so that it won't burn as readily. This is usually done by raking coal and ashes from one side of the pit to the other and putting the fuel where their ashes no longer can burn it. With the fuel pulled to the side, I let the fire die down on its own until my coals turn mostly white. I make sure to soak the fuel I pulled aside in the water trough formed in

Create a water trough in the center of your campfire to soak the fuel in and extinguish your fire.

SKILL #11
FRICTION-FIRE FUNDAMENTALS

the center. When I give the pit a good soaking, I make sure to hover my hand over the pit to feel for hot spots and look for any additional smoke that might be coming up. Only when I know the pit is cool to the touch and I can't see any smoke will I consider my fire to be out.

Making a fire by "rubbing two sticks together" is a true test of your skill. It is also one of the more difficult ways of building a fire, but when you finally get your first coal and blow it into a flame, the satisfaction level is unsurpassed in firemaking. Friction fire starting is one of the last skills I teach, as the lack of success is almost as high as the level of frustration when it just doesn't work. If you recall, I want students to experience success first. Failure and frustration are great barriers to growth and learning. I've watched students toss aside the components of a friction fire set when they gave up on their goal. For some, learning about friction fire and the difficulty and skill level needed to accomplish it simply reinforces the urgency of always having firemaking gear on them. As long as students know they have some firemaking ability, they are able to approach the challenge of friction fire with an open mind instead of one clouded with disappointment and anger.

With friction fires, you must bring the wood dust to a critical temperature for it to turn into a coal. It will be more difficult for those who lack aerobic conditioning, and it will also be difficult for those with limited strength, balance and flexibility. Keep in mind, the friction-fire skill set is elusive but not impossible. Plenty of people have learned it before you, and they came in all different shapes, sizes and abilities. Also, finding all these materials can be time consuming. On a good day, it may take you a minimum of

The bow drill is a proven method to make a friction fire, but proficiency requires regular practice.

30 minutes to find the right wood and that is assuming you already have good cordage. If you need to make cordage, the time commitment is much greater.

The wood you choose for your fireboard and spindle is very important. Both pieces will be made from the same wood to prevent one wood from wearing away the other wood too quickly. You want a wood of medium density, and traditionally this has been tested with a fingernail indentation. If your fingernail goes too easily into the wood, it is too soft. If your fingernail won't mark the wood and it feels like your nail is pushing out the opposite direction, your wood is likely too hard for spindle and fireboard. It is good for the socket piece though. Woods of medium density that

work great for learning friction fire include willow, poplar and cedar. The wood you use should be well seasoned with minimal moisture content. Some geographic areas will be advantageous to you, as desert woods have far less moisture content than those found in the Northern forests.

Whenever I teach friction fire, I become more of a coach than an instructor. I get down in the dirt with my students and pick up on the little nuances that make or break success. I can easily diagnose if a student isn't using enough pressure, if the cord is slipping, if the student is short stroking the bow and when they just need to run the bow drill a little longer to push the wood dust to the critical temperature to become a coal. Since I can't be there in the dirt with you, I can only offer these tips now. Index your spindle so only the bottom of the spindle is making contact with the fireboard. Position your body in a way that you can look directly down over the top of your spindle to see the progress you're making. Add a little sand to your depression underneath the spindle to increase the friction temporarily. Use the full length of the bow when you run it, and don't stop breathing. You don't need to start off fast, but you need to be consistent and run the bow drill until smoke forms. When you see the smoke, you need to move the bow faster, level and long enough until the smoke becomes thicker, and you can see a dark coal pushing out from the notch. You need to finish strong, and when you are finished, you need to keep the spindle in the fireboard temporarily to trap that heat in. When you move the spindle from the board, do so carefully. To protect it from moisture, don't put it down on the ground. Also, make sure you don't knock the coal over as you are moving the

Wood dust from the bow drill needs to reach the critical temperature to form a burning coal.

bow drill parts around. You should take your knife and tap the coal free from the notch. When it comes time to transfer your coal to your tinder bundle, move your tinder bundle close to your coal so you don't have to move the coal a far distance. Pick up your tinder bundle with two hands, and hold it higher than your face when you blow into it to keep the smoke out of your mouth, nose and eyes. Start blowing air slowly into the space between your palms and gradually press the tinder bundle together as you increase the volume and force behind your breath. If you do all of these correctly, you should find success. If you don't, learn from your experience and diagnose it without emotional leakage. All friction fire is science, not magic, and you should be able to determine what you need to do better to achieve victory.

Whenever I teach friction fire, I remind people how difficult the skill is but how those who own the skill are part of an elite segment of the world's population. Friction-fire skills are thousands of years old, and they are highly coveted to this day. Friction fire will impress your friends, but it isn't my primary means of making fire. I like knowing I can fall back on this skill set if my other gear is lost. It has given me confidence in my travels, but it hasn't replaced my pragmatism. Even though I consider myself proficient or advanced in this skill set, I still carry a disposable lighter and a ferro rod with me on a daily basis. Friction fires are cool, but instant fire is better, and primitive man would have killed to have the other fire-starting gear you have access to.

I've heard that experts don't practice until they get something right, they practice until they never get it wrong. With all of these fire skills, you will get to a point that you don't feel challenged. Some of my best students have commented how they "need something challenging" when we reconnect on trips. I pride myself on finding ways to make training more difficult, more interesting and more complex. I have no reservation in saying that I don't run out of fire challenges or ways to test my students' abilities.

Starting with the most basic fire-starting method that gives most students success, the petroleum cotton ball, I challenge students to build as many fires as possible with a single cotton ball. They try lighting it, extinguishing it, lighting it, extinguishing it, as many times as possible or they pull only a few threads from a single ball and light that with perfect tinder. I have students use the cotton ball and burn one as long as possible by shaping it in various ways and surrounding it by wrappers of sorts. Even the most basic fire-starting method can be modified with different handicaps.

Fire starting can be made more difficult by introducing time standards as well as competition against another person. Any of the fire-starting methods mentioned in this chapter, as well as others such as flint and steel, reflective fires and unorthodox methods involving chemicals (potassium permanganate) and batteries (used with steel wool), become more challenging and stressful when you introduce the clock or an opponent. To determine who builds the strongest fire, you can stretch a string across a gap and have competitors try to burn through the string without touching it. You can challenge yourself by seeing how quickly you can bring a cup of water to a boil or how quickly you can find the materials you need to build a fire that will last a set amount of time. The challenges are limited only by your imagination. Just be honest with your results, reasons for success or defeat and the steps you need to take to improve the next time.

One of the more interesting and popular challenges I've had my students tackle is building a fire over water. Most will accomplish this challenge by building some form of tripod platform they can then pile wet leaves and mud on to prevent the platform from burning. Other students will create a "seesaw" and position the fire over water after it is built. The challenge is not so much about building the fire but the thought process and sideways thinking required to come to a solution.

You cannot train fire-starting skills enough. Don't settle and fall into the belief you know it all, because there are so many ways to skin this cat. Fire is absolutely essential to survival, and you should embrace challenges openly. I believe in training hard and fighting easy. Make it a point to constantly seek out challenges in your training, so you don't experience them for the first time in reality. Fire skills not only create warmth and light but character as well. You'll learn a lot about yourself and how you handle adversity through learning how to harness fire on command.

SHELTER SKILLS

"Therefore everyone who hears these words of mine and puts them into practice is like a wise man who built his house on the rock. The rain came down, the streams rose, and the winds blew and beat against that house; yet it did not fall, because it had its foundation on the rock. But everyone who hears these words of mine and does not put them into practice is like a foolish man who built his house on sand. The rain came down, the streams rose, and the winds blew and beat against that house, and it fell with a great crash." —Matthew 7:24–27

Our bodies run approximately 98.6°F (37°C), with some of us running slightly warmer and some of us slightly cooler. This is the critical temperature we must maintain, and the science behind this fact is undeniable. Homeostasis is the key, as swings plus or minus this 98.6°F (37°C) temperature are dangerous to our survival. Drop a few degrees, and you experience hypothermia. Increase that temperature a couple degrees, and you experience hyperthermia. Depending on our body's need, we can exercise or shiver to create warmth and sweat to cool us down. This can help, but our bodies can't fight back the forces of nature on their own. If we have time, we can slowly acclimatize to our environments and learn to operate in warmer or cooler temperatures in relative comfort. We can supplement what our body does naturally with proper clothing given our environment. Our clothing is our first line of shelter, and we should always be prepared to spend the night in only what we wear when we leave home.

According to the well-known rule of threes, you may live an average of three hours exposed to the elements before you succumb to the cold or the heat. This number is only an average; those with less natural insulation (body fat) and those with slow metabolism are probably going to get cooler faster. These factors are influenced by our age, level of activity and genetics. The clothes we wear become critical to our survival and comfort. If we remember and apply the acronym C.O.L.D. (Clean clothes, avoid Overheating, dress in Loose Layers and keep our clothes Dry) to our garments, we will last longer than the person who doesn't.

Nature has many ways to pull the warmth from our bodies, including evaporation (respiration and perspiration), conduction, convection and radiation.

Respiration/Evaporation cooling is easily witnessed when you breathe in and out in cold weather. As you exhale and watch the hot breath leave your body, understand it is replaced with the cool air that you breathe in. Think about the effect of introducing cold, dry air into healthy, warm and moist lungs. You can cool off quickly. Evaporation cooling occurs when our pores open up and release sweat to cool our skin. Our clothing should help ration our sweat and prevent it from drying too quickly in hot temperatures.

Conduction cooling occurs from direct contact with a cool surface. If you have ever taken a seat at a football game in the cold bleachers, you know what conduction cooling is. Conduction cooling takes place any time you have an object of a warmer temperature that makes contact with an object of a cooler temperature. If the object is larger and colder, cooling will happen. Conduction cooling can happen in summer months from the ground. While it won't happen as fast as it works in the winter months, the ground can give you chills on the warmest summer night.

Convection cooling happens when the wind blows, or more technically when liquids or gases pass around an object and cause cooling. Perhaps the most widely understood manner of convection cooling is the concept of wind chill. As air circulates around our bodies, it causes us to feel cooler than the ambient air actually is. In 0°F (-17°C) air temperature, when there is wind 10 miles (16 km) per hour, the wind chill makes it feel like -16°F (-27°C). Convection cooling is actually welcomed on a hot night when the air is stuffy, thick and still. On a winter camping trip, convection cooling can be an unrelenting force to deal with. When you end up with wet clothes in a windy environment, your predicament is even worse.

Radiation cooling is the heat we give off in all directions. Much like a radiator in an old house or wood stove, you don't have to touch it to know it is giving off heat. When this heat is given off, it can be released or it can be trapped to regulate our body temperature. This heat comes from the consumption of calories and the metabolizing of the body's fuel stores. Everyone has a different rate of radiation, and this will impact how warm a person will feel sleeping under a given amount of insulation.

Immersion cooling deserves a category of its own. While experts will disagree on the exact figure, water immersion conducts the heat from your body many times faster than air cooling or regular conduction. Immersion cooling is a nightmare scenario, but even the worst manner of heat loss can be addressed as long as you can pull yourself from the water. More on this later in the chapter.

TYPES OF SHELTERS

The shelters you can make to survive in the great outdoors fall into only one of four potential categories. These categories are divided into heated or unheated shelters and open or closed shelters. Each type of shelter has its place, and you may find yourself preferring one type over another in a given setting and scenario.

HEATED-CLOSED SHELTER
This shelter has the benefit of having walls on all sides and a heat source to change the temperature inside. Traditionally, canvas wall tents with steel hardwood stoves filled this role, but today,

An A-frame shelter can be built with only natural materials.

modern silnylon tipis with titanium stoves like those from the company Kifaru are the top choice of outdoorsmen. Heated shelters allow the occupant to dry clothes and their sleeping bags, heat food and water and sit around in comfort with nothing more than a T-shirt on. Simply put, the heated-closed shelter offers you as close as can be to the comfort you'll find at home.

The heated-closed shelter can also be made with all-natural materials. Large debris shelters and even quinzee shelters can have small fires placed inside them. These, of course, must be carefully lit and monitored as carbon monoxide poisoning, suffocation and accidental fires can disrupt a good night's sleep. The heated-closed shelter requires a significant amount of time to create it, materials to build it and fuel to feed the fire inside.

UNHEATED-CLOSED SHELTER

This option of shelter will protect you from the elements, but there is no heat source inside. Your average department-store camping tent with fiberglass poles and nylon construction is an example of the unheated-closed shelter. In cooler weather, this shelter requires you to provide your own heat and insulation. This is most often accomplished with a sleeping bag or quilt. In extremely warm weather, all you may need is a water-resistant roof overhead and mosquito netting on all sides.

Just like the previous shelter mentioned, the unheated-closed shelter can be made from the land. A-frame shelters made with a removable door and bent-sapling dome shelters are examples of shelters you can stuff with insulation and crawl inside. The unheated-closed shelter isn't entirely insect resistant, but it offers better protection than sleeping outdoors with no cover at all.

HEATED-OPEN SHELTER

This shelter is not fully enclosed, and staying warm is usually accomplished with a fire. If you have no other option, you can drape an emergency blanket over your shoulders and back and sit with your chest facing a small fire. As the heat rises from the small fire, it is reflected back toward you after it bounces off of the emergency blanket. Without a blanket, you must continually do what my good friend Big John calls "the human rotisserie," and turn your body so each part gets warm

A winter lean-to is a perfect example of this shelter with an angled wall behind you and a fire in front of you. The heat from the fire is caught by the overhanging lean-to cover and it reflects back onto you. While not optimal, a large enough fire, on its own, is more than enough to keep you alive in the cold. The heat from the fire can offset the cold from the darkness, precipitation and wind.

UNHEATED-OPEN SHELTER

This is hardly a shelter; it is more like a condition. An unheated-open "shelter" is the worst option for a night out. When you sleep outside unheated and open, you essentially just throw your sleeping bag and pad on the ground and sleep out under the stars. If you have the luxury of knowing what the weather forecast is, you can get by sleeping out this way, but in an emergency, you likely won't know if you will have precipitation overnight or not. Unheated-open shelters are not the most ideal for sleeping in mosquito and black fly country. Unheated-open shelters become compromised in severe precipitation. Anyone who wants to experiment with sleeping out with nothing more than an insulative layer should have an emergency water-resistant cover nearby.

Camping out without a fire is a psychological test. I've mentioned how fire has a comforting effect in the darkness and how the human mind is put into a similar state as deep sleep when starting a fire. When you sleep out with just insulation, you sleep very light. Since your eyes aren't given anything to see other than darkness and shadows, your ears will pick up more sounds and they will be amplified. The unheated-open shelter requires a level of comfort and confidence. It is a test of the mind and the body. Even though insulation is vital in the cold to stay warm, just having a thin layer of nylon around you in the form of a tent or shelter can be the luxury you need to put your mind at ease.

The best option for most survival situations is a closed-heated shelter. With knowledge of the four types of shelters, you can diagnose what kind of sleep situation you have and work to improve it. Be flexible with the type of shelter you can create, as the resources may not be available for the one you want to create. If you are camping in the cold and have the ability to heat up a water bottle or hot rocks in wool socks, you can introduce heat to your enclosed shelter.

If you build a solid A-frame debris shelter but feel a constant breeze from the opening, you can gather a bunch of branches, lash them at the top, forming a triangular-shaped door, and enclose your sleeping area. Each day you spend outside, you should improve your shelter, and each night should become more and more comfortable as you acclimatize to the environment.

PLACEMENT

Shelter building is all about location. My friend and desert survival expert Tony Nester has a simple way to remind students what concerns they should have when selecting a site for a shelter. He calls these issues the four Ws and I have adopted this memory device into my instruction. These Ws include 1) Wind, 2) Wiggles, 3) Widowmakers, 4) Water. You want to be concerned about the wind because if you position your shelter incorrectly, the wind will blow directly into your shelter, carrying smoke with it if you have a fire. Wiggles are the little buggers that crawl, buzz, sting and bite, and you don't want to build a shelter over an insect nest where they reside. Widowmakers are the standing dead trees and the hanging branches of trees that have broken off from a fallen tree but remain hung up on other branches, waiting to fall in a stiff breeze. Water is another concern you should have when building a shelter for multiple reasons.

On one hand, you want to be near water for the importance the resource has to your survival, but on the other hand, you may want to avoid it as it is a breeding ground for mosquitoes. Additionally, when you consider water, think about the precipitation form of water, rain and how it will fall on your area and transform it. Rain can make your shelter leak, and if you select an area to build your shelter where water forms, you could wake up in a puddle. Also, don't forget to drink plenty of water and stay hydrated at all times. Your body needs water to digest food and process calories into heat. The four Ws are a simplified way to remember what to look out for. Experience and awareness will help you refine what each "W" means and why you should heed this advice.

Keep in mind that when you build a shelter, you are going to invest a lot of time and energy in the process. It isn't safe to assume one person could accomplish in three hours the same amount of work as three people could in one. One person will tire much faster than three people would. The reality is, shelter building takes time, a lot of time when you want to do it right, and you need to get started early in the day to avoid running out of daylight. Shelter building also requires burning plenty of calories, and you should always think about how to make your body's furnace burn more efficiently to get you through the night.

SKILL #12

INSULATE FROM THE GROUND

Hot air rises and cold air sinks. Even if you have the greatest sleeping bag in the world with the finest insulation and construction, if you compress the loft of the bag underneath you and fail to insulate yourself from the ground, you will end up cold and miserable at some point in your attempted slumber. When your body comes in contact with the ground, the ground's cold mass starts working to draw all the heat from your body. You need to create a barrier from it and knowing what you can use and how to insulate are essential survival skills.

Starting with what you may already have on you, you can insulate from the ground by using your backpack as a seat. Your backpack likely has some form of foam used to provide rigidity and support to the structure. You can use this foam under your butt to insulate it from the ground. Closed foam of this variety is a popular material for use in sleeping pads sold in camping stores. Air cannot readily pass through this foam and it does a great job in keeping your heat from being sucked away by the ground. To stay warm, you may need to tuck your legs up and next to your body in a cannonball position against a tree for the night. It won't be the most comfortable night, but you will stay warmer than if you attempt to ride out the night by sleeping flat on the ground.

If you have minimal resources with you, perhaps a small emergency kit tucked in your jacket or haversack pockets, you can pair the contents with natural resources to stay warm instead.

Should you have a garbage bag in your pack, it will make sleeping out much easier. With a garbage bag, you can collect dried leaves and create a "bean bag" chair of sorts to sit on throughout the night. When paired with a poncho to cover both you and your chair, you can stay both warm and dry in the worst weather. Also, as long as you don't puncture or tear your bag, you can empty the contents from one location before striking off for another. The best bags you can use are the heavyweight contractor-grade cleanup bags. These will last night after night.

Assuming you don't have a contractor bag or a pack to sit on and you truly have to work with only Mother Nature's resources, you must collect enough insulative material that will keep you elevated off the ground. Natural insulative materials can include leaves, pine needles, evergreen boughs, dried moss, grasses, cattail and milkweed pods. Whenever you gather these materials, you need to gather them in excess. It is not an understatement to say you need about 1½ to 3 feet (46 to 91 cm) of loft to have a comfortable night's sleep on natural materials. Your bodyweight will crush most of it down to only a few inches. That should be enough to keep you off the cold ground and up above the cold air that gathers there. Assuming you spend more than one night in your shelter, you will need to continually add more loft to your bedding area. Unlike synthetic insulation, natural insulation like you'll find in the great outdoors will not fluff back up after you compress it. If you have the means, build a frame to get you higher off the ground and then layer it with insulation.

If at all possible, one of the best ways to insulate from the ground is to create a raised bed with insulation on top of it. Starting with

SKILL #13
BUILD A HOT SEAT/BED

A thick bed of pine needles provides insulation from the ground.

You may find yourself in a situation where there are few resources to pad yourself with from the cold. In a scenario when it appears you have no recourse to stay warm on the ground, the easy way out is to give up. You may have a fire but nothing to sit on. Then again, with a little creativity, you can sit atop a "fire" and stay warm for hours. I don't recommend direct contact with the flames or coals; I recommend building a hot seat or firebed instead.

The hot seat, sometimes called a "hot hole," is created in one of two ways. The first way involves digging a small hole in the ground and building a fire that will create large hot coals. These coals are covered over with approximately 6 inches (15 cm) of earth. As the coals continue to burn, the steam and heat rises from the ground underneath you. The second method of making a hot hole is placing rocks warmed for at least 30 minutes in a roaring fire into a hole and then burying it in the same manner as the coals. This method requires some care as rocks can absorb moisture and heated rocks create expanding moisture that creates steam and eventually explodes rocks. While the buried coals won't last as long, they are safer than heating up suspect rocks. Then again, if you use rocks, you will have a warm seat that will last longer, as long as your rocks are found in dry areas where water isn't known to pool.

If you want to build a hot seat, you should consider the other possible uncomfortable scenarios it can cause. The hot seat is ideally used

two logs about 6 to 12 inches (15 to 30 cm) in diameter, place these perpendicular to where your body will rest, with one at the head and one at your feet. Perpendicular to these two logs and slightly longer than you are tall are the main supports that will create the bed where you will rest. If you find the center of your bed bowing under your weight, you can always add a third log underneath the center of your bed. When you have all of your logs placed, the next step is to turn any logs with branches poking out downward, or you can clip the branches close to the trunk to prevent them from poking you while you sleep. With your initial framework done, you should insulate the bed the same way you did your natural bedding placed directly on the ground. Raised beds, like the one described here, are classic shelters used in the Northern forest and are quite comfortable, making sleep easy.

Buried rocks or coals create a hot seat/bed that can warm you through the night.

only in unfrozen dry soil or sand. If you attempt to build a hot seat in the winter, you may not be able to dig into the frozen ground. Also, that ground can thaw and reveal how damp the soil was before it froze. This will leave you in a muddy mess. If you aren't careful, not only will you be cold, but you will also end up cold, wet and dirty. That is a recipe for disaster. Another potential problem with the hot seat is it becoming too hot. In loose soil or sand, if you don't bury your coals or rocks under enough earth, you could roll over and make contact with something that will burn your gear, your skin and keep you up at night if you roll over on a hot spot.

When used with a poncho, the hot seat not only warms your tail but your whole body too. The heat rises up from the ground and is caught inside the poncho. Another option is the firebed, but you have to consider the amount of effort needed. You may not have the tools to move the amount of earth needed to open up a hole in the ground as long as your body and 9 inches (23 cm) deep. Sometimes you get the skill right and stay warm and dry and other times you end up needing to modify it throughout the night. Ultimately, the hot seat is a skill that takes practice, but it can save your butt if it doesn't burn it.

SKILL #14
THE NAMMY SHELTER

The Nammy shelter can be set up in under a minute.

"You're going to build a shelter in less than a minute that will prevent you from getting soaked in the worst of downpours." If you heard that, you might wonder, "How?" We can barely throw on our rain gear in that amount of time let alone build a shelter. The idea seems impossible, but with a little preparation, you can easily convert a poncho into a 60-second shelter that will, in fact, keep you drier than many others.

The Nammy Shelter is one I learned from Marty Simon at the Wilderness Learning Center, and he told me he used it frequently in Vietnam (hence the "Nammy" name). During courses at the WLC and over the years with Estela Wilderness Education, I have shown the Nammy under the pressure of a minute countdown. With just a poncho, I can usually build it with seconds to spare, and if I have stakes carved or carried ahead of time, I can set up the shelter in half the allotted time.

All you need to do to set up the Nammy is stake out the four corners of your poncho or your small tarp directly to the ground. If you don't have tent stakes, you can improvise with small twigs through grommets or tie-down tabs. If you have more than a minute, you can tie off the hood of your poncho and affix the end of the cord to a low-hanging branch or bent-over sapling. This will raise the center of your shelter. You can also take a small *Y* branch and prop open one side of the shelter for some ventilation. To use the Nammy, all you have to do is crawl underneath the poncho or tarp and lay diago-

nally. The Nammy is not the most comfortable shelter, but you will not get wet as long as you have a quality poncho and you set it up correctly. One additional benefit of making a Nammy is the protection it affords from flying insects. You still have to deal with those underneath you, but at least you aren't getting attacked from the ground and the air at the same time.

The Nammy is a shelter you can use in any season, although it is ideally a warm-weather shelter. In the winter and cooler months, it makes sense to prop up the center of your Nammy by the poncho hood or by bunching up the fabric in the center of your tarp, placing a small pebble in it and tying it from the outside like a button. This will keep the condensation off of you. You should also make sure to keep the ends propped up for better ventilation as you won't have to worry about insects. The winter Nammy also requires proper insulation below, but if you have it, you'll be protected from the wind and light snowfall.

SKILL #15
Ys AND Vs IN TREES

Emergency shelter building requires being very resourceful. Anyone can learn to set up a good shelter with a vapor barrier like an emergency blanket, some cordage and a fire starter. An emergency shelter may require you to build protection from the elements with few resources. This may seem daunting, especially if you are used to creating ridgelines with paracord or setting up your shelter with guy lines and cordage lashings.

Cordage is not easily acquired in all seasons. This limiting factor will require you to think outside the box to prop up ridge poles. A simple solution to the cordage problem is to use naturally occuring hanging points on trees such as branch joints and when trees split into two and grow separate trunks. Just remember, the closer to the trunk of the upright tree you can place the weight of the beam you are hanging, the better. The joint will be stronger than further out on the limb. Also, you will find some *Ys* are stronger than others, especially when the *Y* fork supports the weight of the beam equally instead of on a single tine or branch. Thick forked branches are not easy to pull apart. Try it sometime and you'll see how much weight it would take to snap one in two. When in doubt, if you feel like the *Y* branch won't hold, you can reinforce the branch with a secondary *Y* underneath it, propped up from the ground. If you're making an A-frame shelter, two *Ys* can be used to hold the ridgepole in place. Just kick the *Y* branches out forward some, and when the ridgepole passes through the two junctions of the forks, it will lock in place. By the way, always

Natural Y's and V's supporting a ridge pole in a debris shelter.

use strong green wood or dead seasoned *Ys* and avoid using any wood that feels punky, rotten or too weak.

Forked poles are also good for creating cordage-free tripods. An oversized tripod can be used like a modified tipi shelter if need be. Once you assemble the three legs of the tripod, you can start laying other branches on top of the center and give your tipi more support and structure. If you only have a knife, you can also use your forked tripod with an inverted *J* branch to make a pot holder to suspend a bailed pot over a fire. If you suspend your pot over a fire with a long pole propped up on a log or rock and use a forked branch, driving the two forks into the ground, you will make an anchor point to hold the post in place.

SKILL #16

RIDGELINES AND RIDGE POLES

Setting up a tarp between two trees doesn't sound difficult, but I've had students express disappointment in not being able to tension a line tight enough or having their tarps scrunch in the middle or rip from the grommets. The problem most people have isn't the type of tarp they are using but rather the foundation of a good tarp shelter, the ridgeline. A solid ridgeline, tied correctly, will support your tarp and prevent mishaps throughout the night. All that is required is strong cordage, like paracord or dyneema, and the knowledge of two knots.

When you set up a tarp ridgeline, you need to find strong live trees that are slightly wider apart than the length of your tarp. That is, you want to find a place where your tarp will fit in between trees without large gaps at either end between your tarp and the trees it will be tied to. Your ridgeline can be placed at any height depending on how you want to set up your tarp. Working with a 10 x 10–foot (3 x 3–m) square tarp, I usually start my ridgeline for an A-frame shelter about shoulder height, which for me is around 5 feet (1.5 m) off the ground.

The first knot you will tie is the Siberian hitch, sometimes called the "Even K" hitch. This is a knot that is quick to tie and quick to release. You want to make sure you can retrieve your paracord or lashing line without cutting cordage after you take down your tarp. The Siberian hitch will release with just a tug of one end of the line. With practice, this hitch can be tied very quickly

Top: Rolling hitch with half hitch; Bottom: Quick release

and will become your "go to" method of securing a line to a post or tree.

Securing lines to trees is one essential skill; making sure they have enough tension is another. A common complaint from students is that they cannot tension the line between the trees and that there is too much slack and play in their line. The solution to this is the trucker's hitch. This knot will give you extra leverage to pull your ridgeline taut.

The trucker's hitch is used to tension your line, but you still need to tie it off. The easiest way to do this is with a simple rolling hitch and a couple half hitches. A rolling hitch holds the tension on the line by wrapping over itself. Always back up your half hitch with a second half hitch.

This setup can be tied in a matter of seconds when you become proficient with it, and it takes even less time to take it down. The ridgeline will give you a much greater surface to support your tarp than just tying off from the grommet points. I don't recommend any heavy weight bearing applied to your grommets or tie-down tabs. These can be used to hold your tarp taught to the trees, but the full weight of the tarp should be supported by the ridgeline. A strong ridgeline will prevent the "scrunch effect" where the tarp droops in the center and your living space starts to disappear. The best setup for a tarp is when the ridgeline supports the tarp body and secondary lines hold it in place.

If you don't have enough cordage to make a ridgeline, you can use your cutting tools to cut a post from a young tree and lash this tree to two uprights. You can also just cut a tree about 3 feet (91 cm) from the ground and leave the tree hinged to create a diagonal ridgeline. Before the tree is attached horizontally or cut diagonally, you must remove any sharp branches from where the tarp will contact the tree. The solid post will serve like a ridgeline you can drape your tarp over for secure construction. Make sure your knots are solid on the horizontal and make sure you back up the diagonal construction with some *Y* branches just in case your ridgepost decides to fall on you in the middle of the night.

SKILL #17
FOUR PROVEN TARP SHELTERS

There are some items in your kit that are truly multipurpose. Duct tape, your Swiss Army knife, a handkerchief and your tarp all come to mind. Tarps can be used as rafts, sails, water-collection basins and, of course, shelters. What makes the tarp an excellent choice for shelter is the ability to pitch it in multiple ways. Depending on your situation and requirements, you can use a tarp to provide living space to hunker down under while it is raining, for sleeping in the worst downpour rains, for the most visibility if your situation or mission requires heightened awareness and other options based on how you stake certain corners and raise others. The tarp can be used four seasons of the year, and even if you camp with a tent, you should always pack a tarp for added protection from the elements. An essential skill you should have is knowledge of a handful of tarp shelters you can assemble with a few sharpened wooden stakes and some cordage.

A-FRAME

With a ridgeline tied between two uprights, the tarp is bisected along its width with the longer length being supported by the ridgeline. The four corners are either staked directly to the ground or attached to the ground with a short line that ties to the grommets or tie-down tabs. If there is a strong wind or if you want redundant security, you can stake down the grommets and/ or tie-downs between the corners on the sides of

A-frame tarp setup

Diamond tarp setup

the tarp. If you have a long tarp, you can also tuck some of the tarp fabric underneath your sleeping area to resemble more of a triangular tube tent. The A-frame can be suspended low to the ground to block wind from coming in, or it can be pitched higher when we need more ventilation. The A-frame is a very basic shelter, but it sheds water and blocks the wind well.

DIAMOND

Set up similar to the A-frame in the use of a ridgeline strung up between two vertical poles, the diamond tarp shelter is tied diagonally across the corners. This means you only have to stake two corners to the ground. The diamond tarp setup works great for hammock camping, and it also gives you a lot of living space in camp. If you have a 10 x 10–foot (3 x 3–m) tarp, the length of the fabric supported by the ridgeline diagonally is 14 feet (4.3 m). The diamond tarp shelter provides exceptional visibility of your surroundings and a lot of ventilation. It is my preferred setup for mild evenings in the early spring and late fall. With just a couple of 5-foot (1.5-m) posts, you can also prop up the points anchored

to the ground to give yourself even more visibility. These corners tied to the ground also work great as rainwater collection points for your canteens.

LEAN-TO

The lean-to shelter provides a lot of room for multiple people sleeping underneath it. Often, with an A-frame shelter, sleeping side-by-side underneath it means having a shelter wall in your face and a shoulder that pokes out from underneath the side. The lean-to is pitched at an angle with no bend in the fabric. Assuming your tarp is 10 x 10 feet (3 x 3 m), this means you have a sleeping area of 100 square feet (9.3 sq m). For comparison, a California king-size bed is 6.3 x 6.6 feet (1.9 x 2 m). The lean-to should be pitched in a way that leaves footroom at the base and headroom at the opening. One of the best ways to attach the lean-to to the ridgeline is by passing a bight of line through a grommet hole and placing a wooden dowel between the grommet and inside the bight. This forms a toggle that won't pull through, and attaching and removing is very easy without any knots. Depending how you set up your lean-to,

Lean-to tarp setup

80-20 tarp setup

The overhand loop knot (left) and the bowline knot (right) are two ways to create loops in cordage.

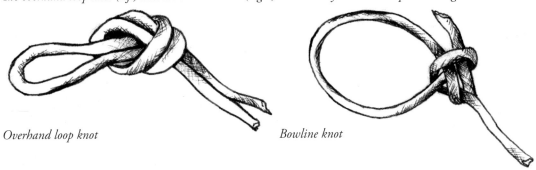

Overhand loop knot

Bowline knot

you can pitch it steeper to sit under it upright, directly to the ground to block the wind at your feet, slightly elevated to be used as a living area or low to the ground to trap heat from sleeping occupants better. When you set up your lean-to, make sure to leave somewhat of a pitch in the design or you will find water pool in the center. You can pull the center of the lean-to down at an extreme angle and all of the water will funnel to this point.

80-20

The lean-to shelter works well with campfires and in rainstorms in which the direction of the wind changes frequently. Similar to the lean-to shelter, the 80-20 is staked either directly to the ground or with cordage that runs to the ground with the tarp slightly elevated from it. The major difference between the 80-20 and the lean-to is the 80-20 is not attached to the ridgeline at the end of the tarp but rather slightly in from it. In other words, there is about 80 percent of the tarp creating the main body of the shelter and 20 percent forming a slight awning on the other side of the ridgeline. This awning has the ability to shed rain coming from the opposite direction of the shelter's opening, and it also works to trap rising hot air. Additionally, in sunny conditions, the awning can give you a little shade if you wish to stay in your shelter during the day's hottest and brightest times. The corners on the side of the awning can be staked diagonally out at an angle or they can be tied at an extreme angle down to close off the opening of the shelter.

SKILL #18
INSULATE FROM THE COLD

You should wear multiple layers if you are looking to insulate from the cold. The layer you wear closest to your skin serves as protection, and the next layer away from your skin works as a trap to the materials you shove in between them. Cattail fluff, milkweed pod seeds and even dried leaves will all work as insulation between your clothes and it will create dead-air space your body will warm. Also, since the fabric is puffed out and further from your body, you won't be as likely to feel the cooling effects of the wind and elements.

The homeless population in cities has long known this trick to staying warm. Newspapers, bubble wrap and packing peanuts can all be used in urban environments. Remember, the key to staying warm is trapping the air between layers of clothes next to your body. The makeshift materials you use as insulation will pale in comparison to the high-end down feathers or synthetic materials used in modern puffball jackets, but they will all be better than not having any additional insulation. This method of insulating is not the most glamourous, but there is no place for fashion when your life's on the line.

Fashion is not a concern when you're stuffing natural insulation between the layers of your clothing but overheating is. Overheating leads to perspiration. This is common when people start hiking or doing work with too many layers on. It is often a better idea and practice to work cold if you expect to sweat. If you have ever been at a trailhead in cool weather and have seen people walking into the woodline with only a base layer while you're sitting in the parking lot with a heavy jacket on, you have witnessed people abiding by this practice. When you sweat and your clothes take on moisture, you have to worry about getting your layers dry. The modern puffball jackets have a special down treatment or are made with hydrophobic (fancy word for water-hating) insulation. What you are using for natural insulation between your clothes will not be like this. Furthermore, your base layer may not be ideal for moisture wicking purposes. You want to be comfortable, not hot. When you are hot, you sweat and that can be deadly.

Assuming you don't have multiple layers on and you need to insulate from the cold, one means of insulating is actually a throwback to childhood: leaf piles. In general, you'll need twice as much insulation above as you have below. Pile up dried leaves and burrow into the center. The leaves will give you some protection from the wind if they don't blow away. One trick is to combine a pile of leaves with live lightweight branches that will hold them in place when placed atop the pile. Depending on your location, you may have to worry about certain insects such as ticks, but you can always remove them after you survive the night.

SKILL #19
SHINGLE WITH NATURAL MATERIALS

Whenever you are constructing natural shelters, you must consider how much material is needed to protect you from the elements above, and you also must think about how to place it properly. Just like the shingles placed on the roof of a house, you should always start your shingling process from the lowest level and work your way to the top. Shingling with natural materials is more than just throwing a bunch of materials on top of a shelter frame. There are some important skills you need to know to make sure your shingling and roofing works as intended.

Shingling with evergreen boughs requires placing the roofing material the same way it is found on trees. Some evergreens, like hemlock, have flat needles. If you examine the top of the needles, they appear dark in color, and the underside is noticeably lighter. When placing these atop your shelter, keep the dark side facing up, as the way the needles are shaped causes them to drip water toward the end of the needles instead of off to the side.

If you have a spare shirt or a trash bag in your kit, it will help you carry shingling material from beyond the immediate area. Pine needles, leaves, chunks of moss and bark from downed or standing dead trees can all be used as shingling material. No matter what you use, don't settle for simply covering the wooden frame of the shelter you created. The more shingling you apply, the more insulative value you'll have. It is not an ex-

Remove sheets of birch bark from fallen trees to create shingles for a natural shelter.

aggeration to say 12 inches (30 cm) of shingling material is the minimum amount needed.

One important shingling detail is covering the peak of your shelter completely. A shelter, like an A-frame, may have the ribs of the shelter body exposed above the base of insulative material. If it rains, water can follow the ribs into your shelter and drip on you. This can be addressed by completely covering your shelter and leaving no wooden structure exposed. Keep in mind, as your shelter gets more and more weathered, the insulative material will mat down and you may need to add more material. Repeat the process of layering it from the bottom to the top. If you can "cap" the ridge of your shelter with solid pieces of bark, you'll add a strong layer of protection from precipitation.

SKILL #20
BE WARM THROUGHOUT THE NIGHT

Even when you select enough wood for your campfire, you may not have the right shelter set up yet that will work with an open flame. No one likes to walk away from a warm fire to retreat to a cold shelter. An essential survival skill is learning how to keep warm throughout the night and get the most out of your fire. Even when your fire goes out, it can keep you warm if you apply some sideways thinking and problem solving.

Firewood is all-important when making a campfire. Softwoods like pine, hemlock and cedar can be used to stoke your fire and get it going, but good hardwoods like oak, maple, beech and hickory are better choices for making coals for long burns. In an emergency situation, you will not have the ability to process large pieces of fuel from thick logs. You will simply need to collect more wood with a smaller diameter. Also, you will find as you burn smaller fuel, you will have to tend to your fire more frequently. Whenever possible, burn large logs if you can find them broken off from dead and standing trees. If you only have small logs, you'll just have to keep your fire smaller and sit closer.

If the average night lasts 8 hours, how long do you need to burn a fire for light, warmth and emotional comfort? If I know I have 8 hours until daybreak and only 5 hours of wood, I'll light a fire while simultaneously heating rocks that will be used to keep me warm. When the fire dies down or when I bank it to preserve the wood

Never underestimate how much firewood you will need at night.

from burning too fast, I transition to warming myself with the hot rocks instead of the flame for the rest of the night. I may even make my fire near a large rock wall to heat it as much as possible before bedding down next to it. You should never make a fire under an overhang and sleep under it, as rocks can fracture under heat, making that bed the last you'll sleep in. In winter months, the nights are longer and you must really be selective with how long you burn a fire and how long you heat with rocks.

You can also fill your water bottle with hot water at the start of the night; it will keep you warm for a few hours. Your body heat will then keep the bottle from freezing for the rest of the night. In the morning, you'll be able to drink water instead of having to deal with ice in your bottle.

SKILL #21
COLD-WATER IMMERSION REWARMING

An immersion kit includes the gear needed to make a warming and drying fire.

Being both cold and wet is the definition of misery. Being cold-water submerged is misery and a nightmare scenario for so many. This nightmare plays out each year as people fall through the ice while ice-fishing, fall off of boats or docks and when people slip on rocks while traversing riverbanks. If you have never felt extreme cold-water immersion, it will come as a surprise to you the first time you do. When the water hits your chest, you almost immediately gasp for air as the shock hits your core. If you end up with your head underwater, you will feel like your face is paralyzed from the cold. Arms and legs don't want to move as easily, as blood is pulled from them to keep your core warm. You have a very finite amount of time to get your body out of the cold and rewarmed. When you end up in cold water, you will fall back on instinct, and if you have enough willingness, you'll make it out to where the real hard work begins.

Clothing, when wet, conducts the cold better than just water on your skin. If you have multiple layers on, you need to ask yourself some important questions. This is yet another example of logical order of thinking and how Sayoc problem solving can be applied to the great outdoors. Some important questions to answer begin with "What layers of your clothing are warm when wet?" These include wool and some synthetic fibers like Primaloft. "What layers of your clothes can you ring out and dry out quickly by a fire?" Your answer may include your base layer and possibly your mid-layer shirts. If you are wearing Merino wool base layers, they will provide some insulation when damp, unlike cotton, which loses all of it. As these layers dry out, you'll notice they steam and get warm to the touch. Be careful not to melt synthetic layers, making them useless when you can't put them on again. "Which layers will take the longest to dry?" If you are wearing a heavy wool jacket, you can't expect to dry it in the same amount of time you will your skin and mid layers. You may be cool or cold when you are drying out your heaviest layer and wearing your damp skin and base layers, but at least you'll be warmer than having all of your clothes soaked on your back. One of the most important questions you should ask before all others is "Where is my immersion kit?" If you are traveling in the great outdoors in the winter near a frozen or not-so-frozen water source, you need to have emergency fire-starters ready to go and within reach for those emergency immersion situations.

An immersion kit should include easy-to-use fire-starting devices. These are tools that can be used with limited dexterity in the fingertips. Your grip may be limited only to grasping with all of

The author using a soft-wood twig bundle to demonstrate the fire capable with it.

your fingers like a mitten. You should also have an easily accessible supply of premade tinder to get a fire immediately. This fire-starting equipment should be used in conjunction with small kindling gathered from the immediate area. Since there is a possibility you won't find tinder, you may want to include an emergency candle with multiple wicks in your immersion kit along with a pocket-sized emergency blanket or two. With a blanket draped around your back and a small candle to huddle over, you'll be able to increase the temperature inside the emergency blanket enclosure slowly to rewarm yourself. Another smart addition to your emergency kit are some disposable chemical hand and feet warmers. The packaging is air tight and will survive a dunking. As you warm yourself by your fire, you can open the packaging and apply the packs to your core to help rewarm yourself.

Another really important method of rewarming is physical activity. You can swing your arms to force blood back to your fingertips, sprint in place, do jumping jacks and push-ups and you'll force your body to fight for warmth. Rubbing your hands together and breathing into them will help bring warmth and dexterity back to them. You can also tuck them underneath your armpits or place them inside your pants near your groin. If you have a more technical piece of outerwear on, like a waterproof layer, strip down and wear only that wind/water-resistant layer: it will trap the heat you create as you move and exercise. Focus on getting your body back to stasis. Then worry about the nonessential gear you may have exposed to the water and need to dry out.

At some point, your clothes will dry out when they will feel damp to the touch. You can survive with damp clothes, and perhaps drying out to a state of damp is all you need to make it to your vehicle to dry out further. Then again, damp may feel safe when you really need to be fully dry. If you are able to dry out your clothes this far, you can dry them out completely. The decision will be up to you, and you must think about your scenario logically. The temptation will be there to cut corners, but unless you know you can get to a reliable heat source to fully rewarm, dry out in place before attempting to move to another.

NEXT LEVEL TRAINING

Like all of the skills in this book, you should always learn what gives you success first and then modify your training with added difficulty until you reach a failure point. From there, analyze how to achieve success and try again. For some people, simply camping outside of their homes is a major hurdle to bound over. For others, sleeping outside in a natural-material shelter is their obstacle. Some people will find camping out in their environment comforting, but the idea of extreme heat in the swamp or tropics or the idea of extreme cold in the North or Arctic has no allure.

Shelter can be defined as your vehicle in a stranded car scenario. The needs are the same, and you can find ways to close off some of the vehicle's compartments with a space blanket and warm yourself with intermittent running of the car's heater, a small candle in a can, chemical hand-warming packs on your body and blankets or sleeping bags. Just make sure you keep the exhaust of your vehicle clear and the windows cracked if you want to experiment sleeping out in your car to simulate an emergency situation.

A fun exercise to practice is building shelters into the natural setting that are not meant to be seen. These hides do not stand out but blend into the terrain. They can double as hunting blinds, and the first time you wake up to find an animal nearby that doesn't realize you are nearby is a unique experience. Think of these shelters like a game of hide-and-go-seek. They are fun to build and fun to find if you are working in a group and looking for where your camping friends have set theirs up. The principles of hiding this type of shelter can be applied to hiding a full campsite you regularly go to off the beaten path. If you can hide a sleeping area, you can hide a campfire. Add a Dakota firepit for a serious stealth camping experience.

Shelter classes always have a time limit allotted to construction. It is almost never enough time for the builder's satisfaction. You can always build a particular shelter untimed, then look at how you built it and see if you can shave time from your baseline. You should always know how long it takes to build a shelter so you know when you will need to start building one in an emergency bivouac situation. If nothing else, learning how long it takes to construct a suitable shelter should inspire you to carry a small shelter like a bivy sack, emergency blankets and a highly compressible sleeping bag with you.

You can always take your shelter skills to the next level; whether you get any sleep is another story. I hope you stay warm, dry and cozy.

KNIFE SKILLS

"All blade, all the time." —*Sayoc Kali Concept*

My interest in knives and the emphasis I place on having a good knife is probably like that of many outdoorsmen. After all, the knife is the most important tool you can have in the woods, and for thousands of years, man has carried this tool on his/her person to address various needs. It makes sense that so many outdoorsmen consider it to be their most important and essential tool. Knives satisfy our primal needs. Knives work better than our teeth and nails for cutting. They can be used for defense, and they can help us build tools to prolong our lives. Knives have value to our survival, which is why I place importance on knife skills in my courses. Students are always eager to learn how to unleash the potential of their cutting tools, and it is sometimes that excitement and enthusiasm that blinds their good judgment.

For that reason, prior to instructing my students, I always provide two very important warnings to mitigate the likelihood of self-cutting. First, make sure you respect the follow-through of the blade. That is, if you are cutting through a piece of cordage, consider where that blade will travel in an infinite line. If you

don't want to get cut, don't cut in the direction of your body parts. The second critical instruction point is to be disciplined with where you place your blade. It should either be in your hand or in its sheath. Sticking your blade in a log when you aren't using it is a bad habit. Leaving your knife on a table is equally bad, as you can accidentally brush up against the edge or drop it off the table. In that case, if you goof and drop it, don't try to catch it, as plenty of people have grabbed the blade and not the handle. Much like a firearm, you should know the status of your blade, and that should include its location. Reducing the number of places it could be to two is the first step in demonstrating good blade discipline.

The knife you choose to practice with should be the best you can afford. Be an educated customer and learn the differences between carbon and stainless steels as well as grind types. You should hold the knife in hand and determine if it fits you. Many knives sold today are made by makers, not users. This becomes apparent when examining the sheath. Many makers simply include a sheath to say one is included. What you consider "the best" will vary from the next

The Gossman Knives Polaris was designed by the author.

SKILL #22
KNIFE GRIPS

There are many grips you can use while holding your knife. Assuming you selected a quality knife with a comfortable handle, it will be easy to hold your knife in various ways to accomplish survival tasks easier. When you watch seasoned outdoorsmen use a knife, you'll notice they transition from grip to grip without even thinking about it. They know how to use a blade, and it looks effortless. While you could probably get away using your basic hammer grip with your knife for most cutting tasks, you'll find the other grips that exist make life much easier.

guy to the guy after that. "Best" is a subjective term. What works best on people and looks tactical won't be the best for working on wood and fitting in at a peaceful gathering of hikers. What works best at fine carving probably won't be best for clearing a jungle trail. Understand multiple knives are needed to address multiple missions, and there is no silver bullet.

HAMMER

With four fingers wrapped around the handle and the thumb closing the grip on the other side, this grip is extremely strong. The hammer grip will be used for carving both hard and soft woods and removing all sizes of wood shavings. The hammer grip can be utilized with knives of all sizes as long as the handle provides you enough room to hold on to it.

Hammer grip

Saber grip

Foil grip

Reverse grip

SABER

The saber grip was a grip traditionally used with heavy sabers. From the hammer grip, the thumb is placed on the back of the blade on the unsharpened tang. When a heavy saber is drawn back to the shoulder, the thumb assist prevents the blade from striking the user in the head and helps move it forward. When you apply the saber grip, you put more pressure on the spine and prevent the knife handle from moving around in your hand. The saber grip is also helpful for pushing the blade through material being whittled; however, the saber grip can lead to blisters on the thumb. When knife/sword makers rounded the spines of their blades, this was not as much of a problem, but since the squared spine is common today and used for sparking a ferro rod, it is wise to use the saber grip sparingly.

FOIL

The foil grip is similar to the saber grip in the use of the thumb in contact with the blade; however, instead of putting your thumb on the spine of the blade, you rotate the blade 90 degrees in your palm and place your thumb on the flat of the blade. This grip is often used when fine carving wood. It is also the grip used when applying a chest-lever motion to cleanly cut through branches. The foil grip can be used with the edge of the blade facing left or right to the inside or outside of the body.

REVERSE

At some point when you are using your blade, you may need to turn the edge of the blade toward you. This is most commonly associated with cutting cordage when you hold a bight of cordage in one hand and cut back toward yourself with the other. I often use this reverse grip when pruning small branches from tree limbs. The reverse grip should look familiar to the grip you

Pinch grip

use when in your kitchen with your paring knife. Simply opening and closing your grip facilitates paring with your knife in a modified reverse grip. Anytime you use the paring reverse grip, make sure to keep your thumb out of the way.

GUTTING AND SKINNING

Whenever you are working with gutting and skinning a harvested animal, you should be mindful of where your tip is. To prevent your tip from sinking too deeply, you can support it with a gutting and skinning grip. This grip is accomplished by placing your index finger forward of the grip and along the unsharpened spine of the blade. The knife is held in place with the middle, ring and little fingers. This grip is also used when a fish is cleaned with a non-fillet knife. Caution should be exercised using any knives while cleaning fish, as the protective slime that covers the fish's body makes holding on to a blade slick at times.

PINCH GRIP

The pinch grip is one used for extremely fine carving with the tip of the blade. The further back from the tip you hold your blade, the harder it is to control. Niche cuts and scoring with the tip are best done by controlling the tip as close to the tip as possible. As the name implies, you pinch the blade between your thumb and forefinger, keeping the edge away from your skin. If you have a heavy handled blade, this grip can be hand fatiguing. For short durations, this grip is not difficult to maintain.

ICE-PICK

An ice pick is held with the point facing down and with the thumb capped over the butt of the handle. This grip is commonly associated with criminal activity and thrusting motions, and while it seems like there is no practical purpose for it in the great outdoors, there may be a time when you need to puncture with your tip or place your blade in a log for one-handed fire starting. The ice-pick grip, when done correctly, prevents you from "riding the blade," a term used to describe what happens when the blade stops moving but your hand doesn't. Depending on whether you have your edge facing forward or towards you, that cut will be on the palm or somewhere along the lower joints/pads of your fingers.

SKILL #23

WHITTLE WITH YOUR KNIFE

Whittling is the process of removing little pieces of wood from a larger piece. Remove enough little pieces of wood in a careful and deliberate manner, and you'll be able to carve any number of tools to help you survive. Whittling is a common activity and is a perishable skill, meaning it degrades over time if you don't practice. You'll find your carving ability will improve as you self-discover. You're probably going to make some mistakes along the way, and these shouldn't be discarded as easily as you'll throw that broken-handled spoon in the fire. Catalog these mistakes and figure out what needs to be done correctly next time to avoid the mistake you just made.

Whittling is best accomplished with a sharp controllable knife. Dedicated whittling knives have large smooth handles for comfort and small blades to work inside tight radiuses and corners. The knife you use for whittling should be as sharp as possible, and you'll find you may need to sharpen it during the carving project you're working on. Sharp knives cut more easily than dull ones and require less effort to remove too much material. Forcing a blade through any material can lead to it slipping and causing a nasty wound. Additionally, never use your knife in the dark without good lighting—for obvious reasons. If it is dark, you most likely will be tired, which is another reason not to use your blade for safety. Also, whittling is a slow process, so take your time and don't rush. Rushing is yet another reason that accidents happen with knives.

Whittling will help you learn how to use your knife to its full potential. It will also help you select a knife that will fit your hand and work best for your needs. What you may want in a knife initially may not be what you end up with. The only way to know is to practice. Instead of simply sharpening points at the end of sticks, which you'll learn eventually has a purpose (but shouldn't be the extent of your carving knowledge), practice making common cuts in wood that will be used in your outdoor travels and in survival situations.

PUSH CUTS

Push cutting is when you use the section of your blade closest to your knife handle. This is the most critical area of your blade if you are concerned with carving. A push cut can remove fine slivers of wood or large pieces. In this area where your hand and cutting edge are close to one another, you'll find there is less leverage working against you than if you try push cutting with the belly of the blade.

STOP CUT

When a push cut is done perpendicular to the wood being cut, it severs the fibers in the wood and it is called a "stop cut." If a push cut is done from above or below this perpendicular cut, a small piece of wood will be removed where the stop cut was made previously. If you repeat the process, carving deeper into the stop cut and removing more material in a ramp leading up to the stop cut, you will create a 90-degree latch used in bushcraft camp kitchen pot holders, figure-four trap triggers and wood-to-wood junctions.

90-degree latch

BEVELING

Wood has a tendency of splintering from the outside in whenever enough pressure or force is put on it. It makes sense to bevel the edges of ground stakes, walking sticks and any other tip of wood that is impacted frequently. Beveling can be done by cutting away from you or it can be done with a paring knife grip toward you. Ideally, you will remove wood at a 45-degree angle to the tip. With the wood removed from the edges, the remaining tip will be much stronger and less likely to crack.

TIP "DRILL"

The tip of your knife is not a drill. Tip drilling and prying are not advised, as they are risky and can destroy part of your most important tool. There is a correct way to use your tip, and that is by leading with your edge. Any time you use the tip of your blade to create a depression or a hole in a piece of wood, use the tip in a cutting motion. Insert the tip at an angle to what you're cutting and cut along this angle in a radius. Cutting with the edge

is safer on the edge than prying with it. A word of warning: avoid holding the section of wood you are carving directly in the palm of your hand as you are working your knife with the other hand. Injuries to the palm of the hand happen when blades slip. It's safer to pin the section worked on against a hard, solid surface.

SPINE SCRAPING

Your knife should have a sharp 90-degree spine for ferro rod scraping. This sharpened spine works well for smoothing out the wood you are carving, and it also works great for removing bark from saplings. With your thumb placed on the flat of the blade, you can scrape with the sharpened spine. Move your blade quickly and with light pressure, or apply more pressure and move slower. Use the spine of your knife for this type of scraping whenever you are working your blade perpendicular against material. Should you use your sharpened edge, you'll quickly dull your knife and risk rolling or chipping the edge.

SLICING

While the section of your knife nearest the ricasso/handle is the most important for carving, it is not the only part of the blade you can use for whittling. The length and belly of your blade are what you can use for slicing. Slicing incorporates the whole length of the blade and results in long ribbons of wood or continuous cuts of other mediums (meat, veggies, other foodstuffs) cut away. Some blades, by virtue of how they are designed, make better slicers, as they have curved blades that always contact the wood being cut at an angle.

SKILL #24
CHOP WITH A SHORT BLADE

The knife I carry on my belt varies, but what doesn't are the general dimensions. For almost twenty years, I've carried a compact blade and have made the most of it. I like a smaller blade just under 4 inches (10 cm) long with a handle that is 4¼ to 4½ inches (11 to 11.5 cm) long. By putting my little or ring finger through the small paracord loop lanyard, I can snap cut with the blade and retain it in my hand. While not a true replacement for a large chopping blade, this extended grip stretches the capability of your blade when options are limited. You're more likely to have a smaller blade on you than a large blade, as large blades are so frequently left behind for their added weight and bulkiness. Having the ability to use your primary belt knife is only possible with strong cordage used as a knife lanyard or fob. Do not attempt this if your knife lanyard/fob is heavily worn.

SKILL #25
CARVE FEATHER STICKS

The feather stick, sometimes referred to as a fuzz stick, is a traditional Scandinavian way of transforming wood resources into tinder. Depending on how fine you carve feathers or fuzz from the wood, you may or may not be able to ignite them with just the sparks from your ferro rod.

Feather sticks test your knife skills and help conserve your supply of premade tinder you should have carried from home. To create one, a small branch of seasoned hardwood is split and split again, leaving you with four quarters. Each of these quarters has an inside edge that should be the driest part of the wood. Using your knife, you carefully carve a thin ribbon the length of the split branch. This is best accomplished by taking the high point of the edge and moving only the knife forward or the branch back against the blade held stationary. After a ribbon is formed, the knife or the branch is repositioned and

Extended grip

Making feather sticks tests your knife-handling skills.

Fine feathers can be lit with a ferro rod.

SKILL #26
CREATE CORDAGE WITH YOUR KNIFE

Cordage is one of the most important resources in the great outdoors. You can use cordage to create shelters, catch fish/game, repair broken equipment and much more. Good cordage requires three attributes: length, strength and flexibility. Your knife can help you create cordage by cutting fabric into long strands or using your knife as a blade in a jig for turning water bottles into a flat plastic cord.

A traditional way of making leather lacing from a piece of buckskin was to drive the tip of a blade into a stump or log and use the fixed knife like a third hand to hold the knife in place while you rotate the leather from the outside in with your two hands. The leather was cut into strips that could be rolled and stretched out to create a single long length of flat leather lacing. The same technique can be applied to modern fabrics found in the woods. Old tarps, contractor garbage bags, old clothing or any fabric can be processed with a knife driven into a log. Using two hands, you can cut the fabric into long strips that can be braided together afterwards. You'll find the fixed blade method of cutting fabric is easier to control than piercing the fabric with the blade and ripping it out, while holding the knife in one hand and the fabric in the other.

Assuming your only knife is a Swiss Army knife with a saw-blade feature and you locate 2-liter bottles, you have all you need to create a jig that will process the bodies of the 2-liter bottles into long, flat cordage. To create the jig, a small

rotated so that the edge contacts another high point and another ribbon is formed. This process is repeated over and over until a bundle of curls is left at the end of the stick. You'll notice that various hardwoods respond differently to your blade and feathers are possible with any suitable belt knife or pocketknife blade as long as there is sufficient skill behind it. Three feather sticks are usually enough to get a fire going when all materials are gathered and assembled correctly.

A water bottle jig converts plastic bottles into strong cordage.

SKILL #27
CUT SAPLINGS EFFICIENTLY

Saplings are used to create many survival tools, and from time to time, you'll need to cut them down to assemble shelters. Rather than hacking away at them, which wastes energy, saplings can be safely cut with minimal effort.

Saplings, just like more mature wood, have grain that runs their entire length from roots to tip. This grain is much like long fibers that can be stretched with enough force. You can exploit the grain of the sapling to your advantage in cutting them down. All you need to do is bend a sapling, using your body weight to pull it down, and create a noticeable bend in the trunk at the base. I prefer to hook an arm over the top of the sapling and use my body to hold it in place rather than holding the sapling with the hand not holding the blade. With a hammer grip and the sapling bent at the base, push down on an angle to trunk and rock your blade back at different angles while applying downward pressure. Since the sapling is

branch 3 inches (7.5 cm) in diameter that is free of knots is cut into a 12-inch (30-cm) log. Using your saw blade, you first cut a notch in the end of the log about a third of the width of it across. Rotating the log 90 degrees, a second notch is cut a third of the way across. What you are left with is a perpendicular cut in one of the quadrants of the log off center. Using your saw, about 1 inch (2.5 cm) from the end of the log, make a third cut down to remove the smallest section of the log created with the two previous cuts made to the end of the log. When this section is cut free, a channel remains in the log where the plastic bottle will feed through after the bottom of the bottle is cut off. By cutting off the bottom of the bottle, a cylinder is left behind that will provide the flat cordage. Take the main blade of your Swiss Army knife and insert it, facing the inside of the notch created about ¼ inch (6 mm) from where the third saw cut was made. When the bottle is pulled through the notch and against the knife edge, it will process the bottle into very usable ribbon. One word of advice: before you pull the bottle through and before you insert the knife into the log, cut a small pull tab in the bottom of the bottle to use as a handle.

To cut a sapling, bend it with your body and cut against the grain.

Under tension, a sapling is easily cut against the grain.

SKILL #28
BATON AND CREATE SPLITTING WEDGES

The belt knife you're carrying lacks both weight and length to be an effective chopping tool, but that doesn't mean you can't be resourceful with what you have around you. If you need to use your knife to chop into and split a piece of wood, you can utilize a small log from a broken branch as a baton and strike the spine of your blade. The added weight drives the blade further into the wood than swinging your blade on its own. Batoning has been considered abuse by some outdoorsmen, but as long as it is done correctly, it puts very little stress on the blade. It's also a skill that has grown in popularity over the years, but it has been around for decades. Just make sure when you baton that you keep your blade in line with the grain of the wood and keep the blade horizontal to the ground. Pointing the blade up or down puts excessive pressure on it. Hold the knife with one hand from the handle and a wooden log with the other. Pound down on the spine of the blade to start separating the wood. Repeatedly hit the exposed blade (if you have a 4-inch [10-cm] knife blade, I'll advise only splitting wood 3 inches [7.5 cm] or under in diameter) until the blade works its way through the wood. To avoid damaging the edge, make sure your blade will not drive into the ground but rather another piece of wood serving as a stopper. If you repeat this process, you will turn a small log into halves, halves into quarters and quarters into small kindling.

stressed, it cuts easily. Should you not be able to cut all the way through at first, simply fold the sapling over in the opposite direction and repeat the process.

When you are done cutting your sapling down, you'll be left with a pointy stump sticking out of the ground. For safety, and if possible, use a saw to cut it flush to the ground. This step isn't necessary in a survival situation, but if you are training or traveling where others may step or fall on this point, it is a good practice to flush cut it.

Top: Wooden baton; Bottom: Hardwood wedges

MAKE A BATON

With the whittling skills presented earlier in this chapter, you can create a baton that is more comfortable to use in an extended camp setting. There's a reason why hammers and other hand tools have smaller diameter handles than large ones. Using a round of wood means gripping it with a partially open and partially closed grip. You'll be able to get more work done if you make your tools more user friendly.

Starting with a small round of wood 3 to 5 inches (7.5 to 13 cm) in diameter and 18 inches (46 cm) long, create a stop cut about 6 to 8 inches (15 to 20 cm) from one end. Remove material around the entire circumference of the log until you have a 2-inch (5-cm) circumference. From the end of the log, on the other side of the stop cut from the 6 to 8 inches (15 to 20 cm) you haven't touched yet, baton down to the stop cut. This will create a 12-inch (30-cm)-long x 2-inch (5-cm)-wide handle with a 6- to 8-inch (15- to 20-cm) heavy baton head. Depending on your level of skill and interest, you can bevel the edges and smooth out the handle to be rounder than one with many bevels. This wooden baton will be easier to use and cause less fatigue than using an untouched log for the same purpose.

SPLIT A LOG WITH HARDWOOD WEDGES

Your knife and your baton are two out of the three tools needed to split a large log. The remaining tool is a set of hardwood wedges. These wedges can be carved from quartered rounds or they can be sharpened chiseled tips of branches. As mentioned previously, make sure to bevel the edges of your wedges to prevent them from cracking along the edges.

As long as a log has a natural crack in it, hardwood wedges can expedite the cracking and splitting process. Starting from the end of a crack, insert a hardwood wedge into a piece of wood. It is pounded in with a baton as deep as it will go, and the process is repeated with additional wedges further along the crack. As the crack begins to widen, the width of your wedges must increase too. Many times, the wedges will fall loose and can be wiggled free. Instead of using your tool in a way that will exhaust you, work smarter and not harder.

SKILL #29
CREATE DIGGING TOOLS

Carved to a chisel point on one end and rounded off at the other, the digging stick will help you access wild ramps and other underground edibles like Indian cucumber and trout lily. A digging stick is used like a probe that is first inserted into the ground and then pried to lift the dirt up. To make a digging stick, all you need is a straight or semi-straight green piece of hardwood about 3 feet (91 cm) long and at least 2 inches (5 cm) thick. Using your knife, you remove the bark from about 2 feet (61 cm) of the stick and carve this into a flat, wide and tapered chisel point. On the other end, your knife is used to round the point to serve as a handle where you can push down on the digging stick with the palm of your hand.

When you have your digging stick carved, the next step is to fire harden the digging end. This is accomplished by placing it in a bed of ashes from your fire where there is plenty of heat but no oxygen. The heat will draw all the moisture out of your digging stick and make it rock hard. During this step, make sure you place your wooden tool in ashes and not in the fire or hot coals. Every so often, check your digging stick to see what kind of progress has been made and if the wood makes a sharp sound when tapped with the back of your blade. A dull sound will indicate more moisture content remains and more time is needed in the ashes.

An alternative digging tool is the digging adze. The digging adze is a one-handed tool that resembles an ice climber's ice ax. It is carved from a tree limb with a secondary branch growing off

Left: Digging stick; Right: Digging adze

of it. Using your knife, the tree branch of approximately 2 to 4 inches (5 to 10 cm) in diameter is cut just below the joint where the secondary branch is growing and about 8 to 12 inches (20 to 30 cm) above. The secondary branch is cut approximately 12 inches (30 cm) from where it grows from the trunk. When this section that resembles a *J* is cut off, it is turned over, with the secondary branch forming the eventual handle and the larger tree branch forming the digging adze blade. Using your blade, round off the end of the handle and the top of the digging adze.

Carve the digging adze blade into a flat, wide chisel point.

Starting from the inside of the digging adze blade, carve the tip to a flat and wide chisel point sharpened primarily on one side. On the back side of the digging adze blade, carve just enough of the material away to prevent the blade tip from terminating at the outermost part of the branch. This will prevent it from cracking when it makes a hard impact with a root or rock. Just like the digging stick, the digging adze is fire hardened in ashes.

SKILL #30
MAINTAIN YOUR KNIFE IN THE FIELD

Use your knife enough and at some point, you will need to sharpen it. Even the strongest and toughest super steels will eventually dull. Sharpening is a skill that requires the awareness of multiple senses. While you can see the results of sharpening, the sound and touch the blade makes as steel is removed is equally important. You'll eventually learn to recognize these signs that your knife is becoming sharper. I'll advise practicing with inexpensive blades before you try any of these methods on a knife for which you paid a considerable amount.

Sharpening is a frequently used term used to describe any process that brings a knife up to acceptable sharpness. However, *reprofiling* is the technical term for removing a significant amount of steel from the blade to change its geometry, *sharpening* is removing steel along the bevel and *honing* is the process of realigning the fine "teeth" along the edge that gives a blade its final touch of sharpness before use. You'll find the more you maintain a blade with honing and stropping with each use, the less you'll need to do a major sharpening job on heavy grit stones.

The best sharpening tools you can use are those you'll pack into the woods with your knife. I believe a knife isn't complete unless it has, nearby, a means to sharpen it. Otherwise, you only prepare to use your knife for a short period or until it becomes less sharp. For traditional steels used in knifemaking, which include 01 tool steel and 1095, you can get by with using various grit

Charcoal from your fire can be used as a mild abrasive to remove stains.

the tip. Sharpening is either done tip to heel or heel to tip depending on your preference. When you near the tip of the blade, you need to lift the handle slightly to accommodate the taper of the blade. The amount of pressure you use is the same as shaving. Start with one side of the blade and build up a "wire." This is a very thin piece of steel left on the edge that is visible with the naked eye. After the wire is built up on one side, repeat the process on the other side. When a wire is built up there, alternating single draws of the blade can be done. If you are uncertain whether you are removing steel where you need to be, you can use a permanent marker (like a Sharpie) to color the blade and see where the stone is making contact with the blade. To test the sharpness, you can use the same Sharpie marker to drag the blade across the marker body at an angle. If your knife is sharp, it will bite into the marker and not skip off. If it does skip off, inspect the blade and look to see if there is an irregularity in the blade like a chip, rolled edge, etc. Work from heaviest grits (lower number) onto the finest grits (highest number). Your final step is to strop the blade to hone and polish the edge. If you have compound rubbed into an old belt, place the belt on a flat surface and repeat the process you used on the stones. Don't hold the belt over a void and allow slack in it like you've probably seen barbers do with a straight razor. Leaving too much slack in the blade will allow the belt to roll back on the edge and dull your knife.

The sharpening processes previously described apply to the equipment you carry into the woods. If Murphy's law comes into play, you will have none of the equipment you need and you'll have to improvise. Just like you should learn how to

Arkansas stones; however, for the most modern steels like 3V, CPM154 and A2, a good diamond stone will make sharpening easier. A small length of an old leather belt impregnated with stropping compound can be carried as a hone for daily maintenance. Wet-dry sandpaper in 600, 800, 1000, 1500 or 2000 grit can be used on a leather backer or piece of mousepad as another means of sharpening in the field.

Sharpening your knife is fairly simple, and the most important detail of the process is consistency. Using either a stone or sandpaper backed with leather/mousepad, place your blade flat on the surface and lift the spine off the stone/paper about as high as your knife is thick while keeping the edge in contact. Drag the knife edge, leading with the spine, across the stone/sandpaper starting with the heel of the blade or sharpen inexpensive knives on modern sharpening equipment first, the same idea applies to using makeshift sharpening tools.

The rocks found in dried river beds will vary in texture. Just like the modern sharpening stone that has been cut and processed, you can use a smooth stone polished by the flowing water to sharpen your blade. Find a river stone that has a flat section you can draw your knife blade across. You can sharpen on a rounded rock, but maintaining consistent pressure is more difficult. If you need a more aggressive texture, you can fracture rocks and use the grit found inside to remove more material. If you are in the tropics, try sharpening your tools on a section of bamboo you rub sand into. A rock can be fractured and ground against itself to create a slurry that can be rubbed into the bamboo. If you're looking to hone your blade in the field without a strop, look for discarded glass bottles. The glass can be used like a ceramic rod and give your blade a fine edge. If you need to remove stains or surface rust from your blade, try using hardwood charcoal leftover from an old fire as a mild abrasive. Just rub it against the stain and see if it will polish the blade. These methods aren't perfect—they'll require patience—but they'll have an effect on the blade. In a long-term survival situation, you'll have time on your side. Take your time to maintain your tools.

SKILL #31
MAKE AN IMPROVISED EDGE

"A knifeless man is a lifeless man." That old proverb is partially correct. A knife does improve your survivability, but not having one doesn't mean you can't fashion one. Don't think of yourself as knifeless. If you have the knowledge and skill along with some basic resources to make a sharpened edge, you always have a blade with you.

When I was a child, my father told me how he would often make sharpened tools out of the lids of old tin cans. He would sharpen them on a rock (as described in the previous skill) and use them like pinch knives. The steel from canned goods can be sharpened, but since it lacks real hardness, it won't hold an edge for long. The same can be said of broken bottles. Glass can be used as an incredibly sharp edge, but a very brittle one that won't last during sustained use.

Should you have nothing other than Mother Nature without litter, you can fashion an edge from any number of natural materials. Rocks can be fractured and small shards can be used as pinch knives. Bones can be cracked, too, and the shards can be sharpened on rocks. Broken seashells along the coastline can be used to gut fish. For thousands of years prior to modern steel, man used natural materials to survive. Studying primitive technology is worthwhile—you never know when you'll have to fall back on it.

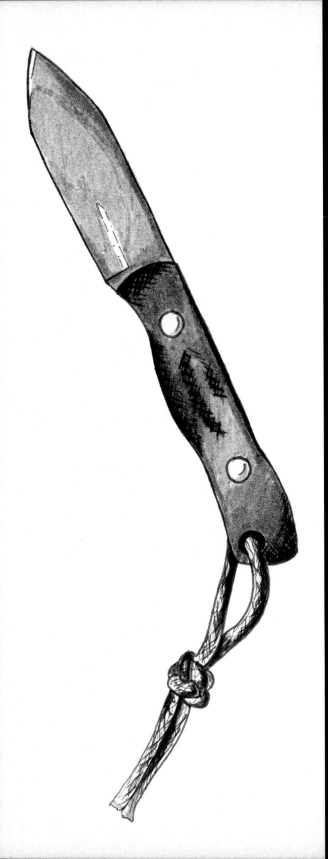

NEXT LEVEL TRAINING

A knife should be an extension of your hand, and after you use your knife for long enough, you'll manipulate it without consciously thinking about it. You'll transition from one grip to the next, and you'll understand the characteristics of the blade and how each inch of the cutting edge performs. The knife you carry should be decided by your needs, not someone else's. Eventually, you'll have a favorite blade you carry, and working with a different knife will feel like you're being disloyal to a good friend. Even though it won't feel right, you should familiarize yourself with as many knives as possible. You never know when you'll need to use a tool that is not your own. You won't always be able to select the best knife, and you'll just have to use the first knife or only knife. Part of your advanced training should include working with tools unlike your own.

Previously in this chapter, I've stated how a small blade can do the work of a large blade. If a 4-inch (10-cm) blade can do some of the work of an 8-inch (20-cm) blade, a smaller blade of 1 or 2 inches (2.5 or 5 cm) should be able to do some of the work of a 4-inch (10-cm) blade, too. During one course I taught, students used scalpel blades and razor blades in camp. This meant creating handles for these blades and hafting them. Using a small blade in a pinch grip, students were able to carve and feather sticks for fire. A razor blade doesn't seem like much of a tool, but when you incorporate training with something that small as your only blade, you tend to use your blade sparingly and more carefully.

Every so often, you should also train with larger blades only. Larger blades tend to be heavier, and working with larger and heavier tools will make your grip stronger for when you return to smaller blades. Larger blades can serve as multiple tools, taking the place of a dedicated chopping tool and a fine carving knife. Larger blades like the machete, khukuri, bolo and golok are often carried as the one tool option by outdoorsmen around the world. Travel to the jungle, and you'll find yourself using your large blade more than any other knife. As a general rule of thumb, the farther you travel from home, the larger your blades should be. I carry a Swiss Army knife daily, but when I go for a hike, I pack a belt knife. When I go on a multiday trip, I have a larger camp knife. When I'm even further from home, I bring a large folding saw and an ax/machete. Learn to use tools of all sizes.

All of the skills in this chapter are essential to your survival. Since many survival situations arise out of emergencies and accidents, it is possible you could have injured one of your hands in a fall. If my Sayoc Kali training has taught me anything, it is the importance of training both sides of my body. When you can accomplish all of the skills described in this chapter, perform them with your other strong side.

As your knife skills improve, you'll find you have better control of your blade. A good test of your ability is to think smaller. Assuming you can whittle a 1-inch (2.5-cm)-wide stick without issue, work to progressively smaller and smaller pieces of wood. As the diameter of the wood you use decreases, the likelihood of breaking what you're working on increases. A great test of knife handling and whittling is to create trap triggers out of wooden match sticks. You may find you need to use a blade with a keener edge to make cuts of that detail. If your skills are on point, the size of the project shouldn't matter.

Think of all knife use as knife training. The more you handle blades, the more comfortable you'll become with them. Even learning how to process food in the kitchen like a professional chef will help increase your blade awareness and handling. Try your hand at competitive cutting challenges and see how well your technique stands up to the pros. Sign up for a knife-making class with a maker or blacksmith to learn more about what makes one blade function better than another. It's all training, and there is value in it if you understand how it helps your overall understanding of knife skills.

CORDAGE SKILLS

"When you get to the end of your rope, tie a knot in it and hang on."
—President Franklin Delano Roosevelt

Long before nails and screws, man lashed materials together with cordage. Good cordage is a godsend, and you'll be surprised what you can do with it. What makes material "good" for cordage are three attributes: length, strength and flexibility. All three attributes must be present in a material for it to be considered "good."

I believe cordage skills are essential to the outdoorsman; you need not be in an emergency or survival situation to use them. We tie our shoes, we police up wires from our electronic devices and we bundle up our garbage bags for trash collection. We use knots and manipulate cordage to some degree in our everyday activities. In the great outdoors, we need to draw upon our cordage knowledge more.

There are many knots—hundreds of knots—you can learn for every purpose. Specific knots exist for tying cargo to roof racks, hooks to fishing line, rope to climber's harnesses and paracord around the shaft of your hiking stick. During survival courses, I teach students at least a dozen knots as a basic foundation, and I've shown upwards of three dozen knots in the course of a weeklong class. While knot names

are important in training to help ensure proper communication, in an emergency, you need not worry about the knot name as long as you remember how to tie it.

Whenever you work with cordage, you should recognize its durability. Synthetic lines are pound for pound both stronger and more durable than their natural fiber counterparts. They will resist exposure to elements better and will also resist abrasion when they come in contact with rough surfaces. When you work with 550 paracord, you will want to carry it with you in your shoelaces, as the lanyard cord for your knife and bundled in short hanks tucked in your kit where you have extra space.

The natural cordage you may work with is prone to failure when it is stressed too much or shock loaded. To make the strongest natural cordage, work with dried fibers that you soak prior to using them. This will reduce the amount of shrinkage you experience when working with green fibers with plenty of moisture content. Keep in mind too that knots weaken line, and some knots preserve the strength of the line better than others. If you struggle with making natural

To make a simple three-strand braid, work from the outside to the center on alternating sides.

SKILL #32
MAKE CORDAGE

There is a lot of trial and error when you first learn to make good cordage. Cordage making is not the easiest of the essential skills you will acquire, and you will get better at it with repeat practice. It is worthwhile to learn from your mistakes and catalog them. This involves writing down what plants you use, in what condition you found them and how durable they were. You may find a plant in the outdoors you have never worked with only to try it out and realize it doesn't lend itself to twisting, braiding or wrapping of any sort. When you find the plants you can consistently turn into good cordage, log them. These are the ones you should actively take note of as you travel through the backcountry. Learning how to make cordage from appropriate materials requires experience and understanding of where to look, how to gather what you need and how to process the raw materials into a finished product.

Cordage can be made from the inner bark of some trees like the basswood, willow and tulip poplar. This requires finding a tree where the bark is ready to separate or purposefully removing it with a knife and expediting the process. It can also be made from invasive vines like the bittersweet and grape vine. Some of these vines can be easily worked when they are living, but as they dry out they become extremely stiff. Some cordage is found underground in root systems of trees with the best being spruce roots. Roots make great quick cordage; I've used them to make fish traps on many occasions. They can be stripped of their outer layer and split easily

cordage, keep practicing and carry more synthetic cordage until your skills improve. Much like the bow drill can inspire you to pack a lighter with you, natural cordage skills may inspire you to carry a lightweight synthetic alternative daily. With some cordage having a breaking strength that far exceeds the strength of human hands, having a sharp knife to cut free in case of entanglement is good practice. With all cordage, make sure you keep it clean of debris as dirt can work its way into it and abrade it from within. Also, whether in the field or at home, keep your cordage away from chemicals and heat, as that will degrade it too.

Milkweed reverse-wrapped cordage.

SKILL #33
REVERSE WRAPPING

By twisting a flat piece of fabric or a bundle of fibers, you can easily create a crude round length of cordage. Twisted fibers and fabrics will unravel and the cordage will come undone if they are not twisted or wrapped around something else. An old technique that uses twisting for creating cordage that will not unravel is called reverse wrapping. This technique is found in countless indigenous communities around the world, and you've likely handled a length of cordage made from it. The technique may seem complicated at first, but after a while, it can be done without looking and while holding a conversation with someone.

Reverse wrapping can be accomplished with natural or synthetic materials. It can be done with natural fibers or existing finished cordage you wish to strengthen by doubling it. The process of reverse wrapping prevents the cordage from unraveling as the two strands of fibers or cords oppose one another. The friction between the two cords is the force that holds them in place. The reverse wrapping process also allows you to create an infinite amount of cordage with natural materials.

You can easily learn to reverse wrap with a small length of paracord. Holding it between your two hands with just your thumbs and forefingers, twist one side away from you while twisting the other side toward you. Make sure you don't start directly in the center of a piece of thread, as you will need one side longer than the other when it comes time to add more fibers or material to lengthen your cord. Continue twisting the paracord until a loop is formed.

between thumbs and forefingers. These can be stored in a container of water to keep them from drying out until they are needed. Cordage can be made from other natural materials like animal sinew and hides. A knife can be fixed in place by sticking it into a log as the animal hide is rotated around to create lacing. Even the litter and garbage left behind and discovered by the survivor can be used as makeshift cordage. Wires can be scavenged from vehicles, spiderwebs of lines can be found along beaches and plastic bags can be cut into strips and wrapped into lines.

As long as you remember cordage needs to be long, strong and flexible, with some trial and error, you will discover it. If cordage can't be broken between your hands, doesn't snap as you wrap it around your palm or forearm and has sufficient length, you should find plenty of uses for it.

This loop is then pinched with the left thumb and forefinger and the fibers are held stacked on top of each other vertically. This usually just requires turning the loop 90 degrees where the twist of the cordage is on the side of your thumb and forefinger closest to your right hand. At this stage, the top cord, and only the top cord, is pinched with the right thumb and forefinger and it is twisted away from you. Without letting it go, the bottom cord is picked up with the back of the forefinger and twisted along with the top cord to where the bottom cord becomes the top cord. If that seems confusing, it isn't when you get the feel for it. Another way to describe this process is by remembering to twist the top one away, and twist two back.

As you experiment and practice with reverse wrapping, you'll find some fabrics will be easier to handle wet and others dry. Reverse wrapping can help you transform plastic bags into incredibly strong rope. You'll find some naturally harvested materials are better left to completely season where there is little to no moisture content left in their cells. This is because green plant fibers will fall apart and loosen as they lose their moisture content. For this reason, I only make quick cordage with green fibers and understand its limitations.

At some point when you reverse wrap cordage, you will need to add more material to make your cordage longer. When you started the process, you left one side longer than the other when that initial loop was formed. As you come close to the end of the fibers on one end, you will need to splice in additional fibers. Splicing should always be done one side at a time. If done correctly, splicing will be very difficult to notice

A strip of cotton from a T-shirt reverse wrapped for a demonstration.

and should be just as strong as the sections of your cordage where there isn't a splice. All you need to do to splice in more fibers is position additional fibers along the length of the shorter piece and extend it past the point where the last reverse wrap connected the strands. Treat the additional fibers and the shorter strand like a single strand and continue your process of reverse wrapping. The twists and wraps will hold it in place until you reach the other side of the original two strands that will need to be spliced as well. When the cordage is ready to be used, you can cut the ends of the spliced in strands from the main cordage to keep it uniform.

SKILL #34
BRAID CORDAGE

A five-strand braid will turn out flat.

Cordage can be doubled on itself for additional strength. Rope can be braided from multiple strands of line and thicker rope can be braided from multiple strands of thinner rope to increase its load-bearing capacity. Braids have the ability to strengthen cordage without stressing it too much. Multiple lengths of paracord knotted every 1 foot (30.5 cm) will be weaker than multiple lengths of paracord braided together. Instead of braiding grass, you can braid jute twine, paracord or flat webbing in case you need rope with more breaking strength.

The braid you use will depend on the number of lengths of cordage you have. The most basic braid is done with three strands. The process is quite simple. Take three lengths of cord and lay them parallel to each other or suspend them from a single point. If you have a small piece of duct-tape, you can hold them together at the end to prevent one end from unfurling. This three-strand braid can be made into a six-strand variation by working with two lines at once that are treated as one. All you have to do is make sure the doubled up lines don't twist over one another for a symmetrical appearance.

Some of the braids you can learn create flat cordage while others create round. The variations of braids for decorative bracelets and long hair are numerous, and some are extremely complicated and detailed. In a survival situation, simplicity should be more important than style. To increase the strength of cordage, additional lines are added to the braid with emphasis placed on simplicity. A four-strand braid is created with two lines folded in half to create four. Starting with the center of each strand, the lines are crossed perpendicularly. The line at the top of the cross is folded down, crossed over itself and then aligned with the line at the bottom of the cross. Working from either the right or the left, the braid is accomplished by following the pattern "behind two, back over one." The same process is done on the opposite side and it continues alternating along the length of the braid. During the braiding process, every so often you can roll the braid on your leg to make it round. This is especially helpful when working with leather lace or rawhide.

The process you use to make a braid with five strands will be exactly the same as the braid you make with seven, nine or eleven strands. The braid you make will turn out flat, and it can be used as a carry strap for your gear, a belt or any other wide strap you may need. To create the five, seven, nine or any other odd-number strand braid, the lengths of line are laid out flat, parallel and adjacent to one another. The strand on the far left of the group of five is then weaved in the following pattern; "over, under, over, under" working to the right. The far left you just worked with becomes the far right. You continue working with the far left in the same manner and each time a line is weaved from left to right, the braid is dressed up for neatness.

SKILL #35
SIX ESSENTIAL KNOTS

Overhand knot

There are knots for rock climbing, boating and tree climbing you may have never heard of and will only learn if you spend considerable time in those circles. Knots were designed with purpose, and some purposes are too specific to be considered essential across all interest areas. After asking some of my students to log what knots they used while addressing bushcraft and survival needs, they presented me with some consistent names. What I realized is that there are a handful of knots more frequently in use than others. I've also found that knowledge of certain knots helps flow into the understanding of others.

THE OVERHAND KNOT AND ITS VARIATIONS

This knot is perhaps the first most people learn to tie. Crossing one end over another (left over right *or* right over left) and pulling tight, the overhand knot is simple and easy to understand. This is generally the first knot you tie when you tie your shoes. You have a right and a left side. There is usually a bow that is tied after it since the overhand knot alone is inadequate to keep your shoes tied. The overhand knot lends itself to an understanding of others. Wrapping one of the ends back through the loop for a second pass results in a surgeon's knot. The surgeon's knot received its name appropriately from the knot commonly used by doctors during surgeries when a quickly tied and secure holding knot is necessary. The surgeon's knot will not come undone as easily as a standard overhand knot, and it has also been used to secure bundles of small fuel for the fire as well as sleeping bags to backpacks.

If you need more of a quick-release knot, you can tuck one end of the surgeon's knot back through the loop you made and pull the half bow to tighten. If you pull the end you passed back through the loop, your surgeon's knot will end up a simple overhand and it will loosen with very little coaxing. If you tie right over left and then left over right, you create a square knot. This is a very common knot that is used for joining line of equal diameter. This knot should always be backed up with a single overhand knot tied on each working end. The square knot is also the foundation for most of the paracord bracelets sold in sporting goods stores. Those bracelets simply repeat right over left, left over right, right over left, over and over around a center core. Should you only tie right over left repeatedly over a core, you'll end up with a spiraling design. Even the simple half hitch, a knot used to tie off bundles of line coiled up, multiple wraps of line around a post or even the legs of a hog in true hog tying, is a version of the overhand knot where the working end is passed over the running end and pulled through. There are other variations of the simple overhand knot, but understanding of the basic knot helps build on the comprehension and learning of the advanced knots that share its simple instructions.

Clove hitch

CLOVE HITCH

There will be times when you need to attach a line to a post or pole to secure an end while you work with the other end. This is an easily adjustable way to secure cordage to one end of a bow drill for friction fire, and it can be used in lieu of a girth hitch (described later in this chapter) for square lashings and tripod lashings. The clove hitch is sometimes used to start a ridgeline for a tarp on one side of two trees, and the bark from the tree around which it is tied will hold it in place securely. It is an excellent knot to know when working with natural cordage you harvest and process from the land.

TRUCKER'S HITCH

There are occasions when you want to tighten some lines as taut as humanly possible. Strapping a canoe to a roof rack and stringing up a ridge line for a tarp are two such instances that readily come to mind. To get the most out of your line and prevent any slack in it, mechanical advantage can be added with the trucker's hitch. The trucker's hitch is made from a loop that is twisted and formed on itself, as the working end is partially pulled through the loop forming a second loop. The working end is wrapped around the fixed pole

you wish to run your line to and pulled through the loop you made. This forms a makeshift block and tackle to give you more leverage when you pull on the line. Use caution when pulling the trucker's hitch tight, as pulling it too quickly can break your line. The working end can be worked back to the post you just tied around and finished in any number of ways to secure it.

FIGURE OF EIGHT

The figure of eight knot is frequently found in climbing circles. The figure of eight knot resembles the number eight and is easily untied, even after a lot of force has been applied to it. Some knots are almost impossible to untie without tools, impossibly small fingers of incredible strength or your teeth. The figure of eight is not one of these difficult-to-untie knots. It is an excellent knot to use as a backup knot and a double figure of eight can be used to create a loop that will not tighten or loosen on you.

Figure of eight loop

A quick release bowline and a tangle-free bundle of paracord.

IAN'S KNOT

If you have swapped out your shoelaces with paracord, this knot will hold stronger than your average shoelace knot. Paracord has a slick outer braid that tends to loosen as you walk. The Ian's knot is a solution to this problem and it requires only a single additional step to your standard shoelace knot. Starting with a simple overhand knot, you generally create a set of loops (sometimes referred to as "bunny ears") or you create one loop with one lace and wrap it with the other. In either case, you pull one loop through the center of the knot while holding the other loop taut. This knot will hold securely on paracord or other laces, and it is the only knot I use to tie my shoes.

STORAGE AND STACKING

A simple way of coiling your line is to work in figure eights. If you hold your line in the palm of your hand, it is wrapped to the outside of your thumb, around it to the inside of your palm to the outside of your little finger, to the inside of your palm and this outside, inside, outside, inside pattern is repeated until you run out of line. The entire bundle is wrapped with the last few feet of your line, and it is finished with a simple half hitch. When the cordage is needed, the end you started your coil with can be pulled out, and it will not tangle as you deploy as little or as much line as you need.

SKILL #36
JOIN LINES OF DIFFERENT DIAMETERS

Whenever we discuss cordage, we need to accept the reality that there is a chance our cordage will come up short. In times like these, you can either rework your cordage, hoping to place that tent peg closer or hoping a single wrap around that load-bearing bar on your vehicle will hold your canoe as a double wrap, or you can use cordage of varying diameters to increase the overall length of your line.

Joining multiple lines of different diameters can lead to problems. The thinner diameter cord has the potential of slipping around the thicker diameter cord. Depending on what cordage is being used, some of the outer braids are slick and don't hold well against other lines. Joining lines of different diameters is an essential skill.

The square knot is most commonly used for joining lines of equal diameter, but it fails when one of the two lines joined together is of a different diameter. With enough pressure, the smaller diameter cord will pull through and around the larger diameter cord. The solution to joining two lines is the sheet bend. The sheet bend relies on tension against itself to hold true. The larger diameter line is formed into a bight, or *U* shape. The smaller diameter line is passed up through the *U*, wrapped around it and then the smaller line is tucked underneath itself. As it is tensioned, the force the smaller line places on itself is enough to hold it in place. If you want to make sure the smaller diameter line is even more secure, a simple overhand knot can be tied in the end as a stopper/safety knot.

A sheet bend joins lines of different diameters.

Square knot

The sheet bend can be used to join paracord to jute or jute twine to bank line or bank line to monofilament fishing line. Whenever setting up a bear bag, I usually use a thinner line tied to a rock to throw over a tree branch. I then attach the thinner line to the hauling line to which the bear bag is attached. There are other occasions you'll discover in which it is easier to throw a weighted line where joining lines of different diameters will be essential.

SKILL #37
THE FRICTION SAW

A friction saw can be made with nothing more than a length of 550 paracord or Kevlar cord about 3 feet (91 cm) long and some elbow grease. Two loops or knobs are tied in the ends of the cordage for use as handles. The cordage is passed around the material you wish to cut through. Using a push and pull motion, the cordage is run back and forth in a single area along what you want to cut. As the friction builds between your cordage and the material being cut, so does the heat. With enough heat, the synthetic material you're cutting will melt. The friction saw will cut through plastic sheeting, climbing rope and nylon webbing to name a few. The longer your cordage, the less your cordage will heat up as the heat will be dissipated over a larger area while still being concentrated in a single area on what you are cutting.

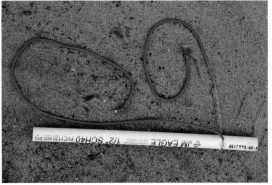

Friction can cut through a synthetic cord and PVC with ease.

The friction saw has been used by tradesmen to cut through PVC piping, and it is a popular skill to teach in anti-illegal restraint courses. For the outdoorsman, it has many uses and also illustrates an important concept. When using synthetic cordage to tie certain knots, you can't pull your line/rope through too quickly or else you run the risk of burning through your line. The trucker's hitch is a prime example of where this can happen. If cordage is to be treated with care, we need to remember what can cause our cord to deteriorate.

Another variation of the friction saw is operated with your legs. If you lack sufficient arm strength or find a situation where your hands are tied, literally or figuratively, you can "ride the bicycle" with each foot placed inside a loop and the saw wrapped around the object you're trying to cut. You may never need to use your legs in conjunction with a friction saw, but carrying the knowledge of how to do so weighs nothing.

SKILL #38
SQUARE LASHING

Using nothing more than paracord and natural materials like branches that conveniently grow on trees, you can build single steps, raised beds and ladders. My students have used square lashing techniques to lash poles across the span between two trees to create seats, raised jungle beds and latrines. Before nails, cordage was used to build structures, and square lashing was the method of tying poles perpendicular to each other.

Square lashing is relatively easy and requires two motions: wrapping and frapping. It requires a good deal of cordage, but as long as it is done correctly, I wouldn't consider the amount needed excessive. A square lashing begins with sturdy poles free of rot and flex. For the purpose of this explanation, let's assume the poles are 3 inches (7.5 cm) in diameter. A girth hitch, also known as a lark's head or cow hitch, is created around one of the poles and close to the other pole. About 1 foot (30.5 cm) of line is left on one side of the hitch with 5 feet (1.5 m) on the other. The wrapping of a square lashing is done by working the 5-foot (1.5-m) length of line "up, around, down, around" three times, never crossing over the intersection of the poles or wrapping completely around any of the individual poles. When three wraps are made, the running end is frapped in between the two crossed poles and over all of the fraps. With each frap, the line is pulled tight. This tightens up the wraps, making the connection very secure. The combination of wrapping and frapping is tied off with the running end to

Wrapping goes around the poles. Frapping goes between them.

the 1-foot (30.5-cm) piece of cordage left behind from the initial girth hitch.

If you are creating a simple step on a single tree, you can tie a single square lashing in the center of a pole, but it will sacrifice some stability. You can climb on it with your hands held vertical and feet horizontal. There will be some movement in the horizontally lashed pole, but you should be fine as long as you keep your feet near the vertical pole/tree. A more secure setup is when two square lashings are made on each end of a horizontal pole. This resembles a more traditional ladder, and it will hold a significant amount of weight without movement. If you square lashed green poles, you will likely have to retie them when the wood seasons, since the wood will contract and the lashing will become loose.

As with any climbing activity, the higher you climb, the greater the danger. The higher you climb, the greater the chance of mechanical injury should you fall.

SKILL #39
ASSEMBLE A TRIPOD

Tripods have been used in traditional camps for hundreds of years. They are versatile, strong, vary in size and can be assembled quickly with nothing more than three stout poles and a length of cordage. Tripod construction changes the way you experience the outdoors. They can be used in the camp kitchen, for raised shelters, to construct smoke generators and so much more. As I tell my students, what you do with a tripod is limited only by your imagination.

There are various ways to assemble tripods, but one of the strongest, described here, uses the same concept of wrapping and frapping as the square lashing mentioned in the previous skill. Depending on how thick your tripod poles are, the length of the cord you use to assemble it will vary. A very lightweight tripod for use in a camp kitchen, for instance, may be constructed out of poles no thicker than your thumb and only require a few feet of cordage. A tripod built from poles as thick as your forearm, on the other hand, may require much more cordage to wrap and frap. The three poles you are using for your tripod need not all be the same length and thickness. You can always kick out the legs at different angles to compensate for the length of one or more poles.

When you have three poles cut from hardwood and free of rot, line them up where two poles are parallel to each other and in line with one another. The third pole is placed in the middle between the other two, with most of the pole's length extending outward and parallel to the other two. You should have only about 1 foot (30.5 cm) of overlap where all the three poles are in line with one another. A girth hitch is placed around one of the outside poles with 1 foot (30.5 cm) of cordage left over on the short end to use later on to tie it off. The longer end of the girth hitch is used to wrap the three poles at three times. It helps if you prop up the three poles on a log so you don't have to fish the paracord out from underneath the poles with your fingers. Once you have three strong wraps, you frap in between the first and second pole three times, pulling tight on the cordage each time to ensure the wraps tighten down. After frapping between the first and second poles, you frap between the second and third poles in the same manner. After pulling tightly on these fraps, secure the running end of your line to the short end of the girth hitch you created on the first pole with a simple square knot. With all three poles secured, wrapped and frapped to create this tripod lashing, you can lift the tripod up and kick the legs out. You'll notice one of the ends will fit on top of the other two poles in the crook created.

The more vertical the tripod is erected, the more strength it will have, but also the less stability. The more the legs are kicked out, the more strength is sacrificed for stability. Depending on your needs, you may want a larger footprint and elect to have the legs spread out farther. If you are using your tripod over a fire to suspend your cooking pot, you might want the tripod to stand taller where the lashing is kept further from the flames. The beauty of the design is the adjustability and portability. Once your tripod is lashed together, you can move it easily and set it up anywhere at varying heights.

Wrapping runs perpendicular to the tripod legs. Frapping runs parallel.

Tripod legs spread out into position.

A tripod can be reinforced with additional poles, and with an added tarp, it becomes a shelter. Two tripods can be assembled separately with horizontal poles square lashed to their legs. Additional horizontal poles can be placed perpendicular to these, and a jungle bed can be created above the ground. A ridge pole can be placed between two tripod peaks, and a tarp can be draped over the top. Tripod legs can be square lashed together to create a platform inside the framework of the legs. This platform can be used as a table, a base for a smoke generator to signal with or used in conjunction with a tarp or blanket on the outside and a smokey fire underneath to smoke food placed on the platform. As mentioned before, you have options and unlimited potential for building essential camp structures when you carry the knowledge of how to build a tripod.

Tripods might seem like a luxury in camp, but once you learn to assemble one, your viewpoint will change and you'll consider them essential camp gear. Even if you don't have paracord or premade cordage, you can assemble a sturdy tripod with natural cordage like bittersweet or spruce roots. You can also use forked and *Y*-shaped sticks to help support your tripod without sufficiently strong cordage. Experiment with tripods as well as how to construct them, and you'll find ways to unlock the outdoors.

SKILL #40
HAUL GEAR

From vehicle recovery to hauling gear up a mountain to removing canoes stuck on rocks, cordage skills can be a lifesaver.

One cordage skill with a very practical purpose is the concept of 3-2-1 anchoring. If you think of a single tent peg pounded into the ground, it is only as strong as the earth around it and can be pulled free with enough directional force. Now imagine bracing that single tent peg by running lines from it to two additional stakes behind it. From these two additional stakes are lines that run to three stakes in another row. The 3-2-1 anchor is a ground anchor system that can be constructed when there isn't a strong fixed anchor in an open field. All that is required are six large wooden stakes, a few lengths of paracord to connect the stakes from the top of the stake(s) in front to the lower part of the stake(s) below and a wooden mallet to pound them in. This anchor system has been used to pull cars with a come-along winch, and it will hold hundreds if not thousands of pounds of weight before pulling free.

I know what you're probably thinking. An anchor system like that is great, but you can't whip up a winch or a come-along out of paracord alone. With good cordage, usually a strong rope, a stout branch is placed perpendicular around a log. A length of rope is wrapped around the log and looped around the branch. The log and branch rotate as one and the leverage on the branch helps spin the cordage around the log. This method is called a "flip-flop winch" or

windlass. Caution must be exercised using this setup since it is under tension, and letting go of the branch can easily lead to a black eye or lost tooth. In the same way this winch is used to pull vehicles horizontally, it can be adapted to lift objects vertically.

What goes up must come down. Simply holding on to a line with your bare hands is a recipe for rope burn. One of the easiest and safest ways of lowering an object is with a munter hitch. This hitch can be tied over a single carabiner or it can be threaded through an exposed root or tree branch that has been smoothed out to reduce friction. The munter hitch positions the cordage used around itself, where tension crushes the line and serves as a brake. The munter hitch and learning how to apply pressure to safely lower objects or a lot of pressure to stop their descent are essential survival skills.

The prusik knot can be used as an emergency brake in your hauling setup should your raising or lowering method fail. The prusik is a knot traditionally used for ascending lines, and it operates with tension that causes friction. When there is no tension on the line, the prusik knot will slip freely along the rope to which it is tied. It can be slipped in either direction freely, but when it is tensioned, the knot tightens around the rope and locks it in place. Traditionally used by alpinists and climbers, the prusik knot was used for ascending a rope should there be no other means of climbing. Cords were tied into loops, and these loops could be tied into prusik knots. One of two prusik knots is attached to the climber's harness, and the climbing rope and the other, attached higher on the climbing rope, is used as a step.

Heavy objects can be hauled with basic knot knowledge.

There may come a time when you need to haul gear or a package on the end of a rope, and along with this need comes the possibility your hands will tire. You can use a prusik knot to give your hands a break. With one prusik loop tied to a fixed anchor like a root of a large tree or around a rock, the other end can be tied to a rope. This skill should be tested and developed with light loads; it would be wrong and dangerous for me to suggest trying to use this knot and hauling method in a manner that could harm yourself or someone else; however, you must make your own decisions in an emergency, and how you use it is ultimately up to you.

SKILL #41
CREATE A FISHING NET

Something you can make with cordage that significantly increases your chances of eating is a simple fishing net. Sized small enough for a scoop net or larger for a gill net, fishing nets are not difficult to tie as long as you have enough cordage and time.

Fishing nets must be tied correctly to work. Smaller fish can escape through the grid pattern if it is sized too large. If the wrong knots or cordage are used, larger fish can damage your efforts. What has proven to be effective in small streams are fishing nets made from 550 paracord. The inner cords are removed and used to tie the net body and the outer braid/sheath is used to form the perimeter of the net. Starting with a length of paracord stretched between two vertical poles and tied horizontally, the inner strands are tied with a girth hitch or lark's head knot to the outer braid at equally spaced-out intervals. For most freshwater fish like trout, bass and perch, these intervals will have to be at least half the thickness of the fish you intend to catch. The inner strands will not stretch, and the knots must be pulled tight. When all the strands are suspended from the horizontal paracord outer braid, they create running lines easily numbered from left to right.

Starting with the second and third lines created from the first and second girth hitch, an overhand knot is tied so the knot falls at the right, equal distance from the horizontal paracord it originated from. Moving to the fourth and fifth paracord inner lines, this process is continued until an entire row of knots is suspended

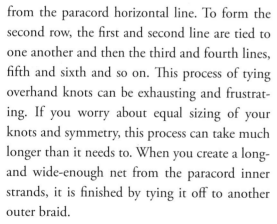

A basic gill net created out of less than 15 feet (4.5 m) of paracord.

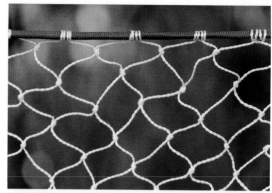

This 550 paracord has all the materials needed to catch fish in a net.

from the paracord horizontal line. To form the second row, the first and second line are tied to one another and then the third and fourth lines, fifth and sixth and so on. This process of tying overhand knots can be exhausting and frustrating. If you worry about equal sizing of your knots and symmetry, this process can take much longer than it needs to. When you create a long- and wide-enough net from the paracord inner strands, it is finished by tying it off to another outer braid.

This paracord net will work as designed as long as it is used in an appropriate manner. Your net need not span the entire width of a creek if you are able to divert the water through a narrow channel by building it up with rocks. You can also use a bent sapling branch to create a hoop the net can stretch across with slack in the center. This scoop net works exceptionally well for catching bullfrogs. As with any trapping device, how it is placed and how it is used are just as important as how it is built.

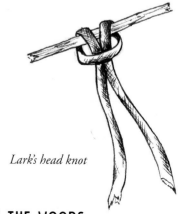

Lark's head knot

NEXT LEVEL TRAINING

I practice cordage making frequently, and whenever possible, I challenge myself to use less of the paracord, Kevlar thread and jute twine I pack with my gear and more of what I can harvest off the land. There are many challenges to help you take your skills to the next level. You can see how strong you can make your cordage, how many feet (30.5 cm) of cordage you can make in a 10-minute period, how many varieties of cordage you can find on a given trip and if you can learn new cordage techniques like leg rolling and other braids.

You can handicap your training by using cordages you are not familiar with that may be sub-par. Instead of using paracord for your bow-drill fire-making practice, try using the bottom hem of your T-shirt or a length of leather lace. See if you can catch a fish with nonstandard fishing line you've scavenged from out of a junk pile or see if that junk pile has what you need to fashion a pack frame with shoulder straps. If you want a better understanding of cordage, learn how to sew and learn how to stitch, as it will help you assemble container crafts. If you can stitch with proper needles and thread, you will understand how to stitch with makeshift bone needles and natural cordage materials.

There are hundreds of knots you can learn to tie, and some are purely decorative. Some knots are specific to boating, others are specific to climbing and others still are found in some areas of the world being used by locals for hundreds of years. The knots you learn to tie can be done holding the running end of the rope with your right hand or they can be done with your left. You can commit yourself to learning a knot a week or finding out how to create a different braid or decorative lanyard stopper knot a month. Cordage kept sailors entertained when nothing else did during the age of the great mariners of history. It still has this potential today. Keep a short hank of cordage in your pocket and you can practice every day to tie the knots that may one day save your life.

ILLUMINATION SKILLS

"It is during our darkest moments that we must focus to see the light." —Aristotle

Something every single human being cannot overcome is our vision. We don't have eagle eyes to see detail at long distances, and we certainly don't have big eyes to see clearly in darkness. For this reason, we must be prepared for encountering darkness. We must always carry a flashlight to make up for our limited vision.

There are some who say carrying a flashlight is foolish or burdensome. A basement can become a dark trap in a power outage, and even in the broad daylight, you can find darkness. Also, for the person who believes a flashlight will be too much to carry, there are some incredibly bright lights available about the size of a standard ballpoint pen and some about the size of a car key fob.

In today's day and age, we must be prepared for addressing both natural emergencies and man-made emergencies. We can't plan for when we will need to see through darkness, fog, smoke or dust. Carrying a flashlight is smart, and I

make it a point to tuck one in my left-hand front pocket on a daily basis. With many options at all different price points, battery sources, output, activation methods, run times and design features, there is a light out there for everyone. Don't get caught up too much in the idea of lumens, by the way. Lumens are one measure of a light and candela is another. If a light has 1000 lumens but can't throw a beam 50 feet (15 m), it may not be what you're looking for if another light of only 250 lumens can throw a beam 100 yards (91 m). Find the right blend of lumens and candela as well as the right beam that combines the spotlight and floodlight in a combination that works for you.

The benefits of having a good light outweigh the inconvenience, if there really is one, of carrying one. My eyes aren't getting any larger, stronger or better equipped to see at night, so until then, I'll have a light in my everyday carry.

SKILL #42
PROPER LIGHT DISCIPLINE

Flashlight technology has become incredible; the most powerful lights of yesteryear can't compare with the average output of a modern handheld flashlight. Modern flashlights are lightweight, easily portable and are usually equipped with LED bulbs that cannot break. They are bright enough to illuminate your path from a great distance and let you visually and facially identify a person in the pitch black from 25 yards (23 m) or more. These lights are a true blessing if you have one, but they can be detrimental to your safety if you don't exercise caution. You must manage light output in some way, or you will end up seeing white spots and ruin your natural night vision.

When you only have a light with a high-intensity setting, it is natural to want to use all the light and see where you need to. We tend to look at the center of the beam instinctively, but looking at the spotlight can ruin how our eyes have adjusted for the darkness. You can walk your light's beam onto your target using only as much light to illuminate it as is necessary. Depending on where you are, you can also bounce the light off of an object nearby and use the ambient light to see what you need to see. By doing this, you aren't looking directly at the light and may even have it facing the opposite direction of what you need to see. The light reflected off the surface may be enough and should not affect how you see in the dark.

Avoid "bleaching" your vision by reflecting too much light off yourself while reading documents.

If you only have a high-intensity light and need to read a document at night, perhaps a map or notes in your field manual, you can press your light against your chest where the bezel of the light is flush with your body. By tilting the light, you can control how much light is released. A similar technique is using your light inside a chest pocket of your shirt or holding a light fabric over the head of your flashlight to diffuse the beam.

SKILL #43

FERRO ROD QUICK LIGHT

The ferrocerium rod is one of the greatest tools in the outdoorsman's tool kit. The ferro rod was created to start fires with an impressive shower of 5000-degree Fahrenheit (2760°C) sparks, and it does so very easily. Those sparks burn white hot, and the light that is emitted from them will wreak havoc on your eyes if they have already adjusted to the dark. This bright light can be countered by squinting your eyes when you are using a ferro rod in the dark to make a fire. The same light can be exploited if you need a quick light to see your general surroundings, snap a mental picture and move until you need to quickly light your area again.

So many modern flashlights have momentary-on tail caps. These tail caps allow the user to activate the light when enough thumb pressure is used. Here is a common scenario: you are using your momentary-on light and for some reason, you end up dropping it to the ground. If you did not have your light dummy corded, it is somewhere on the ground around you. Since you wanted your light to be in a subdued color, when it falls to the ground, it is almost impossible to spot. The momentary-on tail cap activated your light when it was in your hand, but as you dropped it, the light went out. You are now in a scenario where you have no means of finding your way in the dark. If you have a back-up light or a ferro rod, you have a solution to your problem.

Use your flashlight or the ferro-rod quick light.

When students are practicing fire starting at night, they hard focus their eyes on their tinder bundles. They stare directly at the white light, and their night-adjusted eyes take the full flash of light leaving them, seeing white spots as they look around and darkness everywhere else. When you are using a quick light, you can spark just out of your field of vision and still see around you when the area is lit. Spark to the left, right, just below your eyesight or spark high in the air above your head and let the sparks burn the entire way to the ground. As you do this, direct your attention away from your hands. Create a mental image of what you see and move slowly and deliberately until you can't recall your surroundings. If you're searching for something on the ground, be mindful that the ground may have flammable leaves and debris that could catch accidentally. With two people, the quick light really comes into its own. One person sparks in one direction, the other searches.

When students first learn to "see in the dark" with just their ferro rod, they sometimes want to use the skill to the point where their ferro rods wear down prematurely. The quick light is an emergency lighting skill, and it is far easier and smarter to carry a secondary flashlight, even a small LED keychain light, than to burn through your fire-starting device. If your emergency is an all-night affair, perhaps it is wiser to build a fire first and use a torch made from the flames instead. Don't use up your supplies if you have other options at your disposal.

See image on page 98.

SKILL #44
CREATE AREA LIGHTS

When we think about illumination, we tend to think of flashlights and lanterns. A flashlight throws a beam in a given direction, and a lantern throws light in 360 degrees. If you stand to the side of a flashlight as the beam is cast forward, the brightness at the flashlight head shouldn't hurt your eyes. Stare too long at a lantern, though, and you'll begin to see spots. One scenario that comes up frequently in the great outdoors, especially backpacking, is having a flashlight and not having a lantern. An essential skill is knowing how to make an area light with the lights you may have on you. Various forms of lanterns can be made with minimal resources or improvisations.

With nothing more than a small candle, a 12-ounce (355-ml) can and a knife, you can create a windproof candle lantern. All you need to do is cut a door in the side of the can, insert the candle, light it and the interior reflective surface will help cast the light from the single flame toward the open door. You can also cut two doors if the wind seems to blow from all angles. The candle lantern can be suspended from the pull tab or placed on a surface. As with any lit flame used as a lantern, exercise caution and don't let it tip over.

A less flammable option for an area light is made with a headlamp and an opaque water bottle or milk jug. These containers can be filled or empty, and when the headlamp is stretched over them with the beam directed inwards, the light will bounce off the off-white walls and illu-

A simple lantern is made out of a 12-ounce (355-ml) aluminum can and a candle.

minate the area. This type of light is an excellent option when you need to create a nightlight for children on a camping trip. With the battery life of many LED headlamps, you can create a light that will "burn" all night and give kids the sense of security that will let you get some sleep as well. While some would argue this is not an essential survival skill, those doubters probably have never tried camping next to or among a worried child or group of children. I'll kindly disagree with them, and I'm sure plenty of parents understand my sentiment.

SKILL #45
NATURAL TORCHES

Torches are incredibly useful when used correctly. They can also be very dangerous if you don't exercise caution. While the idea of wrapping a knife in burning cloth seems cool, in reality it will destroy the heat treat of your knife, and you probably could find a better torch handle to use in the first place. Also, what looks good in the movies is often not the most practical option in reality.

You likely won't have to escape a team of sheriff deputies and the national guard, like Rambo, but you may need to light your way while fishing in a creek, when the batteries of your lights die out or when you simply want to transport a flame from one camp to another. There are many other scenarios I can't begin to imagine when you will likely foresee the utility of a torch. Your scenario will provide the need; I'll give you the skill.

Your torch handle can be a green sapling approximately as long as your arm from armpit to palm of hand. You want to use green wood as it will burn slower than dried wood. This wood should be straight, and you will end up splitting it down the center about 8 inches (20 cm) to sandwich your fuel source in. One word of warning, when you use a torch: the longer the handle the better, within reason. If your torch is too short, you will more easily breathe in smoke. Also, the right way to hold a torch is at an angle out to the side or angle in front of you to prevent the burning material from falling on your hand.

Z-folded birch bark inserted into a split branch becomes a makeshift torch.

Assuming you have birch trees in your area, you can make an excellent torch with strips of their bark. Folded in a *Z* accordion pattern, birch bark burns consistently and will burn slower than when left unfolded. You can also roll a sheet of birch bark like a newspaper and invert it as the flame weakens to reignite it. This torch fuel won't last forever, and it is a good idea to have multiple strips of bark at the ready for when one is running low. Experiment with a small piece, 3 x 12 inches (7.5 x 30 cm), for starters. Don't crown/girdle a tree if you don't have to, and see how the torch burns. The tighter you fold the birch bark, the longer the torch will burn. Insert your *Z*-folded birch bark into a split at the end of your torch handle. If you run the birch bark perpendicular in the split to form a *T*, you can burn one side of the torch down and then rotate the end to burn the other. You can also run your strips of birch bark in line with your torch handle and fan it out for a larger flame.

Where birch trees may not be plentiful, you may find pine trees with highly flammable resin. Resin, also known as pine pitch, can be found seeping out of pine trees where the tree has been injured, a branch broken off, where pine beetles have bored in or where it splits with growth or from bending in the wind. Pine pitch can be processed into glue sticks, or it can be used for fire-starting purposes. A good dollop of pine pitch can be placed inside the split end of a green sapling torch handle. You'll find pine pitch easier to ignite if you pair it with a good tinder. The pitch will liquefy and feed fuel onto the tinder as it burns. You must be careful, as burning and dripping pine sap can easily fall onto you if you don't hold the torch to the side or angled out in front of you. You can also make an area light with pine pitch by placing it vertically in the ground and igniting it. Since it is stuck in the ground, make sure to clear the area underneath it from anything flammable. This type of pitch torch/lamp is great when you only need a limited amount of light to illuminate your area.

SKILL #46
OIL-SHELL LAMPS

During WWII, my father and his family filled large shells with oil and floated a wick through a piece of cork. The wick soaked up the oil and the cork kept the flame above the oil where it would not go out. Instead of using a large shell, he showed me how it could be made in a shallow pan or using a soda can. My father cut up an old T-shirt, twisted the strips of cotton into a wick, dropped the wick into the soda can after tying it to the pull tab and filled the soda can with some cooking oil we had in our kitchen. I recall him stating how the lamp could tip over and cause a fire, and to this day when I show this skill to my students, I always make reference to this warning.

Oil-shell lamps are a practical way of illuminating your area without resorting to battery power. Many different fuel sources can be used, and as long as a container will hold liquid and is flame resistant, it will be suitable as a reservoir. One word of warning: glass can be an unfit candidate for a fuel reservoir. I have created oil lamps by floating a cork in a shallow dish and that dish cracked as the oil was used up. It simply could not handle the heat of the flame that developed and made contact with the glass. If you end up using old baby food containers, puncture a hole in the lid; or if you only have the small jar, you can suspend the wick with wire over the lid.

You can also make a lamp out of a depression found in a rock. Another container option is to use a log you've hollowed out and don't mind burning if the edges of the bowl get singed. Test whatever container you use with water before

Artist rendering of the oil-shell lamp made by the author's father.

A modern oil lamp. Note the wire wickholders made from snare wire.

you use it. You wouldn't want oil to get all over your sleeping area, gear or you—especially if that oil is flammable. You want to use an oil that will burn, but many fuels, like gasoline, have explosive vapors that could warm you more than you wish.

If you have a small length of wire, you can wrap the cotton wick with this wire along its length, which should give your wick enough rigidity to stand upright. This will allow you to pull more wick out of the lamp or the floating cork and adjust the height of your flame. If you don't have cotton, you can use various natural fiber cordages that are tightly bound. Avoid using any cotton and polyester blend fabrics, as the wick you make will melt and become a bubbling mess.

Other emergency lighting sources include tuna cans with tuna suspended in oil and Crisco cans. With both of these sources of fuel, you

simply poke a hole to the base of the can from the top, insert a cotton wick and light it. The oil will put out a consistent flame until it is used up. If you create more than one channel and insert more than one wick, you can have multiple candlelight flames from a single can. This is usually enough heat to bring water to a boil. When you don't need as many flames, you can snuff out the wicks and return to a single wick solely for illumination purposes. If you want to practice this skill and make a practical lamp to have around the backyard during the summer months, substitute citronella oil for cooking oil. This should help your lamp light your area and keep the skeeters at bay.

SKILL #47

POACH WITH YOUR LIGHT

There are some exceptions to hunting at night for predators, but largely you aren't allowed to shoot after dark for safety and ethical reasons. In a survival situation, you won't have to worry about poaching or breaking any laws.

The common term for using a flashlight in conjunction with a firearm is "jacking." Jacking is highly effective, which is why it is highly prohibited. I cannot recommend you follow through with jacking animals in non-life-threatening scenarios, but you can practice using your light to identify animals by the reflection their eyes make. Animals have a hard time tracking movement when they experience sensory overload through their eyes.

If you are not alone in your survival situation, one person can illuminate while the other uses the firearm. If you are on your own, you may need to adapt to holding your firearm and flashlight, if they cannot be mated, and activated without changing your firing grip. One major consideration of your weaponlight or flashlight is the distance your beam travels. You may have a high-powered rifle, and your light is only capable of casting a beam 25 yards (23 m). Conversely, you could have a powerful light source and only have a handgun you trained to be effective with at 25 yards (23 m). The range of your light and firearm should be complementary.

Poaching is illegal unless you are in a true survival situation.

SKILL #48
CATCH FROGS WITH A FLASHLIGHT

I've caught plenty of frogs with a fishing pole and a small strip of red cloth. On other occasions, I've gone out with no concern for getting my clothes dirty, crawled on the ground toward them head on and tried to grab them from their blind spot, which is right in front of their face. As good as frogs are at swimming, jumping and climbing, they are fairly simple to catch with just a little skill and patience—and even easier prey with the help of a light.

A strong flashlight temporarily blinds frogs and freezes them in their tracks. There are many ways to incorporate a flashlight into your hunting methods, and all yield great results. Starting with the most simple, just holding a flashlight on a frog will enable you to get your hands close enough to grab one. Here are a few tips. Make sure you don't approach a frog with a heavy foot. Even though your flashlight beam makes it so they can't see you, they can sense the vibrations your footsteps make. Also, when you reach for the frog, you need to grab it above the hind legs around the body. This will prevent it from using its legs to push free from your hands. Last but not least, when you have one hand on the frog, get your other hand on it too. You can stretch out the legs to prevent them from kicking free. Frogs can push with their legs better than they can pull. In other words, they can extend their legs stronger than they can retract them.

A strip of cloth can be used on a hooked line to lure frogs.

Another option for catching frogs is using a light and a spear. The spear can be held with one hand if it is not too heavy or unwieldy and the flashlight in the other hand. A spear can also be held with two hands with the hand closest to the tip holding a light on the intended prey. Spearing frogs is best done with a quad-forked spear tip. This method of spearing with the assistance of a strong light will work on many different animals. It will even work on fish in shallow pools in rivers and along the coastline. You don't need to have a projectile survival weapon to incorporate a light into your food-gathering process.

SKILL #49

FLASHLIGHT CORDAGE HANDLE

Most modern flashlight bodies are constructed from heavy-duty polymers or aluminum. These materials make flashlights durable, strong impact weapons and also great makeshift handles to get a better grip on cordage too small in diameter to grip effectively. Since most outdoorsmen will carry paracord, jute twine, braided fishing line, wire and various other types of small diameter line, there may come a time when pulling a line tightly is necessary. A larger diameter line is easier to grab on to and trying to tug on a thin line can be both painful and dangerous. Many times, you'll find yourself wrapping the line around your hand and pulling the line tight. Should your line be attached to something heavy, your hand could become trapped or you could lose a finger.

To pull with your flashlight, use a rolling hitch around the center of the flashlight body. This rolling hitch is nothing more than a few wraps of your line with the last wrap placed over the previous wrap. The rolling hitch will hold your line in place with friction. At this point, you can grab your flashlight with the line placed in between your middle and ring fingers. Unlike wrapping your line around your hand, at any point, you can drop the flashlight and let go of your line should you worry about getting injured. Of course, you don't want to lose your flashlight, so if an alternative is available, use that instead of your flashlight if you anticipate dropping the line for whatever reason.

A rolling hitch used around a flashlight body.

The body of the flashlight is easier to grab than the line on its own.

SKILL #50

FIRE WITH YOUR FLASHLIGHT

A flashlight doesn't seem to have many purposes other than illumination. During courses, I like to show students how to make their flashlight more than a light but a fire starter too. Since many of the modern flashlights use lithium batteries, they have a great power source that can be exploited. Assuming you are carrying fine steel wool in your kit to remove rust from your tools, you can pair it with a lithium battery to start a fire. All you need to do is stretch a piece of steel wool to allow it to reach the positive and negative ends. This will instantly ignite the steel wool when the battery creates a short circuit, and as long as you have additional tinder handy, the steel wool will burn between 800 and 1800°F (427°–982°C), with enough heat to start your fire.

Assuming your batteries are dead, you have a chance to make fire with another part of your flashlight: the reflector. Your reflector found in your flashlight head is designed to concentrate a beam in a single spot. Reflectors are constructed differently, and some will work better than others. You need to have perfect tinder that is supremely dry and the sun needs to be strong enough for this to work. Also, if you have a pair of sunglasses, you should wear them as staring at the concentrated beam of light on your tinder can make your eyes sore. All you need to do to make a fire with a flashlight reflector is to remove the reflector unit from the flashlight head. Hold the reflector in one hand angled at the sun and hold the tinder between your thumb and forefin-

#000 steel wool in contact with both positive and negative sides of a battery will ignite.

ger of your other hand. Experiment with moving the reflector different distances from the tinder until the beam of light is most concentrated. You'll find the beam will start off wide, become narrow and tight and then become wide again when you move too close. Hold the beam on your tinder and you'll hopefully get it to smolder. This glowing orange tinder can then be added to a larger tinder bundle and blown into a flame.

SKILL #51

"MACHETE CARRY" YOUR FLASHLIGHT

When you travel to the tropics, it's common-place to see locals walking around holding their machetes in their hands by the unsharpened ricasso or handle. The machete is usually worn and carried on the left side of the body if you are right-handed and vice versa if you are a southpaw. In the tropics, a cutting tool like a machete could be easily lost if it were to fall from your belt or if it is placed down during a break. Night is especially troublesome as you have to resolve how to hold a flashlight and your machete while still maintaining the ability to draw your machete if needed. If you don't have a headlamp and need to illuminate your way with a standard handheld light, this is where "machete carry" comes into play.

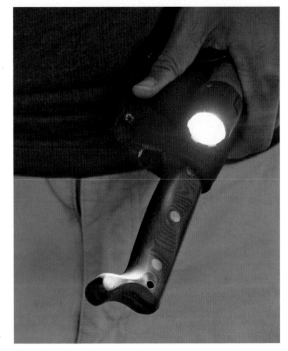

The "machete carry" technique allows you to conceal your machete, illuminate your way with a flashlight and bushwhack with your free hand.

With the flashlight closer to the web of your hand than your machete or machete sheath, you can still retain a hold on the cutting tool with the tips of your fingers and some pressure. By holding your light this way, you can use your free hand to move brush out of the way as you bushwack. You can illuminate your way with the same hand holding your machete and keep your machete in hand and ready for use. By carrying both machete and flashlight in your hand, you reduce the chance of losing one of your most critical tools. If you prefer to wear your machete on your belt, you can tilt the machete backwards and upwards and hold the bezel of the light against the handle facing the punyo (butt). Between the handheld and belt methods, I prefer the handheld version as it doesn't require me to invert my blade as much.

One benefit of this manner of carry is the way the light conceals the blade behind the brightness. I can't tell you when you'll need or want to have a blade in your hand as you walk a trail, but I can tell you it is not always wise to let others know you have one. This method of carrying a light and machete effectively conceals your machete when staying lower profile is important.

NEXT LEVEL TRAINING

A flashlight can be a game changer in the darkness. With just a flip of a switch or lever, you can turn night into day. Darkness is a great training modifier, and during courses at the Wilderness Learning Center, we used darkness to make fire starting more difficult. We gave students nightmare scenarios in which they had to create a fire at night without a light where they had to feel around in the dark for tinder, kindling and fuel. We also had students navigate through a 55-acre (22-hectare) field with their compasses. This required students to charge the luminous bezels of their compasses with their flashlights and avoid accidentally flashing anyone in the face and causing night blindness.

Flashlights can help you gather information in the dark, but they can also provide information to others looking for you. A beam from a flashlight can let someone know your location and what direction you are facing. You may be along a wall, but based on the shape of the light against the wall, a light can give away your place and movement. Learning to navigate with limited light may be an essential skill for those with occupations that require sneaking around for a tactical advantage. If you have a powerful flashlight, you will need to become more aware of where your bezel is in relation to any wall, structure or cover when you are trying to illuminate something beyond that wall. If you turn on your light from behind, you may find yourself getting backsplash and temporarily blinding yourself.

Essential advanced skills also include learning how to use your firearms, all of your firearms, in the dark. Take night courses at reputable firearm training facilities and find out how to use your firearms with attached weapon lights and with handheld lights. Since you can't dictate when you will need to use firearms in self-defense, you should learn how to use them in all settings.

Play a game of hide-and-seek and challenge your friends to light you up with a flashlight before you can get within a given distance of them or even tag them. Games like flashlight tag and hide-and-seek are fun for all ages and are also great to get younger generations involved. Keeping younger generations entertained is a skill in and of itself, but with a few flashlights and the great outdoors, you'll find out how kids can laugh, play and run around in the dark for hours.

NAVIGATION SKILLS

"I will either find a way, or make one." —Hannibal

During the Age of Exploration, the navigator of the ship was more valuable to the crew than the captain. In a mutiny, the captain was expendable if the crew could command the controls. The same cannot be said of the navigator. To this day, the person in charge of navigation holds the fate of the party in their hands. Navigation skills carry a great responsibility. These are the essentials skills I consider to be vital to safe backcountry travel. There are many other skills such as using your compass as an inclinometer, determining latitude, determining an object's height and many more advanced skills that require math and geometry knowledge as well as a firm understanding of fundamental navigation skills. Navigation skills allow us to know where we are going, to create a readiness plan and keep us on track with accomplishing our goals.

Humans take comfort in location. We like to know where we and those we care about are located. Plenty of parents will attest to the peace of mind a courtesy phone call from their teenager brings late at night. "I just want to know where you are" summarizes this sentiment. Comfort in location and comfort in direction allow us to experience the outdoors stress free. We can take in the sights, sounds, smells and the overall experience without worry. Having a sense of place, especially in a large wooded setting, gives us control of our scenario; however, if we lose track of our surroundings, forget to zig when we should have zagged and can't place where we are, we can become afraid. The fear we experience can easily magnify to panic, and when we let our emotions take control of our logic in a scenario like this, our bodies undergo physical changes and we can easily become lost. Being lost is dangerous; being lost can be deadly. If you lack navigation skills, your emergency situation can become a survival situation.

Learning how to use a map and compass requires a strong understanding of the basics, and these fundamental building blocks are needed for the advanced navigation skills that come later. Many emergencies in the great outdoors can be attributed to people losing their way or heading down the wrong path. If a person can remain found, understand where they are and know where they are going, they can mitigate the chances of an emergency. Many skills are perishable, and even the best outdoorsmen become lost if they aren't well practiced in using the basic tools regularly and correctly. Some outdoorsmen believe simply pinning on a button compass to their lapel or having a thermometer/whistle/compass zipper-pull on their jacket will help them navigate. This could not be further from the truth. Navigation skills are not impossible, but they do require a basic understanding of math and logic. Navigation skills, in my opinion, separate exceptional outdoorsmen from amateur adventure seekers.

GEAR

While there are many navigation tools and modern electronics, the most basic navigation setup includes a map and a compass. For most purposes, the map you'll use is a topographic map that shows elevation in contour lines, and the compass you'll want to use is a modern baseplate compass with a sighting mirror. Whenever I teach navigation, I approach it by teaching the map, then the compass and then the map and compass combined. What students need to learn is that each component of a map and compass is invaluable independent of each other, let alone together. While having a map AND compass is ideal, ideal isn't a word commonly used when describing any emergency.

ABOUT YOUR MAP

Your map is likely named after the most prominent feature on the map in the quadrangle (fancy word for square or rectangle area). This map is likely a 7.5-minute series for your area. You learn in grade school about lines of longitude and latitude and each of these degrees is broken down into smaller more manageable units called hours, minutes and seconds. A single minute of latitude represents 1.15 miles (1.9 km) and a 7.5-minute map represents an area of approximately 75 square miles (194 sq km). Don't confuse the 7.5-minute series with map scale. Scale is the relative size or distance on a map with its actual size or distance in the real world. In other words, if the distance between a given point A and point B on a map is 1 inch (2.5 cm), a 1:24,000 map would mean the real world distance between point A and point B is 24,000 inches (60,960 cm). That's 2,000 feet (610 m) or 0.37 mile (0.6 km). Maps can come in many different scales, including 1:24,000, 1:25,000 and 1:50,000 with varying amounts of land represented.

Your map has a few basic colors, including blue representing water, brown representing contours and elevation relief, green representing vegetation, black representing man-made features such as buildings, red representing densely populated areas and roads and purple representing revisions made since the previous edition of the map. The brown lines on your map represent changes in elevation, while those closest together represent steep terrain. When there is a large area with few lines, the terrain is relatively flat. The contour lines never intersect, and they are always the same change in elevation regardless of how far apart they are spread. The change in elevation is referred to as the contour interval with many maps set at ten and others at some interval of it.

Your map contains a great deal of information, but it isn't perfect. After all, your map is a two-dimensional representation of a three-dimensional object. Just as you can't peel an orange and configure the rind into a perfect rectangle, you can't flatten the earth without stretching and distorting the water or land somewhere. This is why Greenland looks enormous on a standard mercator projection of the Earth compared to how it looks on a globe. Always be prepared for inaccuracy to present itself in the great outdoors. Weather can change features found on a map, as can human error. If you use an outdated map, you are to blame. Man-made changes won't be present on the previous version of the map if they were made after its publication.

ABOUT YOUR COMPASS

Your compass is an essential tool for navigation and your primary instrument used to indicate direction. Even when the conditions provide minimal visibility, your compass will read true. If you have ever heard and understood what it means when a pilot "flies by his instruments," then you'll understand how you can navigate the great outdoors in the same way.

Broken down, your compass is nothing more than a magnetized needle suspended or floating somewhat freely in a housing. Since the earth's core is magnetized, your compass needle will point to the direction of one of the poles, usually the north. There are some occasions where compasses are accidentally magnetized to point to the South Pole, so check your compass toward a known direction before you head out. Some compass needles spin freely and take time to settle in one direction, and others are dampened with liquid. Most modern compasses sold at outdoor equipment stores are liquid-filled.

A mirrored sighting compass is a more accurate tool for navigation than a simple button compass.

As compass designs evolved, markings were drawn around the housing. These markings represent the 360 degrees in a flat plane. With a moveable housing and a sighting reference, it became possible to take readings off of where the north needle pointed. To this day, a good navigation compass will have a moveable housing with 360-degree markings called a bezel, a directional arrow sometimes referred to as a direction of travel arrow, an orienting arrow etched into the base of the see-through base and a magnetic needle that points north. There are other features found on a quality compass you may want to consider. Some compasses are equipped with luminous markings that glow in the dark when activated by a flashlight. Others have rubberized feet that won't slide around on your map when you place them on a flat surface. Some compasses have sighting mirrors that eliminate movement and help take more accurate readings. One consideration often overlooked when purchasing a compass is how it will be carried. If your compass doesn't come with a good leather or ballistic nylon pouch, find one and carry it there. This will protect your compass from accidental damage if dropped.

Some compasses will be equipped with adjustable declination. Magnetic declination, sometimes referred to as variance, is the angle found between magnetic north and true north. Magnetic declination is included on your map and aids navigation with a compass. If you recall, maps will be distorted by taking a three-dimensional object and presenting it on a two-dimensional surface. One method of using your compass involves changing the declination by a set number of degrees to correspond to what your map prescribes. While this method works to improve accuracy, I offer a different approach that works with compasses not equipped with adjustable declination.

When you purchase a quality compass, you invest in your safety. Even with the best compass, you must be careful of the forces that can work against it: mainly magnetic forces. Be careful not to use your compass around metallic objects, as they will throw off the compass's accuracy. Even the smallest of screws in a pair of sunglasses can throw off your compass's reading. A degree or two incorrect might not matter over a short distance, but a single degree of inaccuracy results in being 92 feet (28 m) off target after 1 mile (1.6 km); 5 degrees off results in being 460 feet (140.3 m) off target after 1 mile (1.6 km). Whenever possible, you'll want to use your compass on and around a surface free of metallic/magnetic interference.

SKILL #52
MAP RECON

Prior to traveling into an area, you should always conduct map reconnaissance. "Map recon," for short, involves studying the terrain features of an area of operation to determine the lay of the land. You first want to read over your map carefully, looking, sometimes with a Fresnel lens, for features that can be an asset or a liability to safety.

A standard 7.5-minute topographic map contains more information than you or anyone could collect in their lifetime scouting the terrain on the ground. You can read a quality topographic map, prior to heading into the field, to determine where water sources are. You can examine the same map to help locate the nearest road where you could hitch a ride with a passing vehicle. You can look for catch features, which are natural landmarks that will let you know when you've traveled too far in your area of operation and need to turn back. Your map can also tell you where you should set up camp in the flattest terrain and whether or not that terrain is likely to be well drained or swampy. With a topographic map you can take a rough estimate of the distance between two points. Good map reconnaissance is an exercise in awareness. In the same way you research a product before purchasing it or read the reviews others have written about a vacation experience before booking it, you can analyze the work of a mapmaker and use logic to plan where you want to go and how you want to travel there and back. Having a good plan is part of readiness and a good navigation plan starts with map recon.

Studying your map with a Fresnel lens or magnifying glass is essential for familiarizing yourself with the terrain.

Make sure you are looking at the most recent version of your map and not one that hasn't been updated with any changes since the last survey. With a basic knowledge of topography, symbols and scale, it's possible to visualize the area you are traveling to before you step foot there. An essential navigation skill is knowing where you are headed and what challenges the terrain will present and then preparing for them.

SKILL #53
PREP A MAP

Before heading out into the field, the map carried should be prepared. If possible, you should photocopy the map and store it separately from the primary map. If you're glued to your technology, use your camera on your phone to take pictures of your map and store as a tertiary backup. I've seen large maps and charts act like sails when the wind has pulled them from the firm grasp of the outdoorsmen. Be prepared with a spare. The simple act of correctly maintaining a map in the field and making it ready for use is a skill. Far beyond folding a map correctly, preparing a map involves getting the map ready to use and adding information and intelligence to it not already provided.

Your topographic map will have "magnetic north," "grid north" and "true north" arrows. If your compass is adjustable, and you intend to use declination (more on this later), you will focus on using true north. Otherwise, you should focus on using magnetic north for all navigation. Locate the appropriate needle and align a ruler or straightedge along it. For the purpose of explanation, I will focus on using a compass without declination and use magnetic north. Draw a line across the entire map along the magnetic north line. Locate your map scale and measure out how many inches (or centimeters) equal ¼ mile (0.4 km) or other distance you prefer. Draw a parallel line this distance from your original line and repeat this process until the map is covered in a series of parallel lines. These parallel lines can be used as a rough estimate of distance at

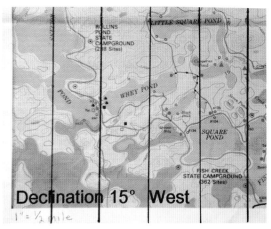

Declination 15° West

1" = ½ mile

A properly prepped map with parallel magnetic north lines.

SKILL #54
ORIENT A MAP (WITHOUT A COMPASS)

A map is more useful if you hold it the right way. The process of aligning a map to the terrain is called "orienting a map." This means lining up the two-dimensional representation of the terrain with the actual three-dimensional world. Without a compass, all you have to do is line up observable features (i.e., a road, river, mountain peaks) around you with your map when it is held horizontally. This rough orientation will help you determine which direction of travel is necessary to reach certain points, assuming you know how to read the map. Orienting a map can also be used with your map recon to determine where resources can be found. When you orient your map, remember it is named after the most prominent feature drawn; look for this feature as the first point from which to orient your map. If you did your map

a given point to the nearest line. Without these lines spaced an equal distance apart, you'll need to open your map to reference the scale. If you already know the lines are spaced ¼ mile (0.4 km) apart, you eliminate one step in the process and avoid exposing your map to the elements outside of its carrier. These lines also allow you to use any parallel line as an indicator of north/south, even if your map is folded and the original north arrow is covered.

Your primary map can be waterproofed with either commercially available sealant, Thompson's WaterSeal or spray urethane or laminated at your local copy store. If none of these treatments are available, you can fold your map and place it inside a ziplock bag with the area of operation facing out. Maps have a tendency to absorb moisture, whether that is in the form of precipitation, the sweat inside your jacket where you store it or the coffee you spilled on it in the trailhead parking lot. Whenever possible, carry your map rolled or folded gently only as small as needed. The more creases in your map, the more difficult it will be to use and the more likely it will rip on you.

Use the magnetic north line with your compass to orient it.

Turn your map without moving your compass until "red is in the shed."

SKILL #55
READ A COMPASS

With just a compass, you're able to travel confidently, relying solely on reading your navigation instrument. A compass will help point you in the right direction, which is read in degrees from north. North is read as 0 degrees. Ninety degrees from that is east, 180 degrees off of north is south and 270 degrees is west. When we make reference to a direction along a line, that is referred to as a "bearing" or "azimuth." Therefore, a bearing of 45 degrees is headed northeast.

To determine the location of a point from your location, you aim the directional arrow on your compass toward that object, holding the compass horizontally away from your belt buckle or anything magnetic (including your watch), and rotate the bezel until the magnetic needle is aligned inside the orienting arrow etching inside your compass. This process of aligning the needle with the etching is called "putting red in the shed" or sometimes "putting the guard in the house." The direction of the object you are taking a bearing off of is read at the directional arrow. Again, make sure to take your bearing far from metallic objects, as they can interfere with the magnetism in your compass's needle. If you plan on taking a bearing off your vehicle's hood or on top of a wooden fence, remember your vehicle is metal and the fence could have nails in it. These mistakes have been repeated over and over. To be safe, place your compass on the ground or a solitary wooden post and double check your bearings with a backup compass.

recon correctly, you should already have an idea of some very prominent features that should stand out before you step in the field.

Without a reference point, you can use the sun and the shadows cast to determine the correct orientation of a map. Prior to noon, the shadow cast by the sun on a 3-foot (91-cm)-tall stick driven into the ground will be in a westerly direction. In the afternoon, the shadow cast will be in an easterly direction. If time allows, you can create shadow sticks and determine a true north/south line from which to orient yourself.

SKILL #56
FOLLOW A BEARING

To follow a bearing, rotate your bezel and put red in the shed.

There are occasions when you will be given a bearing to follow, and you will not be able to utilize a distant reference point from your starting position. You may start off your trip looking into a tall forest with no way to know what is above the canopy and over the horizon. All you may have is your instruments and some simple instructions. Perhaps you are about to settle into a basecamp and want to take inventory of what is around you. It's also not uncommon to scout around your campsite for resources. With this skill, you will be able to strike off on a given path and return on it. In these circumstances, the most valuable tool you can have is a quality compass and the knowledge to follow a bearing.

To follow a bearing, turn your compass bezel to the provided bearing. Make sure to align the bearing with the directional arrow. Without disturbing the bezel, rotate your body holding the compass low, flat and away from metallic objects until "red is in the shed." Take note of what is in front of you as well as behind and walk in the direction of the directional arrow maintaining red in the shed. Avoid staring too much at your compass, as fixating on it will hinder your observation of the natural features around you. In other words, don't trip over something because you're staring too deeply at your instrument. Fixating on your instruments and not being aware of your surroundings in a 720-degree environment can mean you miss a trail marker or the signs of others who tread on the path before you.

Just as important as taking a bearing is taking a back bearing. A back bearing is exactly 180 degrees opposite of your original bearing. Remember this saying, "Over 180, subtract; under 180, add." Assuming you intend to travel in a direction toward an object, you'll want to note the direction to which you will return. Also critical to note are the physical features behind you as you take your original bearing. These can be used as points of reference on your return trip. Get in the habit of determining the back bearing and track this information in a small notebook. Assuming you can't see your distant bearings on your return trip, you will have a written record of the back bearings you need to take to return home.

Hold your compass flat and away from metal as you follow your bearing.

SKILL #57
OFFSET SHOOT

An absolutely essential and potentially lifesaving navigation skill is the ability to offset shoot with your compass. As you recall, navigation exists in a flat 360-degree world. As the bearing increases in number, you rotate more right and as it decreases in number, you rotate left. Assuming you are standing facing due north (0 degrees) and walk 30 degrees (+30 degrees) from your location, you are to the right of where you were originally facing. If you move 330 degrees from your original location (–30 degrees), you moved to the left. If you remember the phrase "Right raise, left lower," the concept will be easy to apply.

One of the scenarios in which offset shooting comes into play is when you are navigating through the woods to a point on a road where your vehicle is parked or where you will be picked up. Offset shooting helps ensure you turn in the right direction the first time. If you are addressing an emergency, you may not be given the luxury of doing it right with a second chance. Many fire roads have twists and turns, which can

Make sure to track what your course will look like on the return trip by stopping in place, turning around and seeing the trail from a different perspective. Depending on what resources are on hand, you may bend branches, create small cairns, leave surveyor's tape or some other visual reference to help you return along this path later. If you are walking through a thick stand of trees, you can always cut a very long pole and pass it through the trees: a straighter line than alternating going left and right around trees or always going right. You want to make sure you don't always walk around trees on the same side as you walk a bearing; this can take you on a parallel path or a different heading.

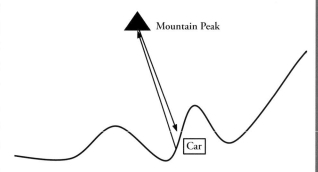

Deliberately offset shoot to know which way to turn when returning to your vehcle.

make seeing a distance down the road impossible. If you parked your vehicle along this windy road and walked an initial heading of 70 degrees from your car to a campsite, your back bearing should be 250 degrees (original 70 degrees plus 180 degrees). If you deliberately offset your back bearing 5 degrees more (255 degrees), you should return to the road and find your vehicle to your left. The actual amount of offset you use in your back bearing is up to you. In this scenario, if you offset your back bearing by subtracting 5 degrees, making it 245 degrees, your vehicle would be to your right when you hit the road.

SKILL #58
TRACK DISTANCE TRAVELED

Humans are not equipped with on-board odometers or GPS. The only way to estimate the distance we've traveled is with pacing. This method has been used for thousands of years and dates back to the Roman era. It is still in use by militaries around the world and with practice, it can be very accurate over long distances. Pace can relate to the distance traveled in a set amount of time or the number of paces in a given distance. The method of measuring distance every outdoorsman should know involves using the latter of the two.

To establish your pace, you must first determine your pace factor. The easiest way to determine this is to determine how many paces you take in a 100-foot (30-m)-long course. Walk 100 feet (30 m) and count your paces. Repeat this process 10 times and take the average of all these trials. This number will be different from one person to the next as countless variables can impact it. Divide this number into 100 and you'll likely come up with a number between 4 and 7. What this number represents is your pace factor. My factor, for instance, is 5.5, meaning that for every pace I take (a complete stride with the right and then left leg) I travel 5½ feet (1.7 cm). Using this number as an average, I can determine how many paces I need to walk to travel $\frac{1}{10}$ of a mile or $\frac{1}{10}$ of a kilometer. A great place to work on your pacing is a high school track where one lap is ¼ mile (0.4 km).

Pace beads can be used in one-tenth kilometers or one-tenth miles.

With an understanding of pace, you can keep track of how far you've traveled and estimate how far it is from where you are to your destination. Just keep in mind, your pace will be impacted by many variables, and you should familiarize yourself with how darkness, fatigue, extra weight and others will impact your pacing. In order to keep track of your number of paces, a simple counter made from pony beads and paracord can be made. These "ranger beads" found in many equipment catalogs were originally created by Army Rangers to visually track their distance in paces when the number they counted reached the equivalent of 100 meters (109 yards). With nine beads on the bottom of a paracord strand and four on top with a knot separating them, you can count the first $9/10$ of a kilometer or mile $1/10$ at a time. When you reach your pace count for $1/10$ of a mile or kilometer, you pull one bead down. When you reach 1 mile (1.6 km), you return the nine beads to the top and pull one bead down from the top four beads above the knot to indicate the mile (or kilometer).

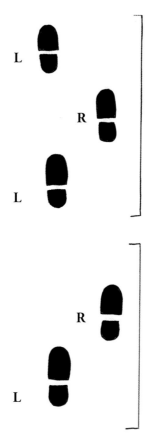

A pace (top) is measured between steps on a single foot. Steps (bottom) are single beats.

SKILL #59
PLOT A COURSE

Plotting a course using a map and a compass is an essential skill to backcountry navigation. It lets you determine which direction to set your compass to when you arrive at a particular point and strike off in that direction to your destination. With an understanding of taking bearings and measuring distance with pacing, you can navigate around objects or through dense woods without any visual references on the landscape.

The first step in plotting a course is orienting your map. This time, instead of using visual references, you simply align the side of your compass with the magnetic north lines you drew previously. (Note: If you prefer to set your compass's declination, remember to use the true north arrow. Since some compasses are not equipped with adjustable declination, I prefer teaching the method that uses magnetic north instead. Your compass needle is magnetized to point to magnetic north constantly. It makes sense to stick with constants and use the drawn lines for magnetic north.) When your compass is on the magnetic north line, rotate the map without lifting up the compass until red is in the shed. When "red is in the shed," your map is oriented. You can tape down or weigh down the corners of your map. Make sure you don't place your map on anything metallic (even screws in a table will throw off your reading).

Now you can find a location on the map pertinent to your outdoor activity. Place your compass along this point in a straight line to your next waypoint, and draw a line connecting

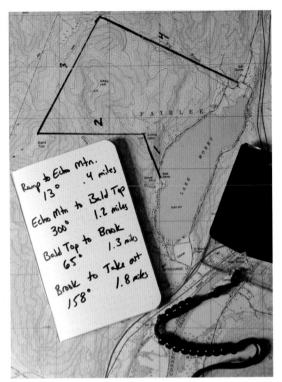

Record plotted courses before you leave home.

the two. Make sure the direction of travel arrow is pointed in the correct direction toward this new location. Without moving your map, rotate the bezel of the compass until red is in the shed. The bearing at the directional arrow is what you will set your compass to at the start of your trip. Measure that line you drew, and relate it to the map scale. This is the distance, as the crow flies, between these two points. The actual distance will vary with changes in elevation. That distance from point A to B can now be calculated in paces using your pace factor. Repeat this process from B to C and so on, plot how far you have to travel in paces following a bearing before you have to make a directional change. Keep all these notes in a small notebook and you'll be able to fall back on them in your backcountry navigation.

SKILL #60
BOX AN OBSTACLE

Unless we sprout wings and learn to fly, we will not be able to avoid some obstacles on the ground. Swamps, cliffs and rapid sections of river are among some of the obstacles you can face if you walk in a straight line in the woods. The question always comes up, "How do you get around that and stay on course?" As long as you have a firm grasp of pacing and knowledge of how to shoot bearings and walk them, you can create a solution to any obstacle by boxing it.

Boxing an obstacle works on the concept of 90-degree turns. This navigation method has been used by outdoorsmen and the military for years. Basic boxing only requires four course changes, and it is not complicated as long as you are proficient with some basic addition and subtraction. Assume you are walking an original heading of 110 degrees. You come across a pond you cannot walk through. Walk as far as you can without getting your feet wet and when forward travel is not possible anymore. Set your compass to 200 degrees, and follow this bearing to your right (or subtract 90 and go to your left if a right turn isn't possible) until you walk past the object. Make sure to keep track of your paces on this right turn. When you walk just past the object, set your compass to 110 degrees, turn left and walk just past the object again. This second leg of boxing an obstacle takes you along your original heading on a parallel line. When you get past the object, set your compass to 20 degrees and turn left again. Walk the same number of paces

on this leg as you did on your first. (Note: The number of paces counted on the first turn and the last must be the same or else you won't be on the same line you originally were walking.) When you reach that number, set your compass to 110 and continue walking on your original heading, having just successfully boxed the obstacle.

You may find you have to box an obstacle multiple times. This is where tracking your paces in a small notebook is extremely helpful and a simple sketch of your route on a blank sheet of paper will help you remember where you are in the boxing process. Some objects in the natural world are oblong, asymmetrical and inevitably will be in our paths. As long as you trust your compass and your pacing, you will be amazed how easy it is to accomplish navigating around them.

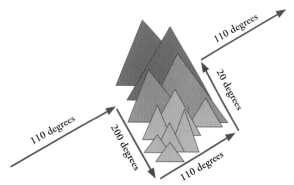

Turn right → Raise
Turn left → Lower
Use 90-degree turns to "box" around an obstacle.

SKILL #61
RESECTION

You may find yourself in a scenario where you have a map and a compass for your area but you can't determine where you are. Perhaps you lost your bearings, your pace was off or you genuinely can't recall how you lost your way. A less threatening scenario is finding out where you are on a map back home after stumbling onto a great fishing hole, a camping spot or buried treasure so you can get back there. You'll find some navigation skills are needed after you get out of the field under your own power or with the assistance of a rescue crew. If you have a clear line of sight to at least two objects in the distance, are equipped with a map and a compass and know about taking bearings and back bearings, you can use the principle of resection to calculate where you or where the rest of your party are (or were).

By sighting to one object, perhaps a distinctive mountain peak at 250 degrees southwest, you know the back bearing is minus 180 degrees, which is 70 degrees. If you have your map, you can first orient it with your compass and shoot a bearing 70 degrees from that mountain peak, assuming you can locate it accurately on the map. With a wet-erase marker or a grease pen, you can draw directly on your map, assuming you prepped it correctly. Good news: you are somewhere along that line you just drew. With a second object in sight, a noticeable break in a mountain ridgeline at 340 degrees northwest, you can shoot a bearing to that and calculate the backbearing. A second line is drawn, and where these two back bearings intersect is your

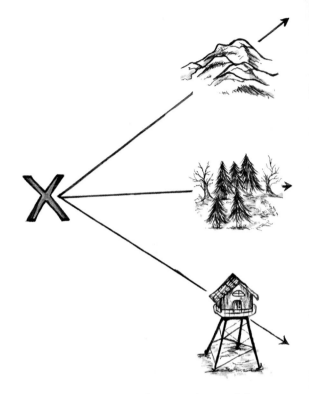

Resection uses back bearings from two objects, while triangulation uses back bearings from three.

location. This process of determining location with two back bearings is called resection. Utilize one more back bearing and you have the process of triangulation. The more points you can shoot back bearings from, the more accurate the calculation of your location on the map you're carrying will be.

NEXT LEVEL TRAINING

Navigation skills are easily trained, and there is simply no excuse for neglecting them. The goal is to decrease the chances of getting lost and enhance your experience outdoors. It doesn't take much to practice navigation, and with just a compass in your backyard, you can shoot bearings to objects and let someone else verify them. You can try pacing in new shoes or at a different rate. You can work on your awareness skills and always keep a known directional indicator in the forefront of your mind as you travel. Simply put, you will never run out of content to study. All of this information and data can be recorded, and your navigation logbook will be a living record of your skill set. You may find that your pace factor, for example, will change. Perhaps you create a list of information to record in your given area and this changes with development or relocation. Record what you discover, and refer back to it before you head out again.

Many of the skills presented in this chapter are introductory or intermediate level. Professional outdoorsmen will tell you it is impossible to have enough fundamentals training. There are ways of making each of these skills more difficult to increase the level of skill needed. The following are some ways you can modify your training to improve your overall performance. Some of these drills can be done solo and others are best accomplished with a partner or training group.

- Partner drills involve following a course someone draws on a map, bearing verification done with two compasses to the same point or checking tape-measure distances marked by one and paced out by the other.

- Pacing with different shoes, after activity, in different weather, over different terrain, at a jog and at a run will help you gather different data for your pace factor.

- "Bushwhacking" a safe course through the woods under controlled conditions to a known point will gauge your ability to follow a bearing. It will also test your fortitude if you cross waterways or rip your clothes.

- Drawing a map of an unknown area and confirming the survey with an actual map will test your scouting ability. Look to see if you are focusing on the small or the large details and what details you overlook.

- Orienteering courses and treasure hunts (for the kids) work well to help others get interested in navigation. My father made treasure hunts for my siblings and me that subtly reinforced how to read maps at a young age.

- "Lost man" drills for locating someone with provided bearings using resection can combine navigation skills with medical training. What frequently comes up in this activity is the lack of preparedness. Your training partners will have compasses, but they may not have essential first-aid and trauma gear at hand.

- Night navigation is a whole other animal, but not terribly difficult. Practice in an open field using compasses to follow bearings to flags or cones placed earlier in the day.

- Teams can practice navigation through dense woods using "leap frogging." Instead of shooting a bearing to a fixed point, use your partner as the bearing and send them off in the direction your compass points off their back. Have them go 100 feet (30 m), and stop. Walk to their location and repeat. You'll find it very effective when it is difficult to identify a single point.

SIGNALING AND COMMUNICATION SKILLS

"What you do speaks so loudly that I cannot hear what you say." —*Ralph Waldo Emerson*

Nine out of ten emergency situations do not extend past 72 hours. You don't want to try your luck to find out if you can avoid being the one out of ten that does. Many of these emergencies terminate with a rescue because someone was able to call for help. Signaling for help is most effective if you can relay certain information rescuers will find useful. The number of people in your party, your location (exact, near or last known), the physical and mental state of the group, the nature of the problem, the supplies at hand—all of this information can be useful. Unfortunately, you may only have a whistle and a signal mirror or your cell phone may not be in service or it could have a dead battery. You need to have a solid set of skills to alert others to your location and to the seriousness of your signal.

When we look for someone in distress, we look for the break in the norm. If the baseline of a setting is calm and tranquil, a person blowing a whistle or sounding a car alarm/horn will draw our attention.

One group of people who must learn to signal when they are in trouble is small children. Many small children are taught from a young age not to speak to strangers. If a child becomes lost, their parent may not be the one tasked with finding them in the woods. This may fall on the shoulders of search and rescue personnel who wear strange-looking clothing with radio wires, flashlights and reflective stripes on their clothes. If you have children in your group, you must tell them it is OK to speak to some strangers.

When we think about signaling, we can break the act as a whole into various types of signals.

Visual Signals are meant to attract the attention of someone by reflecting light, casting light or contrasting against a backdrop. Some popular visual signals include signal mirrors, marker panels, sea dye, surveyor's tape, aerial flares, strobes and smoke signals/signal fires.

Auditory Signals are designed to make a noticeable noise for either human or dog ears to hear. Whistles are common, as are compressed-air horns and battery-operated sirens. Screaming is not a very effective means of signaling as it can cause laryngitis and limit your ability to communicate after a couple good bellows.

Electronic Signals are sophisticated and highly effective. They are also prone to breakage, weak broadcast signals and dead batteries. Electronic signals, when they are functional, are great ways of sending detailed messages and location. Electronic signals can include emergency personal locator beacons, GPS units with text-message capability, cell phones and tracking devices.

Day/Night Signals are the two variants of visual signals. Day signals are most effective in clear conditions with great visibility. Night signals require some form of man-made illumination from either a battery operated device, chemical reaction, sparks or a flame. Some common night signal devices include flashlights, chemical light sticks, signal fires and emergency strobes.

Active/Passive Signals. Active signals are any of those that require your attention and action. These can include signal mirrors, whistles and even tending to a signal fire or smoke generator. Waving your arms over your head or using a flashlight to signal SOS are also examples of active signaling. Even though you don't expend much energy, making a phone call or sending out a text message are also examples of active signaling. Passive signaling

Buy the best signaling devices you can afford. Your life may depend on them.

methods are those that you set up one time and rely on it being discovered. A passive signal could be leaving a note behind on a stranded vehicle, setting up large letters from contrasting materials in an open area, hanging reflective devices that will swing in the wind or anything else that just needs to be created once and will work for you when you are attending to other tasks.

Of the two, focused-active signaling will likely be more effective. Countless stories have played out in the past of people yelling and screaming while waving hands when they have realized help was nearby. Anytime you can direct both auditory and visual signaling in a focused manner, you will increase your chances of being recognized.

SKILL #62
CREATE A "FLOAT PLAN"

Trekking off solo into the wilderness gives you the ultimate sense of freedom. You are your own boss and travel at your own speed. There is no one to hassle you and you can do what you want when you want. Freedom is just a couple doorways and a turn of the ignition key away, but that doesn't mean you should leave home without telling someone where you will be. This step takes only minutes, yet it can save you hours or days of frustration and suffering if you do it correctly. Telling someone where you are going is what we at the Wilderness Learning Center refer to as a float plan. In Sayoc, we always communicate travel plans to the members of the tribe in the immediate area. In my family, my parents always wanted to know where I was going and who I was going to be with. The float plan is absolutely vital yet so frequently neglected. The essential skill is in providing the essential information to the right people.

When you file a float plan, you want to leave the information about your travels with at least three responsible people. Responsible is a relative term. A young child might be responsible enough to use the bathroom on their own, but they are not responsible enough to write down information or remember important details of your trip. Responsible people should be those who will notice your absence. They should also be willing to follow through contacting the appropriate authorities if you do not return home on time. You can inform these people with an email, text

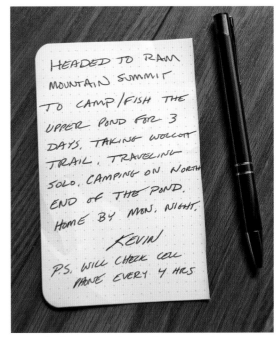

A simple float plan is better than no one knowing your wherabouts.

message or in person. Ideally, you should wait for a confirmation they have received your message and replied to you.

When you leave a float plan, think of the five W's you probably recall from high school writing/composition classes. These are the "who," "what," "where," "when" and "why." You should include your destination and direction of travel. In the Northeast on Mount Washington for instance, there are multiple routes to the summit from the Pinkham Notch Shelter. If a search party were to set out after you, they should know not just where you are going but how you are getting there. Another bit of information you should always include is when you intend to be back. This is important because you don't want a search party formed for your absence prematurely. Both of these details, direction of travel and expected return, are points you should include. If you stray from your float plan, rescuers may not be able to locate you.

Furthermore, you want to let others know some personal information. This includes your driver's license number (authorities can find most information about you with just this), physical health, medical issues and allergies and the information of others in your party. The other W's may also prove useful if included in a float plan. This includes why you are in the woods (i.e., to hunt, to fish, to camp) what gear you are carrying and the provisions you have. Search parties should know what your physical description is as well as the predominant colors of your gear. If you can draw a map or provide a topo map of the route and destination, even better.

In addition to telling close friends and associates your float plan, you should also leave a copy of your plan in your car. Should you go missing, authorities will gain access to your vehicle and search it. You should not leave your float plan in plain view for predators to exploit. If you are seen walking into the woods and leave a message stating you will be back in a week, the predators can return during the week, steal from your vehicle and know you won't be around until the end of the week to find out. For this reason, you also want to make sure you don't leave any expensive gear out in the open. Somewhere in your car, you may want to leave an aluminum foil imprint of your hiking boot treads. All you have to do is place a sheet of kitchen aluminum foil on the ground and stride over it with your boots on. This will help rescuers decipher your footprints from someone else's. You may even want to notch a unique cut into one of your boot treads to make them stand out even more.

Some backcountry trails require you to sign in prior to heading into the backcountry. Do not disregard these points. Rangers keep track of the number of people in and out. Also, if you leave the backcountry and forget to sign out, don't forget to call the park office and let them know they don't need to search for you.

One other float plan you may file is with a wounded member of your party. Assuming someone is injured and unconscious and you have no other choice but to leave them and look for help, you will need to leave a note on them to alert whoever finds them should you not return with help first. This is why carrying a good notepad and pen is important in your emergency kit. You should include details about what injured them, when it happened, how you rendered aid, when you left, where you are headed and how you are getting there. Leaving a stranded friend or family member is not a good scenario for anyone, but accidents happen and this could play out.

SKILL #63
LEAVE A "BREADCRUMB" TRAIL

Hang colorful surveyor's tape at eye level for an effective breadcrumb trail.

A very lightweight option for marking trails is surveyor's tape. This colorful tape is available in rolls of a couple hundred feet, and just a few feet are needed each time you tie a length to a tree branch. I prefer carrying one of two colors in my pack depending on the season. Red or orange stands out fantastic in the winter, as they are unnatural colors and contrast with the frozen backdrop. In the summer, I carry neon green or bright blue. Surveyor's tape should be tied about eye level from the ground. Even though humans tend to look down when they are walking on trails, those looking for you will likely scan the area for signs of you, and eye-level markers will be easier to see. Aside from surveyor's tape, you can also pack reflective tacks hunters use to mark trails in the dark. These are extremely light and easy to spot when illuminated with a light.

One way to use surveyor's tape that has proven very effective is by creating a chevron pattern about head height in the woods. I've used this in the thick woods when first getting into camp right before I set out to scout my surrounding area. A single length of surveyor's tape stretched between two trees might go overlooked if you are walking in line with it. However, if you make a V or an L placed horizontally, you will always see at least a straight line no matter what orientation you are to it while walking towards it. You don't need to create a closed triangle as the shape from the two lengths of tape are visible without the third length.

The alternative to using manufactured breadcrumbs is to make natural trail markers instead. Indigenous people from all over the world have developed their own methods of marking their paths, and so can you. On many alpine routes and established trails, elaborate cairns have been formed. These rock piles take time to build, and more important, energy. You shouldn't expend more energy than you are putting in, and moving a lot of rocks probably won't be a good strategy for marking your trail. However, a few rocks stacked high or placed conspicuously may be all that is needed. Another natural option for marking your trail could simply be breaking branches and turning their leaves upside down. If you are comfortable and competent with noticing this difference as you travel, you can use this method. Be forewarned, though: in a strong wind your broken and twisted upside-down branches can blow back over and look like all the others. If you are in a rocky canyon, you can carry a small chunk of charcoal and mark the walls you are traveling by. The charcoal will stain the wall as long as it doesn't rain, and you should be able to follow these black breadcrumbs back to where you started.

SKILL #64
GROUND SIGNALS WITH NATURAL MATERIALS

For a signal to stand out, it has to contrast. Audibly, be loud when it is quiet. Visually, be bright when surrounding colors are dull. If you are in an area where an aerial rescue is more likely than a ground rescue, you will need to signal the helicopter or small plane where your location is. A whistle is not likely going to be heard over the helicopter blades. Depending on the time of year and the ground cover, you'll have to adjust how you contrast your visual ground signal. You can use Mother Nature's resources to your advantage.

Ideally, your ground signals for aircraft should be large enough to stand out. If you can, simple arrows can be created on the landscape, and these can be 10 yards (9.1 m) or longer.

During the summer, when the ground is green, you can remove a layer of earth to expose the brown underneath. Or better yet, use birch bark logs. During the winter when the ground is white, you can contrast with brown tree bark or evergreen boughs. At any time in the year, you can use clothing or brightly colored gear to draw arrows to your location. Simple symbols are better than complex ones, and anything that appears symmetrical or man-made will stand out from the natural terrain. A large *X* or ➡ should be noticeable against a consistent backdrop of greens, browns or whites.

Ground signals like these are passive, but you should not be. Wind, rain and other natural factors can deteriorate your signal, and you must routinely check on it to make sure it hasn't blown away, washed away or become obstructed from view. Place your signal in a prominent location and build active signaling measures to back it up.

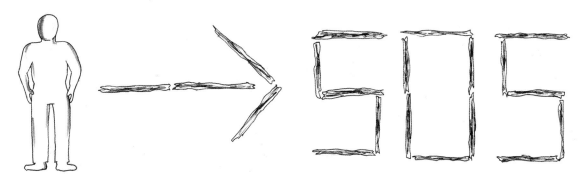

A ground signal should be at least as large as an average-size person.

SKILL #65
SODA-CAN WHISTLE

With aluminum cans littering the woods, you always have the materials to make a simple whistle.

With nothing more than your knife or a pair of scissors and a single aluminum soda can, you can construct a simple whistle that can be heard at quite some distance. Since cans are found all throughout the great outdoors as discarded litter, this soda-can whistle can be made almost anywhere people travel. One word of warning: The soda-can whistle requires handling jagged aluminum. There is a risk you can cut your fingers while making this. Exercise caution with your blades and the aluminum can. If you have a flat surface, this process of converting a can to a whistle will be much easier.

Using your knife or a pair of scissors, poke a hole in the can and proceed to cut around the body of the can, removing the top. Repeat this process to remove the bottom of the can as well. Cut the cylinder down the middle to create a single sheet of aluminum that forms a rectangle. Using your blade or scissors, trim up the rectangle as best as you can to remove any sharp points. You can work the aluminum rectangle with your fingers or across a log to flatten some of it to make handling easier. Just avoid putting any creases in it.

The whistle you are making has two strips that are joined at the mouthpiece. The first part of your whistle will resemble the letter *b*. A single strip of aluminum can is cut about 3½ inches (9 cm) long and 1 inch (2.5 cm) wide. This piece is rounded, and a straight portion is left for the mouthpiece. A second piece of aluminum, about 2 inches (5 cm) long and 1 inch (2.5 cm) wide, is cut, and this piece is placed perpendicular on the straight mouthpiece of the first. The overlap is folded un-derneath the mouthpiece. The rounded portion of the first part holds the second piece in place and a small fold is made in the mouthpiece at the end to keep the second piece from falling off. (See visual.) Using the tip of your knife or a small twig, you can open the mouthpiece by separating the two pieces of aluminum can that form it.

To use your whistle, you must pinch the sides of the rounded section to seal the chamber of the whistle. If you have small fingers, you can use your thumb pads instead. You will have to tinker with how much of a gap you leave between the mouthpiece and the end of the curved section. When you blow through the mouthpiece, you can adjust the opening of the chamber until you hit the sweet spot. If you cover the chamber with your hand, you can adjust the pitch of the whistle too.

This whistle can either be made in the field with scavenged materials or with a piece of light-weight aluminum flashing precut and scored for easy breaking. If you are packing the materials into the field, you can tuck this aluminum strip virtually anywhere as it will lay flat. Keep in mind, this whistle is not as powerful as dedicated whistles like the Fox 40, Acme Tornado or Storm whistle. You must decide if the value of signaling with a dedicated whistle is worth carrying the extra bulk on a daily basis or if carrying the knowledge of how to make a whistle will suffice.

SKILL #66
SIGNAL SOS WITH MORSE CODE

Dot-Dot-Dot, Dash-Dash-Dash, Dot-Dot-Dot. That is the short answer to the question, "How do you send an SOS?" Morse code was created by Samuel Morse way back in 1836. Originally intended to be used with the electric telegraph, you can use Morse code in other ways today. SOS can be sent by keying the microphone of a radio if you are too weak to talk. It can be sent visually with a flashlight that has a momentary on/off. Or it can even be sent by drumming it out loudly on a metal surface or pipe with a metal drumstick of sorts.

If you are stressed and somehow forget S is represented by Dot-Dot-Dot and replace it with Dash-Dash-Dash, don't fret. SOS is a repeating cycle, and whether you use dots or dashes, the message should be read loud and clear. I highly doubt anyone will read "OSO" and not realize it is anything but a distress signal. Repeat the cycle as long as it is appropriate and reasonable given your circumstances.

S.O.S.
▪ ▪ ▪ ▬▬ ▬▬ ▪ ▪ ▪

Dot, Dot, Dot Dash, Dash, Dash Dot, Dot, Dot

Simple to remember, S.O.S. is a widely recognizable distress signal.

SKILL #67
IMPROVISED REFLECTIVE DEVICES

One form of visual signaling is the use of reflective devices. Depending on your situation, you may need to use reflective devices to signal your location. A common survival scenario that comes up is that of the stranded vehicle after an accident. Think of all the reflective objects in your vehicle. You have taillights, multiple mirrors, metallic reflective surfaces, as well as glass. Your vehicle may also include plenty of wires, straps and cords you can strip from it. Your vehicle is an incredible resource for reflective and visual parts you can utilize to make passive signaling devices.

Visual signaling is usually portrayed as an active means of signaling, but it can also be passive. Your car may catch the attention of a person who sees it somewhere it shouldn't be. The same goes for your tent if it is brightly colored or if you can make it so by draping an aluminum-colored space blanket over it. Depending on your resources, you can suspend mirrors or reflectors like wind chimes to twist, spin and catch light from different angles. If an aerial rescue is a possibility, reflective surfaces can be scattered on the ground at different angles.

Plenty of roads are situated in places where going off-road by accident can put you in a blind area. Passersby may have trouble seeing you. Another likely scenario where the improvised reflective device would come in handy is when you are too weak to continue actively signaling. Passive signals in the backcountry can be clothes, pots and pans or an emergency mylar blanket hanging in the wind at eye level.

Correct reflective mirror position.

SKILL #68
DEDICATED SIGNAL MIRROR USE

Dedicated signal mirrors feature a small peephole in the center of the mirror body along with a grid you will notice when you look through it. Studies have shown this mirror is extremely accurate in sending a beam of light to an object and more accurate than the standard *V* notch. These mirrors are common in military survival kits. They tend to be made from real glass and while they are heavier than their polymer counterparts, they generally are more reflective and worth the extra weight.

Assuming you have a reflective surface, you can use it to signal for help by directing the beam of light that reflects off of it. You won't be able to see where the beam of light is hitting at any great distance. What you will need to do is use the *V* notch method of signaling with a mirror. Using one arm, extend it out in front of you at full extension and create a *V* with your index and middle finger. Place the object you wish to signal inside this *V*. Holding the mirror or reflective device in the other hand, put it close to your face under your eye. You want to keep your eye, mirror and notched fingers all in one line. This will ensure the beam is sent along the same line of sight as your sight picture through your fingers. To signal with the beam of light, reflect the light from the sun off the mirror or reflective surface onto your notched fingers. Work the light back and forth from one finger to the next and back again. If the object you want to signal is in between your fingers, the beam should hit it as long as it is hitting your two fingers too.

Look directly through a dedicated signal mirror and place the bright spot on your target.

To use the dedicated signaling mirror, hold the peep sight close to your eye and face in the direction of the sun but not at it. Even looking directly at the sun with this peep sight is not a wise move. If you are in direct sunlight and for some reason can't acquire the sun—it sounds ridiculous—make sure you don't have a hat with a brim on, as it can block the light you want to reflect. When you are certain you have the sun, look through the peep sight and find your intended recipient in the grid pattern in the sight. Move the mirror until you acquire the white dot. The white dot can then be walked in the peep sight onto your intended recipient.

SKILL #69
SIGNAL FIRES AND SMOKE GENERATORS

You've probably heard of First Nations smoke signals in some form of story or classroom instruction. Smoke has been used for hundreds of years to convey simple messages over great distances. There is truth in the expression, "where there's smoke, there is fire," and you will be able to improve your chances of rescue by having fire-starting gear on you. What is also sometimes true and tragic is where there is no smoke, there may not be fire. It is better to have it and not need it than need it and not have it.

Smoke generators require knowledge of fire starting and construction of the log-cabin fire lay. Since your smoke needs to contrast, remember to use white smoke in the summer with green vegetation and dark smoke in the winter against a wintery-white frozen background. Evergreens work great to make white smoke, while birch bark smokes black. In a bind, to create the thickest and darkest smoke, burn rubber tires if you can find them or anything petroleum based like plastics, polymers and oils. Throwing wet greens and leaves on a bed of coals will create white smoke, but you want the ability to keep that fire going underneath the green vegetation for larger plumes of smoke. To make this happen, what you are going to make is a fire lay that will serve as a platform for material that will smoke as fire is burning underneath it. Think of a smoke generator as a log-cabin fire made from green wood, so as not to burn through easily with a tipi fire inside of it. The green wood will support the material from falling inside the fire, and the spaces between the "lincoln logs" will help fuel the fire with plenty of air.

The signal fire is more of a night signal, as fire will burn bright and smoke is not easily seen. At night, think bright. In other words, you want your signal to stand tall and cast a lot of light. The log-cabin fire used for the smoke generator is ideal for providing a consistent flame that will burn long and steady. For a night signal fire, you want to build a tipi fire that will catch with a single strike of your ferro rod or a single lit match thrown at its core. Your signal fire is one you can build up over days and add more and more tinder and kindling to that will fully engulf faster than large fuel, which takes more time to burn. You can use heavier fuel along the outside as a frame or cage to hold all of your lighter fuel in place. A signal fire is a onetime deal, and you have to remember you may only have one chance to grab someone's attention with your fire. A 6-foot (1.8-m) tipi fire is the minimum height I would make a tipi fire, as the height of the flames should be double the height of the structure and a near two-story high should be easy to spot.

With both signal fire and smoke generators, always be prepared to add additional materials once you realize you have been spotted. If your fire dies out, those looking for you might assume they simply "saw something that wasn't there." If you can add additional material to keep that flame burning or smoke billowing, you can help your rescuers validate your existence. This means having a second fire setup or smoke generator ready to go when the first one dies out.

A smoke generator is built from a log-cabin fire.

Greens are placed over the log-cabin fire to create white smoke.

SKILL #70
CHEMICAL LIGHT STICK SIGNAL

Chemical light sticks have been around for a few decades. Break the inner glass capsule inside the plastic bendable body, and the chemical inside the vial mixes with the solution in the plastic body. These chemical light sticks create no heat and are safe to use in emergencies where an open flame is a risky proposition. Variations of light sticks are available—from those that let off a green glow for hours to high-intensity white and yellow light sticks that have a "burn time" of only minutes. While these lights give off significant illumination, there is a way to increase their visibility with only a length of cord.

By tying a short length of cord to the lanyard hole in the end of the light stick, you can swing the light stick around your head or at your side in a circle. This will turn a single light stick into a circular pattern that will stand out. That short length, say 3-feet (91-cm) long, creates a 6-foot (1.8-m)-wide circle that will be more visible than a single point of light. This manner of signaling is done in the military with infrared chemical light sticks, but it is applicable in the civilian world too. Even if you are not signaling for an air rescue, you can alert others in your group to your position in the same manner.

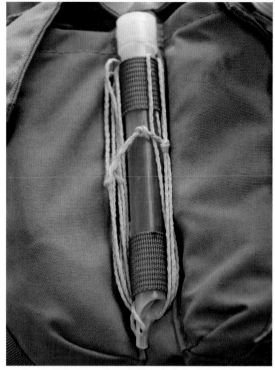

A chemical light stick and short length of Kevlar cordage are carried on a canteen pouch for use as a night signal.

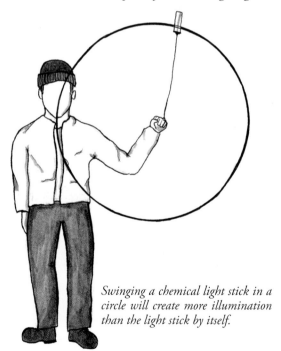

Swinging a chemical light stick in a circle will create more illumination than the light stick by itself.

SKILL #71

TURNBUCKLE RATTLER PERIMETER ALARM

Watch yourself when constructing this spinning alarm system.

Sometimes the signals are not meant to alert others, but you instead. Alarm systems can signal when an animal disturbs your food supply as well as when someone, perhaps a rescuer, walks across a nearby trail where they would otherwise miss you. One very effective audible alarm is the turnbuckle rattler made with a few lengths of paracord and discarded cans.

The turnbuckle rattler is constructed between two sturdy trees separated by no more than a couple feet. These trees should be approximately 3 to 6 inches (7.5 to 15 cm) in diameter. Although thicker trees can work, they require more cordage than you may have. The first step in building this alarm system is stringing up salvaged cans between the two selected trees. A length of cord can span the gap between the trees, and the cans can hang from this cordage on drop lines. The cans can be filled with small pebbles to increase the rattle effect.

A second loop of paracord is tied below the hanging cans around both trees, spanning the gap with the line just touching the bottom of the cans. Make sure you have a strong knot tied in this second loop, as it will be tensioned with a wooden dowel. A double overhand knot will hold up well. Place a 1-inch (2.5-cm)-thick section of a branch in between the second loop and make sure it will make contact with the cans as it is twisted. Do a practice run of your alarm system by twisting this branch like a turnbuckle until the line is tensioned. When you release the wooden dowel, it should spin wildly and strike the cans.

Believe it or not, the most difficult part of making this signal is devising the trigger mechanism. While there are elaborate ways of setting up triggers that require carving, running a simple loop of paracord over the tensioned turnbuckle and then around a tree and across a trail is the easiest. The loop holds the turnbuckle in place until the cord is pulled on or tripped. When the cord is disturbed, the tension on the turnbuckle slips it off and frees the turnbuckle to spin.

The turnbuckle rattler doesn't require many resources to build, but it does require some time and caution while setting it up. The turnbuckle is a concept that has advanced uses in building bow saws as well as striking traps for rodents.

NEXT LEVEL TRAINING

It is said that the universal symbol of distress is the number three. This is mostly true unless you are somewhere when hunting season is taking place. Three gunshots in succession could simply signal that someone is a bad hunter instead of someone in need of assistance. If you can build one signal fire or smoke generator, you can build three. These should all be sized up and spread out so they do not appear as one from a distance. When you first learn skills, you may struggle to keep one fire or one smoke generator operating, but remember you should train until you can build, light and manage all three. When you can manage three fires, you should do some self-discovery to determine what plants in your area will produce smoke and what woods will produce the fastest fire.

To send a flash of light in the opposite direction the sun is facing, a dedicated signal mirror can be used in conjunction with the small mirror found on the inside of the compasses carried.

The skills presented in this chapter are largely focused on how to attract attention with the bare necessities and running gear in your kit. There are improved ways to send signals that require skill sets of their own.

RADIO SKILLS

Depending on your location, you may choose to pursue a HAM radio operator license or purchase a marine band radio that boaters use. Both of these radio-communication methods will offer you an advantage of a person relying on the cellular network, but they do have limitations. The radio can transmit and receive, but it is not open like a phone where you can both speak at the same time. Also, your radio may be limited in range or by the surroundings, which can limit the effectiveness of this form of communication and signal. You can take communication classes and become licensed while learning proper radio etiquette along the way.

FLASHING STROBE

Signaling skills should take into account the entire 24-hour day. Visual signaling is more than reflecting sunlight. At night, you can attract attention visually if you have a bright enough light. You can use your flashlight and strobe it with a fast thumb or turn it onto the strobe function if it is capable of that. You can also use a dedicated strobe that serves that single purpose; it will flash for days of battery life and can be seen for miles. A dedicated strobe can be a small keychain model or a larger style like those carried by the armed forces, boaters and pilots. Whenever I travel solo, I pack my strobe, as it weighs very little and ensures I can send a signal in the darkness as I try to catch up on sleep.

SATELLITE DISTRESS BEACONS

If, at some point, you decide to take the search out of "search and rescue," you may decide to purchase a personal locator beacon (PLB) or a survival emergency notification device (SEND). These devices are more expensive than your whistle and mirror but can get you rescued in as little as a few hours and will significantly shorten your survival experience. With just the press of a button, they notify authorities of your distress and provide your location. PLBs operate on the 406 MHz international distress frequency, sending your signal to a government monitoring agency. SENDs are equipped with an "SOS" button but also allow one-way or two-way text communications depending upon the model. They require a subscription to their service. They utilize commercial satellite services and a private specialist monitoring company. If you want the best option for rescue in the shortest amount of time, you should consider a PLB or SEND.

FIRST-AID AND TRAUMA SKILLS

"When seconds count, help is minutes away." —Anonymous

There is no substitute for good training, and this includes medical training. If you're looking to learn all there is to know about first-aid and trauma skills in this chapter, you're seeking out information from the wrong Estela. My father received comprehensive medical training during his career as a physician. I can enhance your understanding of common practices and provide some essential skills, but what I can provide in the following chapter should not be the end of the road in your medical training.

During the basic survival course at the Wilderness Learning Center, we never spent too much time covering the first-aid skills students could acquire in a dedicated first-aid class. We believed our students came to the WLC to learn survival, and while we could present information on first aid, we knew first-aid instructors could not present information about fire starting, navigation, edible plants and so on. During the basic course, we covered emergency medicine

that could save a life that might not be covered in a basic first-aid class. In that same respect, this won't be the longest or most detailed chapter in this book. There are definitely many more skills you can learn from a qualified first-aid instructor or dedicated first-aid manual. If you need to have a handful of useful skills to prolong life, this chapter will give you a breakdown of those skills.

Many emergency situations result from medical emergencies. Falls create broken bones and accidents with knives, axes and saws lead to bleeding. Not drinking enough water makes people dehydrated, clouds their judgment and leads to bad decision making. Accidents happen, and you need to be ready to respond to them appropriately. Just as many firearms enthusiasts carry blowout kits with trauma gear to respond to negligent and/or accidental gunshot wounds, you must carry gear appropriate to address the injuries that can result from using your gear incorrectly.

SKILL #72
PRIMARY SURVEY SKILLS

Everyone should learn first-aid skills, as the life you save could be your own. The ABCs—Airway, Breathing and Circulation—are critical parts to surveying a patient's vital signs, but something many forget to include is surveying the scene prior to entering it. This is critical for those of you who will rely on these skills in the great outdoors, as you will have potential threats to identify before helping a patient. As an outdoorsman/woman, you'll have to worry about unstable terrain, loose rocks/ice overhead, swarms of bees, sharp briars, wild animals and many other variables. Prior to checking vitals, look for dangerous conditions above, below and behind you in the 720-degree world we live in that could create another injury for you.

If, after you check the consciousness and vitals of a patient, you recognize the need to call for help, do so as quickly as possible and don't delay. Remember, when seconds count, help is minutes, hours or even days away. In the great outdoors, you might be miles from the nearest hospital or ranger station. If you readied yourself before leaving your house, you should have no issue communicating with the outside world. In civilization, you can make a phone call, wait for help or drive someone to the emergency room. In the great outdoors, you may have to send a runner from your party, leave your patient in a recovery position after marking their location or transport your patient if movement won't cause additional injury.

Estela Wilderness Education Instructor Mike Travis demonstrates a primary survey on a patient.

Assuming you've checked out the scene and alerted someone to bring additional advanced care, your next step before you perform a primary survey is gaining a patient's consent. If a person is unconscious, this step is unnecessary as it is assumed an unconscious person gives you their consent. If a person is lucid, alert and able to communicate with you, make sure you identify yourself, your ability and your intentions and ask if you can help them. Consent is important if you plan on returning back to civilization at some point. You never can be too careful in a litigious society. After gaining consent, you can ask your patient what is wrong with them and listen to what they have to say. You can run questions and answers before deciding what to do. If you are dealing with someone who is unconscious, you won't have the luxury of instant feedback to your questioning.

When you finally go "hands on" during your primary survey, work deliberately and be thorough. Look, listen and feel for vital signs. What this means is relying on your senses to gain a sense of awareness as to the condition of your patient. Following the ABCs, when assessing an airway, get close to your unconscious patient and physically look into their mouth to see if the airway is restricted. If you suspect the patient has a spinal injury, under no circumstances should you move their head. In fact, you should take spare clothing and immobilize their head or enlist a partner to hold their head still. What you should do is open their jaw by moving it forward. The jaw moves independently from the spine and accessing the airway this way reduces the chance of further injuring the patient. To "look, listen and feel" for breathing, watch for the patient's chest to rise, listen for air coming from their lungs and feel for that breath with the sensitive hair/skin in and around your ears.

After checking the airway and breathing, you want to assess your patient's circulation. This means checking for a heartbeat where you can feel a pulse. This is commonly done at the carotid arteries on either side of the windpipe, at the wrist on the radial artery and by the ankle on the posterior tibial. These are not the only locations where the arteries are near the surface of the skin, but they are common locations easily accessed on most people wearing a variety of clothing. If a person has a pulse and is breathing, move on to checking their body for signs of trauma. If a person has a pulse but isn't breathing, check to see if their airway is obstructed—if not, begin rescue breathing. If a person has no pulse and is not breathing, begin CPR. Rescue breathing is simple enough: pinch your patient's nose shut and breathe into their mouth (ideally with a rescue mask barrier) by making a seal over it with yours, and breathe for a second, removing your mouth when inhaling back in. Repeat the process for two breaths and reassess the patient's ABCs. Assuming your rescue breathing does not work, begin CPR. Since CPR standards are continually changing, I will simply advise you to consult the most recent standards and apply them at this point.

Part of your primary survey should be a thorough scan of your patient's body. This may require removing or looking under your patient's clothing. Be professional in assessing someone, so that they may maintain their dignity afterward.

SKILL #73
STOPGAP PRESSURE

A time-proven method for dealing with bleeding is the application of direct pressure to a wound. There have been more than a few instances when I've seen direct pressure work effectively on cuts to fingers and hands when a person has had an accident while carving with a knife. Often, these cuts are quick and glancing and don't penetrate too deeply. Direct pressure does work on shallow cuts, those that don't bleed too heavily and those that haven't cut an artery. There are other times when blood loss is more extreme. In car crashes, for instance, when there is a risk of amputation or when using a heavy cutting tool like an ax or machete, you won't be able to apply enough pressure to a wound or the area that is bleeding with just your hand. You'll need a different method of keeping blood in the body of your patient. You'll need to apply stopgap pressure.

Stopgap is a term used to describe a temporary solution to a problem. Stopgap pressure is what you can do to stop bleeding to an extremity until you can apply a tourniquet (described in the next essential skill). Stopgap pressure is applied to the femoral artery at the crease between the thigh and the pelvis and to the brachial artery on the inside of the arm near the armpit. Instead of using your hands, stopgap pressure is applied with your knees, shins, forearms or elbows, allowing you to free up your hands to prepare your tourniquet or makeshift tourniquet for use. Also, blood is very slick. If you have never had your hands covered in blood (an animal's, your own, someone else's), it makes gripping an object difficult. When you temporarily stop the bleeding with a stopgap, you keep your hands clean.

Don't worry about being gentle when applying stopgap pressure to your patient's body. The inside of the body (inner thighs and inner arm) as well as the pelvis and armpit are extremely sensitive to pressure. You must be prepared to make someone uncomfortable to address the bigger problem of bleeding. You need to remember you are choosing pain over death, and if you are proficient in stopping blood loss with a tourniquet, you will only be applying the stopgap until you can get that tourniquet on. Tourniquet pressure, as you'll read, is not pleasant either, but again, as long as you stop bleeding, prolong your patient's life and get them to an emergency room quickly, the discomfort is worth it.

SKILL #74
APPLY A TOURNIQUET

At one point in history, if you even mentioned "tourniquet" in a medical discussion, it was controversial. Before modern advanced medical care, applying a tourniquet to someone or yourself was an almost foolproof way to ensure the patient's extremity would be lost and need to be amputated. Tourniquets cut off circulation and at one point, medical professionals did not have the understanding or technology to save the limb. As time passed, tourniquets came back into favor, and the lessons learned overseas on the battlefield have become common practice in the civilian world. Modern medicine has allowed doctors, like one of my former survival students Dr. Ian, to remove tourniquets up to six hours after they have been applied. As long as a patient is moved to advanced care quickly, applying a tourniquet in the modern era no longer means amputation is always necessary.

Tourniquets stop bleeding and dedicated purpose-built tourniquets do it best. You can certainly make some improvised tourniquets work, but with the right gear and training, a dedicated and purpose-built tourniquet will work better. A single strand of paracord makes a horrible tourniquet as it can do damage to tissue, blood vessels and arteries. Multiple strands of paracord used as one that spread out the pressure are better but nothing beats something built to be a tourniquet. Even if you don't operate sharp tools, visit the firing range or work in an occupation where the likelihood of self-care is high, you could need to stop severe bleeding from a car accident or other

The author applies a tourniquet high and tight.

mishap. I carry a purpose-built fire starter instead of creating fire-starting devices in the field. I use a purpose-built compass to navigate through the woods instead of relying on makeshift wayfinders. I carry a tourniquet because it is designed to stop bleeding and I want the best device to address a life-threatening situation.

There are many tourniquet designs you can use that apply tension with elasticity, turnbuckles or ratcheting action. Always assess the quality of your gear and seek out what the professionals use. Avoid untested and unproven tourniquets, as well as those that are unauthorized copies, as many counterfeits are sold each year. Also, determine what tourniquet will work with most scenarios and those where you will not be able to move the extremity where it is applied. I personally

SOF-T tourniquet

carry the Combat Application Tourniquet (C.A.T.) and the SOF Tourniquet. Both utilize a twisting turnbuckle and can be applied easily with one hand. Both can be applied to the arms or legs, and each can be folded and stored in a manner for quick deployment.

Tourniquet application is a skill, and you must practice how to self-administer one and learn how to apply one to a patient in diverse conditions. You must learn to apply a tourniquet with two hands, with only your right hand and with only your left hand. You must practice to quickly apply one as seconds matter if you or your patient are losing blood. You never can predict when or where you'll need one or what limitations and conditions will exist requiring you to modify how you access, make ready and ultimately apply your tourniquet.

What doesn't change is where you place the tourniquet. Remember to apply your tourniquet both high and tight. This means high up on the arm, not on the forearm, and high on the thigh above the knee. You can't be certain if the bleeding is isolated to one area or if it is found internally inside the arm or the leg far from the point of bleeding. Don't worry about removing clothing; just get your tourniquet on as soon as possible. Keep applying more and more pressure until the bleeding stops. When the tourniquet is applied and the bleeding stops, make sure you mark when the tourniquet was applied as advanced care will need to know what they are dealing with. Under no circumstances should you remove a tourniquet once you apply it.

In case you're wondering, you can test out a tourniquet on one of your extremities and gauge its effectiveness by taking your pulse below the application. I don't recommend leaving a tourniquet on for any significant length of time. You should remove it when you start to feel slight numbness in your fingers or toes. You should know how much pressure to apply in an emergency, and there is no better way than learning firsthand. You will also recognize that you will have some mobility in that extremity for a while until the tourniquet reduces the sensitivity of the extremity.

SKILL #75
IRRIGATE A WOUND

A water bottle can easily be turned into a makeshift irrigation device.

Not all cuts are caused by a sharp instrument. Sometimes a cut happens while something unsanitary is being cut. Kitchen knives slip while processing raw meat, chainsaws kick back while cutting wood, random sharp metal cuts us after being exposed to bacteria and countless unknown substances. We can't assume a bleeding cut is a clean cut, and putting a bandage on it will just trap in what shouldn't be there. When you can, you need to irrigate wounds with a steady stream of purified water. By the way, I make the point of stressing purified water to reduce the chance of infection. In terms of infection, if you have a choice of using nonsterile dressings or no dressings at all, use the nonsterile dressings. You can always treat infection after the bleeding stops, but if the bleeding is severe enough, you can't treat death.

Irrigating wounds is simple at home. I've accidentally nicked my fingers, have made my way to the kitchen sink while holding pressure on the cut and winced at the pain as the steady flow of tap water has run under and into the cut I just caused. In ideal conditions, irrigation of wounds is done with a large-volume syringe filled with a sterile irrigation solution. In the great outdoors, you won't have access to an irrigation syringe or solution unless you packed them with you. If you have other resources available, you can exercise your resourcefulness and make do with what you have. A simple disposable bottle of water can be adapted to suit your purpose. By poking a hole in the cap and squeezing the body of the bottle, your disposable bottle of water is now an irrigation device that will squirt water. To some degree, the same can be done with a plastic bag, but depending on how hard you squeeze the bag, the spot you cut or punctured can tear more easily.

If irrigation syringes, plastic bottles and bags are not available, you can simply use gravity to help irrigate a wound. Pour a water bottle out and place the cut portion of the body underneath the flow far enough from the source where the falling water will force its way into the cut. Avoid intermittent irrigation flow if possible by using copious amounts of water in a steady flow.

When the cut is properly cleaned out, the wound should be covered with a clean dressing. If the cut is clean, the wound should knit (the term used to describe what happens when a cut closes and heals on its own), but if it is ragged, it may need direct pressure to help it along its way to healing and eventually scabbing over. If possible, you should change out your dressings and keep the cut area dry. If you have it, an antibiotic ointment will help the cut area from becoming infected and can help the healing process.

SKILL #76
MAKESHIFT SNOW GOGGLES

Winter conditions can be brutal. Cold is uncomfortable, and the lack of sunlight can be a serious blow to your morale. One problem associated with winter blizzard conditions is snow blindness. On sunny days, snow reflects light very well, and unprotected eyes can lead to headaches and/or pain when looking out over the landscape. There can simply be too much light entering your iris. A quick fix is simply squinting, but this can lead to eye fatigue too. You may not have the luxury of a set of sunglasses, but this doesn't mean you are without any other options. You can always create makeshift goggles to address the problem of snow blindness.

Assuming you have no materials on hand other than what you can access off the land, a time-tested way of creating goggles is with birch bark. Birch bark can be cut into a strip and two slits can be cut for the eye apertures. The entire strip can be worn around the head attached with natural cordage or a small length of paracord.

If you have some resources, you can repurpose a disposable emergency blanket into an emergency set of goggles. If you cut a small strip of emergency blanket and hold it up to your eyes you'll see that you can see through it slightly. If you are struggling to see through your blanket, poke a couple of pinholes for each of your eyes. Much like a peephole on a door, you need to put the holes close to your eyes to see through them. You can also use duct tape, adhesive side pressed to adhesive side, if you are without an emergency

Held close to the eyes, emergency blankets can be seen through to prevent snow blindness.

blanket. Just like the birch bark goggles, you can use cordage or a ribbon cut from the disposable emergency blanket or duct tape twisted into line to tie the goggles onto your face. You'll see some versions of these goggles referenced elsewhere with a nose cutout much like a regular set of sunglasses. You can leave a flap over your nose to provide additional sun coverage if you like.

SKILL #77
CATTAIL ANTISEPTIC

Even those who don't study plants can likely identify a cattail. Normally found in wetlands, they are ubiquitous and have a very unique flowering spike. Cattail really is unmistakable with its distinct head and fluff that forms when the seeds are ready to spread. The seeds that form look very much like a cat's tail stretched straight. This plant is nicknamed the supermarket of the swamp, and depending on what time of year it is, there is something you can take from the plant to get some caloric value.

From a first-aid standpoint, cattail has an incredible antiseptic quality. Depending on the time of the year, cattail has a gel-like substance that can be found when you pull back the leaves toward the base of the plant. This gel can be used on fresh cuts as a topical treatment.

In an emergency, anything you can do to boost morale will potentially keep you from heading down the path to depression, despair and defeat. As outdoorsmen, we don't want to ask for a bandage or sweat the little cuts and scratches we get as we carry out our tasks in the wild. This pride can hurt us if one of those cuts gets infected. It doesn't hurt to treat what we can and know we are controlling one element of our existence and fate. Cattail has many uses beyond treating cuts. For instance, the cattail seed pods can also be used as effective insulation between two layers of clothes. Not only is this plant incredibly nutritious, it can save your life and make you more comfortable when you get the occasional nick or scratch.

Harvesting cattail from a pond.

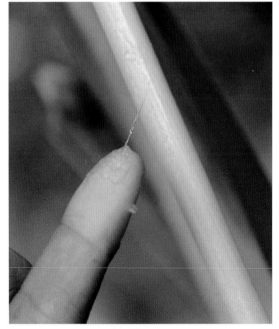

Cattail gel is a natural antiseptic.

SKILL #78

SELF-EXAMINE WITH TWO MIRRORS

I always recommend my students carry at least two mirrors on them. One of these mirrors is their dedicated signaling mirror and the other could be a duplicate or perhaps the mirror from their sighting compass. Two mirrors let you signal in more directions than one, regardless of the sun's position. The other benefit of having two mirrors is being able to self-examine the back of your head and body.

Mirrors work great if what you need to see is on the front of your body or if you can turn your head enough to see your back, but you need at least two mirrors to see the back of your head and your neck. Ticks have the tendency to embed in your hairline and in places you can't see easily. I can trust the tips of my fingers or a comb to feel blindly for any foreign objects, or I can visually confirm I'm tick free. With two mirrors, I can hold one behind my head and outstretch my arm in front of me holding the other. I can also set one in place on a rock or tree branch and hold the other until I get a good picture of what I need to see. Ticks are not the only problem you can identify with two mirrors. After a slip and fall, you can assess how bad a cut is to your head or after an insect bite, you can look for swelling or redness. When you need a second set of eyes, don't forget you have them with two mirrors.

Two mirrors let you examine the back of your head and body.

SKILL #79
HYPOTHERMIA BLANKET WRAP

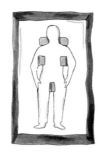

A hypothermia wrap using a tarp, a blanket and hot rocks.

Cold on its own is not that bad. Wet on its own is not that bad. Both cold and wet combined is a recipe for misery, and add in a little wind or lack of food and/or mobility and you'll find your body heat is pulled from you very quickly. Your body's temperature hovers around the 98.6°F (37°C) temperature mark. When it rises only a couple degrees, you experience hyperthermia and when it decreases a couple degrees, you enter into hypothermia. Both conditions can be extremely dangerous to your health, and both are treated in the same way. Ideally, you want to move the patient to a location where their body temperature can return to normal—into the shade if treating hyperthermia and near a fire for hypothermia. You also want to introduce liquids in small quantities: warm water for hypothermia patients and cool water for hyperthermia patients. Ideally, intravenous fluids are administered for hyperthermia victims, but the necessary hardware won't be available in an emergency.

Assuming someone is showing signs of hypothermia that include lethargy, mumbling, slow breathing and cold-pale skin, you may need to utilize the resources around you to make a thermal cocoon for them. This is sometimes referred to as the "hypothermia burrito" or "hypo wrap," and it is how you can use a blanket to trap the air around a patient while you treat them. If you have ever felt your bare leg sneak out from under the covers on a cold night, you know how quickly you can become cold. With nothing more than a sleeping bag or two, sleeping pad or two and a tarp, you can assemble a thermal burrito to help treat a patient of hypothermia.

Starting with your tarp, lay it on the ground and place your sleeping pad(s) in the center of it. On top of the sleeping pad, place a sleeping bag down and another sleeping bag on top of that (not inside of the first) where you will place your patient. If you can boil water and warm the bag with hot water bottles, do so or use hot rocks tucked inside of socks. Chemical hand warmers will also work if they are available. These heat sources should be placed near the crotch, under the armpits and near the neck of your patient. Place your patient inside the sleeping bag and zip it up. Fold one side of the tarp over your patient followed by folding the bottom of the tarp up on the feet and legs. The last step is folding the other side of the flap over the first and second folds. If possible, tuck this flap underneath the patient to prevent it from opening up. Do not cover your patient's face or mouth to avoid suffocation and condensation from their breath forming on the tarp that could eventually get them wet and make them even colder. When you are done wrapping your patient, remember to monitor them and provide warm water in small quantities.

SKILL #80
SPLINT A BROKEN BONE

Broken bones vary in severity from hairline fractures noticeable only by X-ray to compound fractures where the bone has actually been exposed through the skin. You will know you have a broken bone when you feel a sharp pain at first from the suspected area and then deep pain throbbing from that area. If you or your patient notice increased sensitivity or pain to the touch in the suspected area, you have even more cause for concern. If you also notice discoloration from bleeding, you can be fairly certain you're dealing with a broken bone.

The treatment for a broken bone out in the field is immobilization. This means applying a splint to the affected area that secures the break above and below the suspected area. Broken bones are supposed to be reset in a controlled environment where advanced care is available. I don't advise resetting bones in the field as you can cause more harm than good. Without advanced training, you can't know the necessary precautions to take, the correct order of events or signs to look for to know you did it correctly. Your best course of action is splinting your patient and getting them help right away. You may need to wait for help to arrive to you in the backcountry, or you may need to move your patient.

Splints can be fashioned from many makeshift materials. Closed-foam sleeping pads work well, as do hiking or tent poles, composite or aluminum backpack stays and even branches. In urban areas, you have more options to use for

Support breaks above and below the injury and immobilize the limb with splints.

makeshift splints, including cardboard boxes, magazines, building materials and so on. If you can or when it is necessary, apply padding to prevent your splint from cutting your patient in transport and to aid in comfort. Splints should be placed to the left and right of a leg injury and to the outside of an arm injury. Fingers should be splinted above and below the joints of the finger. You can use tape or strips of cloth to secure a splint in place. Make sure to use only enough pressure to keep the splint in place. Too much pressure can result in a loss of circulation to the extremity; this is why you need to monitor the pulse of your patient every hour while the splint is on. You also want to look for any worsening conditions while the splint is on.

You may have to self-administer a splint or apply one to a backwoods companion. Keep in mind, if mobility is not a concern, you can always splint a broken leg to the opposite leg, assuming it is not broken. Like all the other emergency medical advice given here, do what you can on your own, but seek out advanced care to ultimately address the medical issue you're treating.

SKILL #81
USE MEDICINAL PLANTS

Five teas you can learn and start using as soon as you learn to identify them confidently are white pine, yarrow, hawthorne, willow and St. John's Wort. I'd recommend finding a local expert who can help you verify each of these is what you believe it to be, and you should always check the plant against three reference books to make sure the information overlaps and is redundant. Start off trying medicinal plants slowly. You may eventually prefer using them to modern medicine. As with any change to your lifestyle or routine, you should consult your physician before starting any of these. They know you better than I do. Also, these recommendations are just that, recommendations. You should learn what works for you.

WHITE PINE

This pine tree is easily identified by the five needles that grow from each cluster. Simply take a handful of needles and place them in a cup. Pour boiling water over them (decoction) and let the tea steep for a few minutes. You'll notice a slight film develop over the water. These are the oils found in the plant that are filled with both Vitamin C and Vitamin A. It was traditionally used to treat scurvy and can be used today to change the flavor of your treated water or make it have some flavor to boost your morale. (Wintergreen can also be used in a similar way for Vitamin C.)

Yarrow flowers and leaves

YARROW

Yarrow is a small flowering plant with feather-like leaves that alternate and have incredible medicinal value. Throughout history, this plant has been used both internally and externally. It was chewed on to relieve toothaches, the fresh leaves were placed on wounds to help with healing and teas were made to help digestion, fight fevers and treat the common cold. The leaves and flowers can be used green, or they can be dried.

HAWTHORN

Hawthorn is a tree with many uses. The small "thornapples" are edible (just avoid the seeds), the extremely long and ominous-looking thorns are my choice for gouge hooks and the barbs used in forked fishing spears. From a medicinal

Wintergreen tea is flavorful and loaded with vitamin C.

aspirin-like flavor. You can, like all of the plants recommended here, make a tea from steeping the stripped bark from young willow twigs. When used properly, salicylic acid is effective as a treatment for both high fever and headaches. It can also be used to address minor aches and pains. Like aspirin, you don't want to ingest too much willow. Too much of either aspirin or willow bark can lead to stomach cramping and bleeding.

ST. JOHN'S WORT

St. John's Wort is a low yellow flowering plant that grows in sunny, well-drained areas. Take one of the yellow flowers and crush it in the palm of your hand and you'll notice a red to purplish color that looks like the "blood of St. John." If you are still not certain you are looking at St. John's Wort, hold the green leaves up to the sun and examine them. You will notice light working its way through the leaves through many tiny "pinholes." St. John's Wort is an excellent sedative and a few of my friends harvest it, dry it at home and keep it on hand when the winter blues and mild depression settle in. In an emergency situation, when you feel you need to calm your nerves or address feelings of despair, you can make a tea out of St. John's Wort. By the way, if you are concerned about drinking a tea from a plant called "wort," don't worry. "Wort" is just an early term used to describe a plant.

aspect, hawthorn is an incredible plant from which to make teas for all matters of the heart. Some guides will recommend using hawthorne for low-blood pressure and others for high-blood pressure. Evidence suggests it can be used for both. It can be beneficial for those with high cholesterol, too. Hawthorn has other benefits for indigestion as well as for anxiety, diarrhea, menstrual pains and stomach pain. This plant contains flavonoids that relax the body. To make a tea, steep the leaves and berries in boiling water.

WILLOW

Before there was aspirin, there was willow. The willow tree has an ingredient found in its bark called salicin. Salicylic acids, synthesized, become acetaminophen. Chew on the bark of young twigs and you'll notice a distinct medicinal and

NEXT LEVEL TRAINING

This chapter is far, and I mean really far, from a substitute for formal medical training. Even your most basic first-aid course will be useful day to day, as you never know when you'll need to draw from your training to treat cuts, broken bones, burns and so on. As I was writing this chapter and speaking with my father, he stressed how important it is for me to encourage you to seek out advanced training. You should look into your local community centers; many programs are free to the public or extremely inexpensive and taught by volunteers. I skipped over the basics you can find elsewhere because courses and informational resources are so plentiful and easily acquired. I would rather present material not commonly found that will enhance your understanding of treating problems in the wild. I suggest you read up on what you can carry in your first-aid kit and talk to your physician about what s/he recommends you should have. Maybe your physician has information about a training opportunity in their network you can participate in.

First-aid courses, including wilderness first-aid courses, will provide you one perspective for addressing medical issues. You shouldn't limit your training to one source, though. Even if you don't consider yourself a firearms enthusiast, you should participate in a firearms training course that places emphasis on treatment of gunshot wounds. In the twenty-first century, in and out of the woods, there is the possibility of encountering trauma from those who wield firearms improperly, negligently or illegally. You should learn when to apply a tourniquet, how to pack a junction and how to seal a sucking chest wound. You should also learn CPR and be up to date on the current standards for administration. Seek out qualified instructors and get certified. First-aid and trauma responsibilities don't begin at the trail and end when you walk off the trail. You're more likely to need the skills after a car accident getting to the trail. Understanding this reality will hopefully inspire you to make first-aid and trauma gear part of your daily carry.

WATER SKILLS

"You must be shapeless, formless, like water. When you pour water in a cup, it becomes the cup. When you pour water in a bottle, it becomes the bottle. When you pour water in a teapot, it becomes the teapot. Water can drip and it can crash. Become like water my friend." —*Bruce Lee*

The human body is composed mostly of water. We need water for digestion, for circulation, for padding our brain from the inside of our skulls, for coating our eyelids and for countless bodily functions. Water is life, and proper hydration is something many take for granted. As a general rule, you should consume at least half your body weight in ounces of water each day. On active days, this number almost doubles. For many, the idea of constantly drinking water is a burden, and there are many people walking around already in the early stages of dehydration. Dehydration is a real threat to the outdoorsman during all seasons of the year. It can inhibit your body's ability to cool itself, make digestion painful, cause headaches and blur your vision.

In an emergency or a survival situation, your water consumption will be critical. Hyperventilation, sweating and the possible fight, flight or freeze response of "pissing your pants" all mean you are releasing water from your system. This needs to be replaced. After extended physical exertion, it is common to see a thirsty person down an entire water bottle, gulping all of its contents before stopping. Drinking too quickly doesn't let your body absorb the water the way it needs to. While you should drink copious amounts of water, and more in times of high physical activity and heat, you should drink frequently and sip your water to let it absorb slowly. Just be careful not to consume too much water. When you drink too much water, you dilute the amount of salt in your body and place yourself in a condition known as hyponatremia. Also, in cold conditions, drinking water can feel painful against the throat. This is why having the ability to heat water over an open fire will make hydrating more pleasant and warm drinks will encourage you to consume enough water. The water you consume must be greater than the water you put out.

In some circumstances, such as those involving coastal survival or scenarios where you are surviving at sea, there may be a temptation to drink salt water. This can cause your kidneys to shut down. Your urine is less salty than salt water and your body will attempt to urinate more frequently to remove the excess salt from your system. This will dehydrate you more quickly.

Always be aware of water resources and where they can be located.

For similar reasons, you should not drink your own urine. While this practice has been shown in movies and television shows, it is bad practice. Your body excretes toxins in your urine, which is meant to leave your body, not enter it. Fresh water can be created from salt water, but this process is not easy. Keep this in mind: not easy but also not impossible.

When we look at our water needs, we need to break down and address them in four stages.

I. FIND WATER

Depending on your environment, locating water will mean looking for it based off of the natural cues around you. Water can be in liquid form or it can be found in the snow and ice around you. Water can be found above us in the form of precipitation, it can be found trapped in naturally forming pools or it can be found below ground by digging. The water you find may be fast moving or it could be the remnants of the lone drinking hole in the middle of nowhere with plenty of animal signs around it. It could have an earthy, fishy or mineral taste, or it could be better tasting than the water you purchase in bottles at the convenience store down the street. Don't be

turned away from seeing creatures living in your water, and remember when you eventually treat the water it will become safe to drink.

II. COLLECT WATER

With the exception of some survival straws that let you drink straight from the water source, you will either pump purified water into a container or place untreated water into a container to boil it or treat it with tablets, drops, boiling it or by other means. Water collection can be accomplished by dunking a bottle under water, by setting up a drip system where water slowly collects one drip at a time or by sponging it with an absorbent material like a pack towel, a bandana or that dirty T-shirt you're wearing. In cooler months, you may have to collect water by melting snow with a water generator that drops water into a vessel. In tropical conditions, you may collect water from the local vegetation.

III. TREAT WATER

Water can be treated in a number of ways to make it safe for drinking. This can be as simple as boiling or can include using chemical drops, iodine tablets, UV light or mechanical pumps. Treated water should never come near untreated water and vice versa. Even a single drop of contaminated water has the potential to spoil good drinking water. The nasties found in untreated water, including giardia and cryptosporidium, are too small to see with the naked eye. This is why the threads of water bottles are of concern and why the instructions on iodine tablets usually include loosening the cap, turning the bottle upside down and letting some of the treated iodine water drip out of the cap along the threads. Ideally, a two-container system with a nesting cup and sealable bottle or canteen is the best option. Treat water in the cup and pour it into the bottle.

You will eventually find or be forced to use any number of water treatment options. Boiling has been used for centuries (knowingly and unknowingly when making tea) and it is the simplest. Opinions will vary on boil times (30 seconds, 1 minute, 5 minutes), but as long as you bring water to a roaring boil and see big bubbles, your water will be safe to drink. Iodine can be used in drops or tablet form, though some find the aftertaste unpleasant. This is why modern iodine tablets come with a secondary neutralization tablet to add after treating the water. You can also mask the smell and taste with a vitamin C drink mix. Other means of treating water involve mechanical pumps that either filter (removing particulates), micro filter (removing bacteria and protozoa down to 0.2 micron) or purify (removing viruses) water. If you travel to developing countries or places with high-human traffic, there is always a chance for encountering more viruses than a remote mountain stream in a developed nation. Keep in mind, mechanical pumps have moving parts and are vulnerable to breaking. While they produce safe treated water from questionable sources, they do require pumping and occasional maintenance.

Another option you may have in your kit is an ultraviolet device to treat water. This tool uses ultraviolet light to sterilize the water. Unlike a filter, the UV light won't remove any particulates from the water. Also, those same particulates may inhibit the light's ability to treat the water. Furthermore, in cold conditions, you have to consider the battery power and output and if it will have an effect on the safety of the water you're drinking. You will have to evaluate and decide if this option is right for you.

IV. CARRY WATER

Unless you plan on remaining in place near a reliable water source, you will need some means of carrying water from point A to point B. Whenever you can, carry water in your body *and* on your person. Water containers come in many shapes, sizes and compositions. Pocket emergency kits have included containers made from unlubricated condoms to Reynolds oven bags. Personal-sized water containers include disposable water bottles, 32-ounce (1-L) Nalgene bottles, stainless steel canteens and my personal favorite—the titanium canteen from Heavy Cover. Group-size and base-camp water container options include jerry cans, gallon-sized (3.8-L) "milk" jug containers and flexible bladders. With increased capacity comes increased weight, as a gallon (3.8 L) of water weighs a little more than 8 pounds (3.6 kg).

I find a good combination of water containers is a small personal water container set made from metal (stainless or titanium) and a larger container that can collapse and roll up when not in use like a flexible bladder. I transfer water from my flexible bladder to my smaller canteen until I have to treat water and refill the bladder before setting off from camp. This is my way, but it's not the only way you can carry water. Find what works best for you.

SIMPLE MATH

I previously stated that water consumed must be greater than the water you expel. There will be times in the water process when you must

The author's favorite container, a Heavy Cover titanium canteen.

SKILL #82
FIND WATER IN DIFFERENT ENVIRONMENTS

You can't refill your canteen if you can't find water. Finding water will largely rely on your area of operation and the conditions you're in. If you are in a familiar area, you'll likely know the locations where water pools or where running water can be found. If you are in an unfamiliar area, you will have to fall back on recognizing universal concepts, past experience and some trial and error to find what you're looking for. Finding water requires using your senses as well as a hefty dose of common sense. The idea of dowsing or water divining has largely been debunked by scientists. If you think subsurface water is going to react with metal rods held in your hands, perhaps you should not read on.

Water can be collected first thing in the morning in the dew that forms on grass in open woodland fields. All you need to do is tie a handkerchief or spare T-shirt around your ankle and walk through a field. The cloth can be wrung out into a container. Water can also be found in the form of condensation on rocks. Hot weather and cold rocks will create damp surfaces you can also gather water from. Since water only drips down, tall rock faces can have significant amounts of water at their bases. Rock crevices can also trap water and it is in your best interest to check them too. Just be careful and look inside crevices to feel for moisture as insects and animals may house there.

Water can also be found by looking for water-loving vegetation. A prime example of this

monitor and judge how much you are sweating and how much water you are getting in return. A classic example is that of the solar still seen in so many survival manuals. The solar still has been reproduced and written about in many manuals. I take issue with it as it requires materials you are not likely to have on you, including a large plastic sheet, a long drinking tube and a shovel. Also, it requires you to dig a large hole in the ground, which can cause you to sweat profusely. In return, if you are able to maintain a proper seal on your still and have adequate sunlight, you may get a small amount of water in your collection cup.

Water supports life, and if we follow the average found in the rule of threes, we know we need to consume water or die in three days. Keep in mind, the rule of threes is an average, and while there have been people who have lasted longer than three days, there are people who have died in under three days as well. Your water needs will be determined by the clothing you are wearing, the temperature of the air, the amount and type of food you are eating and so many more factors. Water is life—you need to hydrate or die.

Pay attention to the physical landscape, as it will help you locate water.

is the willow tree in desert environments. Willow trees signal water, and they have a distinct shape and color that stands out from the rest of the more commonly found low-lying vegetation. From a vantage point, you can spot these color variations on the landscape and reduce the amount of scouting you need to do to find water. Another water-loving plant is cattail. Next time you see it along highways or in your backwood travels, note where it is growing. It could be found in swampy areas or in extremely saturated marshland. Water is not far away.

If you are in mountainous terrain, water collection can require some serious physical exertion. Mountains can hide ponds, and ravines found between peaks can represent places where running water can be found. When scouting areas with my map, I typically look for ravines as potential seasonal water sources. After all, when the map was drawn, it could have been a drier season when no water was present. Look to the terrain to give you clues. Another clue to look for is animal behavior. Birds tend to circle not far from water sources, and you may find animal tracks leading to water as well. Insects are similar; an abundance of mosquitoes may signal a water hole or pool of water nearby.

In winter conditions, you may be surrounded by snow in all directions. While it is tempting to grab a handful of snow and consume it, eating snow will lower your body temperature and it is a dangerous practice while trying to maintain your core temperature. Snow can be collected and turned into water in a number of ways. A large snowball can be stuck on a stick and angled toward a fire with a container underneath it. A tripod can be constructed with a cloth suspended between the legs and snow placed on the fabric. When this is placed near a fire, the snow begins to melt and drip through the bottom of the cloth. Should you have a metal pot, you can melt snow very easily, but you should always place a small amount of water in your pan first. This will keep your pan from burning, and the snow will melt more easily.

Digging down into dried riverbeds can be a fruitless exercise as the soil, sand and rocks found in riverbeds may not hold any water or moisture content. You have to remember: water in and water out. Digging in sand along riverbeds where damp sand can be found may be beneficial, but it should only be done when the sun is not high and you can regulate how much you are sweating by moving slowly.

SKILL #83
GATHER WATER FROM WET ROCKS

The reality of finding water will be less than ideal. You may not find an abundance of water but rather a trickle rolling down the side of a rock in a thin coating. You will try to place the lip of your canteen against the rock face but will find it difficult to get the water in your container. You can take advantage of this water that refuses to drip with nothing more than a small length of string.

With only a piece of cordage and a water bottle, you can set up a drip water collection system to fill your canteen. All you need to do is afix one end of your cordage to the rock face and place the other taut end in the bottom of your bottle. If the rock face you are working with has fissures and cracks, you can tie a knot at the end of your paracord and jam it in one of the cracks where the water is running over. Make sure to place your water bottle lower than where the paracord is attached to the rock, and keep the angle of the cord steep. With this setup, the water from the rock will follow your cordage down into your bottle while you work on other tasks around your camp. This setup doesn't require constant vigilance. If you don't have cordage, you can still wipe down the rock surface with a cloth and wring out the water into a container. Either way will help you utilize this resource instead of abandoning it and searching for that oasis that may not exist.

By the way, as an additional tip, if you are a hammock camper, to stop the water from dripping down onto the body of your hammock, all you need to do is tie a couple small lengths of paracord to your suspension lines. The knots will serve as water breaks, and the water will fall to the ground before it hits you.

Water will drip down a string attached to a wet rock and will drop into a cup placed under a knot tied in the line.

SKILL #84
TRANSPIRATION BAGS

Transpiration is the process by which trees absorb water through their roots and then give it off through their leaves. In layman's terms, transpiration is when a tree sweats. According to USGS Water scientists, a large oak tree can give off up to 40,000 gallons (151,400 L) of water per year, which averages out to slightly over 100 gallons (379 L) of water per day. This number is probably much higher on warmer days and less on cooler days, as heat is a factor. The amount of available water in the soil is also a factor, as is the plant variety as some plants slow down the rate they transpire in drier environments. Transpiration is a process you can take advantage of with just a large plastic bag and a small length of cord.

Starting with an edible deciduous tree like maple, birch or beech, find a branch with an abundance of leaves. You want to avoid trees or vegetation that are poisonous or that contain anything toxic that could impart a bad flavor to your water—or worse. For example, you wouldn't want to start with a cherry tree, as it contains cyanogenic glycosides that wreak havoc on the human body, causing headaches, vomiting and dizziness. Using a large bag, like a contractor's cleanup bag many people carry as an emergency vapor barrier in their kit or a clear garbage can liner, place it over the branch with the bundle of leaves inside. One word of warning: Be careful what bag you select for your kit that could be used for this purpose. Some bags come with an added chemical fragrance that also is meant to prevent insects infestation during shipping.

Place transparent bags over the leafiest branches to generate the most water.

Select bags that do not have this. Before you tie off the bag, place a small pebble in the bottom corner of the bag and place this corner at the lowest possible point. This will help collect all the water at this point. Using cordage, tie off the bag to the branch and walk away. As long as you selected a branch that is exposed to the sunlight for the majority of the day, the transpiration bag will work while you focus on conserving energy or dealing with other tasks. The temperature will rise inside the bag, increasing the rate at which the tree will transpire.

In only a few minutes exposed to the sun, you will notice beads of water forming on the inside of the bag. After hours exposed to the sunlight, you will notice water formed at the bottom of the bag. At this point you can either remove the bag from the tree or cut a small spout in the corner of the bag. You can always make a clothespin from a split branch or tie a knot in your bag to reuse it again. As for the branch you are using, transpiration will eventually kill all the leaves used inside the bag. For this reason, it is wise to rotate to greener and healthier leaves when you notice the reused leaves turning color.

Transpiration water may have a slight green color to it, but this is harmless. You may also detect some particulates in the water or even small insects. You can strain them out with your teeth as you drink the water. This method of water collection takes seconds to set up and yields a respectable amount of water considering the little effort needed on the front end. Compare this to the solar still that requires digging a hole, having a large sheet of plastic to cover the hole, a container to place in the center of the hole and a digging tool, and you can clearly see why I prefer transpiration bags to the more labor-intensive solar still.

SKILL #85
MOSS WATER COLLECTION

Collecting water from moss is easily accomplished with a handkerchief. All you need to do to access the water inside of the moss is to squeeze it. You can also grab a chunk of moss, squeeze it in your hand and drink right from the source, but there is no way of straining out the particulates without a cloth. What you want to do is place more green moss inside your handkerchief and remove any bits of dirt or mud if possible. When you have a sizeable amount of moss, gather the four corners of your handkerchief and twist them in your hand until you have a bundle in the center. As you squeeze this bundle, you will extract the water from the moss. If you did not remove the mud and dirt before you squeezed the bundle, the water that comes out of the handkerchief will be muddier in appearance. The handkerchief will strain the water and filter it for you, but you will still want to treat this water by boiling, mechanical water filter or chemical treatment.

Moss can be squeezed to extract water.

SKILL #86
FRESH WATER FROM SALT WATER

Salt water should not be consumed under any circumstances as it will shut down your vital organs and dehydrate you faster. Salt water is water, though—you just have to find a way to separate the water from the salt. Short of a portable desalination unit that will cost you well over $1,000, to make fresh water from salt water you only have a few reasonable options. Simply digging a seepage basin in the sand will not filter out the salt. Boiling salt water will just evaporate the water and leave you with a sludge of salt on the bottom of your pan. If you have no fresh water, you can still get it from salt water, but it will require both resources and resourcefulness.

A pot of salt water can be placed over a fire with a cloth suspended over the top to catch the steam that boils off. The easiest way to suspend the cloth over the pot is with a tripod to hold the cloth horizontally. This steam dampens the cloth with fresh water and it can be wrung out into your mouth or a container. The process is slow, but it does work. Just make sure to avoid accidentally dropping your rag or letting it sag from the added water weight into your pot of salt water.

Another method is more complicated, but it is a great water generator. A sheet of plastic or a tarp is suspended at an angle low to the ground, forming a vestibule. At the base of the vestibule, you place a collection cup. Underneath the tarp, you build a small fire and bring a pot of salt water to boil. As the steam rises, it catches on the underside of the suspended vestibule and condenses. The water will begin to drip down the inside angle and down to the collection cup at the base. The trick is getting the angle of the vestibule and curving it just right to drip to a single collection point at the bottom.

The final method is the dreaded solar still. I really do not like this method, but if I have no other option, I don't mind digging in sand as much as I do in hard-packed soil and rock. The solar still in this case will require the same large sheet of plastic, a large collection bowl and a weight to create a single low point in the center of the plastic cover sheet, where condensation will be drawn before dropping into the collection container. This requires a lot of elbow grease, and you'll experience frustration if you are attempting to hold the plastic sheeting in place with just sand. I recommend using heavier rocks, as they are less likely to dislodge from their location and slip to the low point in the center of the tarp. The location of your solar still can also become compromised as you may find your still underwater if it was built during low tide and the tides have changed. Remember, you don't need a pool of water inside your still to make condensation: even damp sand or random green vegetation inside will help the process along.

You may never travel to a location where you will need to know this skill. You may, however, be placed in a scenario where boiling off the water from other ingredients is all you can do to create clean drinking water. Just remember: Some chemicals will not boil off, and the water that evaporates will create steam with these chemicals still in it. This concept is good to know, but you should also know when to apply it and what its limitations are.

SKILL #87
TAP TREES FOR SAP

Maple syrup comes from maple sap. This is the clear liquid that runs just under the outer bark and is mostly water with very little sugar content. Maple syrup comes from boiling this water off, leaving behind the concentrated sugar in different colors of amber. You generally need 40 gallons (151 L) of sap to create a single gallon (3.8 L) of syrup. You can tap trees when the daytime temperature rises above freezing and falls below freezing at night. The temperature swing forces the sap to move within the tree. Depending on where you live, this could be in February, March or April. Commercial syrup tappers will use power drills to predrill the holes before inserting metal taps. You are not going to have dedicated taps or tools with you in an emergency, but you can learn from the commercial syrup producers and find a reliable source of hydration that requires just a collection container, a knife and a twig to set up. As a bonus to hydration, the sap you will collect has some sugar in it that is a source of carbohydrates.

In an emergency situation, you don't have to worry about selecting the most mature trees to tap. Mature trees of 12 inches (30 cm) in diameter may be too large to make tapping practical. You can more easily access the inner bark on smaller trees with less effort; however, the smaller trees will not produce as much sap as the larger ones. To tap the tree, use the tip of your blade and carve a small hole in the tree at waist level on an upward angle. If the conditions are right, the sap will begin to drip out almost immediately.

Maple syrup is boiled down from maple tree sap, which is edible and mildly sweet.

All you have to do is insert a small twig about 2 inches (5 cm) long, and this will direct the sap into your container. That container can be tied onto the tree with cordage.

If you tap your tree in the morning, by the late afternoon, you should see some sap in your container when you check it later. The tap you created may freeze overnight, but the tree can be retapped the following day. The sap you collect might have a slight yellow color and a very mild, sweet flavor. The process of tapping trees takes very little effort, and the return is worth the energy investment you put into it. As previously stated, you'll find both birch and maple trees can be tapped, and these can be found in many environments. You can also tap beech, sycamore and hickory trees, too. If the conditions are right, you'll end up with a hydrating reward in your canteen.

SKILL #88
SEEPAGE BASIN

Suspect water can be strained with a seepage basin.

Assuming you don't have a bandana or handkerchief to strain the water, you can dig a seepage basin to filter out what you don't want floating in your cup. Also known as an "Indian well," it is just the first step in making water cleaner, better and safer to drink.

In some survival manuals, an alternative filter is shown with a plastic bottle or pant leg tied off with various layers of porous materials inside. These include sand, small pebbles, charcoal and grass usually. The idea behind this filter is to clean the water and trap the sediment like a strainer works with pasta in your kitchen. The charcoal helps remove the odor of the water and the system works well when you have all the materials at your disposal; however, it is not field expedient and if you are without resources, you will need an alternative. The seepage basin utilizes the terrain as a filter. It will not create water ready to drink, but the water will have almost no particulates if done correctly.

To dig a seepage basin, all you have to do is find a spot about 2 to 3 feet (61 to 91 cm) away from the edge of a swamp or body of water and ideally just beyond vegetation on its border. Ideally, you want to dig your seepage basin in a relatively flat spot, as if there is a slight bank. You will need to dig down past the level of the body of water, since water will not drain against the forces of gravity. Your seepage basin will not collapse in on itself as readily if you can dig in an area where there is a healthy root system from nearby plants. Even if you end up with muddy water, let it sit for a while and the dirt and sediment will settle and your water will be clearer when you come back to it.

This seepage basin may help you hydrate those in your group, but remember it will not affect the smell of the water. That can be changed if you have knowledge of the plants you can make teas out of. As stated before, this skill is just one of the essential steps in making water cleaner, better and safer to drink.

SKILL #89
BOIL WATER WITH HOT ROCKS

In your survival or emergency situation, you may not be left with a strong container you can place on the fire without fear of it burning. You may find a natural depression in a rock that will hold water or maybe you have a water-resistant bag that will hold water. You may also scavenge a large plastic container from a shoreline or discarded along a trail. It is very possible you will have the means to hold water but not boil it. If you can't bring your container to the heat source, bring your heat source to the water in your container. Rather than boiling with fire, utilize hot rocks and a set of tongs to treat your water when you can't put a pot over your fire.

Starting with a green sapling, remove the branches, leaving a 3-foot (91-cm)-long section. Carve down the material on the inside of one side of the sapling to allow it to bend without breaking. Your goal is to make a set of tongs, with both ends touching, that you can hold in one hand. The connected section will help "spring" the ends open as you release tension on them. These will help move your hot rocks from the fire to the container of water you're using. Also, instead of just plunking your hot rocks into the container that might melt the container, a good set of tongs can be used to hold the rock in the water without dropping it before replacing it with another hot rock. If your container is resistant to the heat of the hot rocks, you can place them inside and just use a couple forked sticks to maneuver them around.

Forked sticks holding hot rocks in a carved container for boiling.

A quart (1 L) of water might take four to six rocks about the size of a small apple. The exact number will vary based on the size of the rocks you are using and the temperature of the water you start with. Select rocks that have not been sitting in water to avoid them exploding. Heat these rocks in a small fire for at least 30 minutes. To avoid muddying your water, you can quickly rinse your hot rocks in one container of water before placing them in a second container. This quick rinse will not draw too much heat from the rocks you're using and you'll appreciate cleaner water in the second container. You'll be surprised how quickly these rocks bring water to a boil. Make sure to use caution placing your spent hot rocks, as they can retain a lot of heat after getting the water to boil and can cause burns to exposed skin.

SKILL #90
BARK CONTAINERS

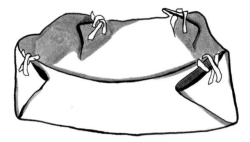

A simple container can be folded from a square of bark.

Bark functions to keep the sap of a tree against the cambium layer; it can be bent and formed to create reliable water-holding containers. Two very common trees found throughout the United States are the tulip poplar and the birch. Both trees are easy to work with, and the bark from both is not difficult to remove with a simple folding pocketknife.

You can use the tulip poplar for everything from fire starting, to cordage, to making containers. The tree is easily identifiable by its long, straight, limbless trunk and uniquely shaped leaves. When tulip poplars are dead standing, the bark can be easily separated and the inner fibers can be turned into cordage. On a recently downed tree or living tree, a section of the bark can be removed and turned into a bowl with careful bending. If you attempt to fold the tulip poplar without scoring the material on the inner bark where it should bend, you will crack or tear the material and put a hole in your container. The folds you make will be slightly rounded, and the walls of the water container will not be that tall. This shallow container can be used for hot-rock boiling, and the shallow walls make it easy to move the rocks around.

Birch is another favorite tree to teach for carving and whittling projects. It can be tapped for sap and as mentioned in a previous tip, the young leaves are edible, the bark can be peeled and used for fire starting and the bark of the paper birch is perfect for making containers. Birch bark has been used for arts and crafts of indigenous peoples

for years. It can be fashioned into knife sheaths as well as dipping spoons and larger bowls. Due to the high oil content in birch bark, it is incredibly water resistant. When collecting bark for the purpose of container making, select a section of trunk with few branches and imperfections. If you are concerned with the life of the tree, do not remove all of the bark around the entire circumference. This is called "girdling" or "crowning," and it will kill a tree; however, if you are in an emergency, your life is worth more than the tree's. Birch bark, especially paper birch, has many layers, and you want the sturdiest of the layers found next to the cambium layer. Much like the tulip poplar, when working with the bark, avoid folding it with hard creases. If the bark will break open, this is how it is weakened. A simple cone can be rolled or folded into shape and pinched shut at the seams with a secondary twig.

These two trees are extremely common but are not the only trees that can be used for containers. I'm told by friends who travel more frequently to the tropics that similar containers can be made with trees in that area. An essential skill is learning how to fashion a container from the most common resources in your area. Bark containers are found around the world and throughout history. Learn how to make one in your neck of the woods.

SKILL #91
FIRE-BLOWN BOWLS

If you only have a knife and a fire starter, you can make a container to hold water. A method of container construction you need to know about is fire-blowing. You can make a fire-blown bowl on the end of a round of wood or you can burn directly into the side of wood you are working with. This same technique can be used to make the shallow bowl of a spoon if you are into spoon carving or need to make an eating utensil.

The key to fire-blowing bowls is having good coals to work with. Create a fire and burn hardwood until you develop a good bed of coals from which to draw. These coals can be grabbed with the same tongs used for hot-rock boiling or they can be balanced on forked sticks. When you have a coal, place it on the wooden surface where you wish to create a hollow. Hold the coal in place with a small green twig, and lightly blow down onto the coal. What you are attempting to do is burn the surface where the coal is resting. If you have access to a small piece of tubing like a plastic straw, tent pole or even a small section of bamboo or Japanese knotweed, you can use it to focus your breath exactly where you want it. When the coal burns out, you simply replace it with a hot new coal and repeat the process.

At some point, you will want to use your knife blade to scrape away the charred section of the wood. This will help you burn deeper faster. Depending on how neat you want your work to look or how important symmetry is, you can attack the goal of making a deep bowl by sacrificing the appearance of your fire-blown bowl. If, even

Burn a depression into a piece of wood to create a fire-blown bowl.

in an emergency, you are the type of person that wants your fire-blown bowl to have a symmetrical appearance, you can dampen the charred section with some water to prevent it from burning right away. There is always a chance, by the way, for the fire to crack the side of the bowl you are burning. It makes sense to use a larger piece of wood and keep the sidewalls thick.

I suggest positioning yourself in a way where you are comfortable, not strained, and working slowly at a smooth pace. You don't want to stand up, pass out, get injured and turn a container-making session into a first-aid or trauma event.

NEXT LEVEL TRAINING

Water skills fall into the four categories mentioned at the onset of this chapter. Finding water, collecting water, treating water and carrying it. Training modifiers can be set up for each of these broad categories of skills. Water-based training modifiers are challenging, considering the nature of water. If you drop your fire starter, you can pick it up and it won't absorb into the ground. Water can be unforgiving, and it is one resource that may induce stress. Since water is vital to our survival, it is always wise to have an emergency supply at hand while you are training. You can always fall back on these reserves if you can't accomplish a particular skill or come up with a solution to a problem.

FINDING WATER

If you are comfortable finding water in your home environment, try traveling to a foreign destination and learn how to find it there. You can also try following tracks of animals and determine which, more often than not, lead to waterways. Additionally, you can look for water in various edible plants and determine which have the most water content.

COLLECTING WATER

Gathering water can be made more difficult if water is located just out of reach. A simple length of cord can help you reach otherwise inaccessible water. Additionally, you can challenge yourself by using suboptimal containers. As mentioned in this chapter, condoms have been used in emergency kits, and unless you have a large body of water to forcefully pull the condom body up through or a deluge of water to open it up as it is poured inside, you will be limited to the volume it can hold. You can also experiment with siphoning methods and finding water in the urban landscape that isn't contaminated.

TREATING WATER

Water treatment is not an area I like to experiment with. I will try out various filters and purifiers in the backcountry, but I don't want to chance accidentally ingesting bad water if I can help it. I don't suggest you try drinking water you aren't absolutely certain you have treated correctly, and the only method you can visually verify in the field is boiling. You can try boiling water in a plastic bottle as well as in a paper cup. You can also see how quickly you can get water to a boil and experiment with making lids for your containers to decrease the boil tie, and thus the amount of fuel needed to get it there.

CARRYING WATER

Water seems to have a life of its own when you are moving it. It has a tendency to spill, leak and slosh around, potentially soaking you, your gear or putting out your fire. Creating water containers is a challenge. Moving water can be a greater challenge, and if you are working to fill a container separated from your water source by a great distance, this can be difficult. Carrying water can get heavy, but you can experiment with ways to comfortably pack a gallon (3.8 L) or more without straining yourself. You can also track your water consumption and learn to carry more water in your body than you do on your person.

FOOD-GATHERING SKILLS

"You don't seem to want to accept the fact you're dealing with an expert in guerrilla warfare, with a man who's the best, with guns, with knives, with his bare hands. A man who's been trained to ignore pain, ignore weather, to live off the land, to eat things that would make a billy goat puke." —Colonel Samuel Trautman on John Rambo, First Blood

The rule of threes states a human being can live three minutes without air, three hours without shelter, three days without water and three weeks without food. These are all averages, and you can't assume what is true of one person will be true of you. You should note how food is not your first priority and it isn't as urgent to find a snack in the outdoors as it is to find some warmth in the cold. If you have fewer fat stores on your body, you cannot endure or slowly starve as long as a person with a few extra pounds on their bones. Calories are, after all, a measure of heat, and the fat from our bodies is stored energy to keep heating our natural furnaces. Food is not that important in short-term survival situations, and many emergencies are resolved within 72 hours, never becoming full-blown life or death struggles. Still, food-gathering skills inspire confidence and better prepare you for long-term survival. What are the chances your survival sit-uation will not extend past the point where food becomes a major concern?

Food gathering incorporates various fishing, hunting, trapping and foraging techniques. These essential skills have been modified over the years with better technology. Fishing poles, once made from cane and bamboo, are now made from graphite and carbon fiber. Spears and primitive projectiles have been replaced by modern firearms and sophisticated optics. Simple natural cordage snares and deadfalls aren't as popular today as commercially made dedicated snares and conibear traps. What hasn't changed is the relationship between the fisherman, hunter, trapper, forager and the land. You still need to know your prey, how to find it, get close to it and harvest it. Modern technology will not replace the time-honored skills those who came before us have passed down. What also has not changed is the chance of coming up empty after a long

Wild berries make great trail nibbles if you can identify them.

Before I describe how to learn plant identification properly, please understand you may be tempted to try out an alternative method of deeming if a plant is safe to eat. The universal edibility test was originally designed for the military and only the most select members of the military. It was intended for someone who may have food taken from them in a prisoner of war situation. It was not meant for regular use and was only meant for the most extreme circumstances when no other possible food was available. Even if you discover an edible plant, you may receive little to no calorie value from it. Since the military published the steps of the universal edibility test, it has been reproduced, in part and inaccurately, many times in multiple reference books. If you wish to learn it, seek out the first appearance of it in older US military survival manuals. If you know your area of operation and learn the plants in it, you should have no trouble locating what you can and cannot eat without risking poisoning yourself with a plant following this highly specialized test.

day in the field. We want to be excited with a successful harvest, but we must also be prepared for the blow to morale of being unsuccessful. All of the stalking and trekking require consumption. While you can go home and grab a slice of leftover pizza from your refrigerator, getting skunked in the great outdoors can be demoralizing with nothing to eat back in your camp.

We don't realize it, but consuming food is a very emotional process. We appreciate a good presentation of a plate at a restaurant. We savor the aroma of our food, and the flavors make us smile. So much of our food satisfies our minds before it reaches our stomachs. In a survival situation, you must separate your emotions from your needs. You ultimately need more calories in than you expend. These calories don't need to taste great, as long as they get the job done. So much of our food we can gather from the great outdoors may offend your refined palate used to eating food purchased in stores and prepared for you. You must remember the importance of eating and suppress your gag reflex as available calories are consumed.

There are some constants you can begin with that will keep you safe in North America. For starters, all segmented berries (think blackberries you see at the grocery store) are edible when they are ripe. These include raspberries, cloudberries, salmon berries, mulberries and any other berry that has multiple seed pods attached to one another. Many of these berries can only be found in the summer months, but you still use certain segmented berry plants year-round for different

All segmented berries, which have multiple seed pods attached to one another, are edible.

many people consider weeds are actually great plants to know for emergency food. In your average backyard, you'll find dandelion. This bitter plant is great for salads as are wood sorrel and sheep sorrel. Sorrels have oxalic acid, which has a slight lemon taste to it, and these can be used to stuff the cavities of freshly caught fish. You also likely have plantain (broad and narrow leaf varieties) that can be eaten like spinach when it is young and before it becomes stringy. Furthermore, you possibly have clovers in your backyard that contain very sweet nectar commonly found in store-bought honey. These clover flowers taste incredible dipped in tempura batter and fried. If you make it a point to learn the plants in your yard or a nearby place you frequent, you'll be able to recall the names of each of these plants without a supplemental guide, and you'll be able to recall the names and purposes of each when you identify them elsewhere.

Learning plants requires knowing how to use reference books and field guides correctly. These guides will have either line sketches, color illustrations or photographs. Many times, these are all too perfect, and the books represent the best possible example you can find of a given plant. You want to make sure, as you are uncertain of a new plant, to cross-reference the information you find in three guides if you have them. There are some edible plants that resemble poisonous plants, but as long as you have a good guide, you should be able to differentiate between the two in person.

A good practice, if you can, is to place markers in your yard or hide them in a park where you find plants in various states of growth. The plant you find will be represented in a particular season

purposes like barbs for forked fishing spears and tea leaves. Another constant to remember is that any plant that has the scent of garlic or onions is edible. Garlic mustard, an invasive, is edible along with wild onion and leeks. Some of these plants are found earlier in the spring season and some last long into the fall. Crush a section of the plant and smell it. If it smells like onion, you are safe to try it. These constants are reliable in the United States, while other countries may have plants that break this rule. Consult local experts to verify this fact.

If you are looking to learn plants and start your wild-plant education somewhere, look in your front yard and your backyard. If you don't have a yard but live near a park, start there. What

and throughout the year, it may not look the same in person as it does in the pages of a book. By marking your plants with surveyor-tape flags, you can track what each plant looks like at any time in the year, adding to your understanding of what to look for.

When you are first learning plants, you can either read up on the plants and seek them out or find one in the field and research it in the books. In either case, you need resources and, ideally, a living, breathing guide to give you some pointers. Plant knowledge can be found at local science centers, through conservation groups, on social media meetups and sometimes through farmers' markets. Plant studies are most interesting when you have someone to bounce ideas off of. Remember, when you start, the whole plant world will look green, but if you commit to learning a single new plant each week for a year, at the end of the period you'll already have a strong understanding of what to look for while in the field. Plant skills are essential skills, and I completely agree with my friend and mentor Marty Simon that plant knowledge separates the hobbyist survival practitioners from the real deal outdoorsmen/woodsmen.

SKILL #93
EDIBLE BARK

A couple hundred years ago, some of the First Nations tribes found in the Adirondacks earned a reputation for eating trees. During hard times, the Adirondack people (roughly translated to "bark eaters" in the Mohawk language), would seek out the nutritious inner bark of the white pine. Some say, the term "barkeater" was meant as an insult in an area so rich with wild fish and game. In other words, why would you need to eat a tree when you can eat animals? You must be a bad hunter/fisherman. While the exact roots of the term are not certain, as much of the First Nations history is passed down through oral tradition, eating bark is worthy of your consideration.

Bark may be the only food you can find in the great outdoors. You may be too tired to hunt, fish, trap or seek out nutrition elsewhere. According to Marty, not only can you survive on bark, you can thrive on it. The bark he is referring to is from the white pine tree. White pine is easy to identify as the needles are usually found in a cluster of five, one for each letter of *white*. Once you identify white pine, don't grab a branch and bite into it. You must process the white pine by removing the outer bark of a branch and exposing the softer inner bark that rides above the woody center. The white inner bark will have a distinct "car air freshener" scent to it as you chew it. Consumed right from the tree, you'll definitely get that strong pine taste in your mouth. Mixed with soups and bouillon cubes, you'll find that finely shaved strings will thicken broth to some degree and give your soup more texture.

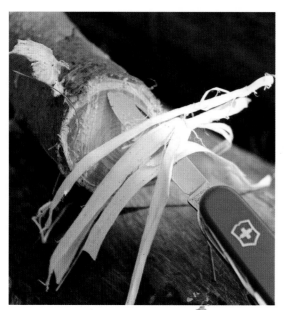

The inner bark of white pine is easily accessible and edible.

SKILL #94
TIE A LONGLINE

Since the world is covered primarily with water, it makes sense to have fishing gear in your emergency kit. Modern steel fishing hooks weigh next to nothing and are unrivaled in strength. There is no comparison to their effectiveness to carved gouge hooks made from wood. Fishing line can be wrapped around containers or coiled and tucked anywhere. I literally carry fish hooks and fishing line with me on a daily basis in my wallet. Fishing weights can be carried in small quantities and weights or they can be fashioned out of rocks when more weight is needed. With just hooks, lines, sinkers and bait you harvest from rotten logs, you can catch plenty of panfish in ponds and slow-moving stream pools.

The longline is a method of fishing commonly used in the ocean. A single longline is let out behind a boat, and attached to this longline at spaced-out intervals are secondary lines that have baited hooks or lures on them. As the boat trolls, the longline is at work. After a given amount of time, the longline is reeled back in and fish after fish are pulled into the boat from a single longline. You may be able to improvise a longline with the resources you do have and yield similar results.

If you have a length of paracord, this will become your main line. At one end of your paracord, you should attach a heavy weight that will secure it to the bottom of the stream pool or pond. This is usually accomplished by finding a rock of sufficient weight. At the other end of your longline, you can secure your paracord to a wooden stake, tree, branch or otherwise secure

By the way, just as you can learn local plants, you can learn local trees. Find out what the bark of common trees look like as well as leaves and the structure of each type of tree. Learn to identify trees based on their structure and overall shape. Learn to recognize old signs of what the trees may be such as nuts that have fallen in past years that are still lingering on the ground. Start off with the conifers and work your way to deciduous trees. Remember you can eat the young leaves and twigs of maples, birches and beeches. You can also drink the sap when the days are warm and the nights are cold.

Hopefully times won't be tough enough that you have to resort to eating trees, but should you, know that many people who came before you did the same thing. If they could survive on it, so can you. It may not taste like you want it to, but it will give you something back and offer you some nutrition.

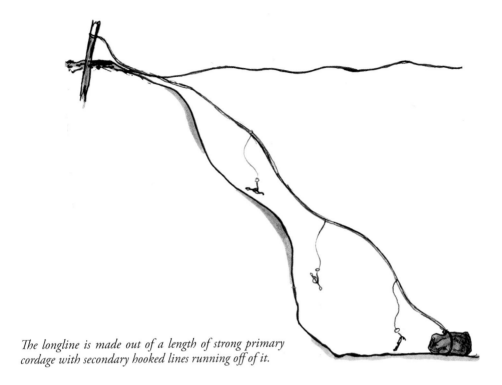

The longline is made out of a length of strong primary cordage with secondary hooked lines running off of it.

anchor. Before you throw your longline into the water, you must attach the secondary lines to the main line. If you have snap swivels, all you need to do is push the gate of each snap swivel through the outer braid of the paracord. If you don't have snap swivels, you will need to securely tie your fishing line to the main line in a manner where it will not slip down the main line. I suggest a variation of a self-tightening knot like a clove hitch followed up with a couple half hitches. From each of these lines, you attach your hooks and smaller weights to present each line at a different depth. When you attach your secondary lines, make sure they are not able to touch when stretched toward each other. If they are able to touch, you run the risk of having one caught fish tangling with another caught fish and losing one or both as they struggle against each other.

The longline can be placed diagonally down in depths of water or horizontally across a slow moving stream. When you handle the long line, be careful of the hooks. If you used snap swivels, don't be afraid to remove each secondary line by unsnapping it from the main line braid as you retrieve it. You don't want to have multiple hooks exposed along one end of your line as you handle fish on the other. If you are not having luck with your longline attached to an object on shore, you can also float a log or bottle out from shore and drop your longline off the side where deeper water can be found. One benefit of the longline you'll recognize is the ability to fish different depths at the same time. Perhaps the fish aren't biting at 10 feet (3 m) but they are at 15 feet (4.6 m). The longline will maximize your investment by working multiple lines in the same time that you could fish a single line.

SKILL #95
HOBO FISHING

Fishing is one of my favorite pastimes, and it is an incredibly effective way of filling your stomach if you have the right gear. Walk through a fishing store or a large outfitter, and you'll find thousands of different rods, reels, lines, hooks, lures, artificial baits and many more accessories for the pursuit of the big one. This gear is highly specialized, species specific and many times extremely costly. With all the great equipment available for the angler, having only basic equipment can seem insulting, especially if you are used to holding a $300 rod and reel combination in your hands. If you look around, you might be able to improve your fishing ability with some resourcefulness

It's one skill to underhand cast a baited line into the water, it is another skill making sure your standing line doesn't tangle as it "spools" out. Fishing line maintenance is tricky, especially in high wind or when you are working in a tight area with plenty of brush in which to tangle your line. Another popular way of fishing is to tie your line to the end of a pole and use a pendulum type of motion to swing your baited hook into position. This method is effective when conditions are right, but if your luck is like mine, you'll end up in a spot where using a long pole is impractical or where there are no long, straight poles to use in the first place. An alternative way to maintain your line and make casting easy is to use an aluminum can or water bottle. With a little skill and some foraging, you can equip yourself with a "hobo reel" and improve your

A hobo fishing "reel" made out of a cylinder container.

chances of hooking dinner.

Hobo fishing, sometimes referred to as "beer can fishing" requires very little equipment, and those trying it for the first time will become very proficient with the method in short order. All you need to do to set up your fishing reel is to wrap the outside of the can or bottle you are using with fishing line. The end of the fishing line opposite the hook should be attached to the bottle around the throat or around the thumb tab for security. The other end of the line is your standard hook, line and sinker, if you have them. To cast your hobo reel, hold the bottle/can in one hand with the "spool" facing the direction you want to cast. As you underhand toss the hook, line and sinker, the line wrapped around the can spools out freely. To retrieve your hook, pull the line in from the

To cast a hobo line, throw the weighted end and let the line unspool.

SKILL #96
CREATE A GAFF HOOK

A solution to lost fish is a fishing net, but these aren't always packed in backcountry gear. Many pocket emergency kits are equipped with hooks, line and sinkers but no aides to landing fish. While you could simply retrieve your fish quickly and toss it up on shore, sometimes you don't want to risk snapping your line or a hook if the fish you've caught is on the larger side. Without a net, without the ability to toss a fish high on the shore and without taking any chances trying to grab it with your hand from the water, you can create a gaff hook to secure your fish and pull it in.

A gaff hook is most easily created with a large saltwater hook. This hook is secured to a pole with the barb facing outward. It is attached with wire, line or a nail, and you'll find the makeshift gaff is even more secure when you carve a small groove in the pole you're using to accommodate the width of the hook's shaft. Ideally, your gaff pole should be straight so the force of your pulling motion is easily controlled and predictable. When it comes time to use your gaff, you want to pull it quickly back toward you, aiming for the underside of the fish where the belly is softest. Warning: Gaffing fish is not meant for catch and release and the practice should only be done on fish you intend to keep. By gaffing your fish, you eliminate the stress on the hook and line that caught your fish. You also have a secure "grip" on a fish that otherwise might have sharp teeth or a slimy body.

water and work your can/bottle in a circular motion to wrap the line before you cast it out again. If you have never tried fishing this way, the sensation of a fish tugging on your line held in your hand is exciting. Just be careful if you are using braided fishing line and you hook a large fish; that fish could run, pull the line held in the palm of your hand and the braided line could cut you. Never wrap your hand or fingers around the line; keep tension with the bottle or can instead.

Another way of using a plastic bottle with hooks and line is the floating turtle trap. This trap can be set up if you have a small length of paracord, a large enough float and a heavy-gauge hook. When a turtle takes the bait, it becomes hooked and it cannot dive as the bottle keeps it near the surface. This type of fishing/trapping should only be done in an absolute emergency as it often results in foul hooking that will kill the turtle caught.

Gaffing fish need not be done only when you have a hook and line in the water. A gaff, on its own, can be highly effective in snagging fish from

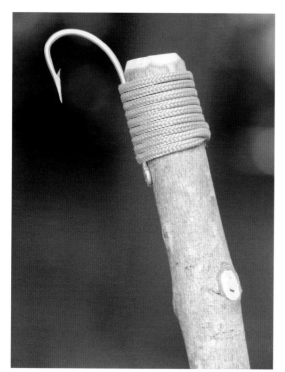

A gaff hook reduces the chance of lost fish.

SKILL #97

SNARES AND PLACEMENT

If you want to make a reliable snare, all you need are a short length of wire, 18 inches (46 cm) should do, and a single small twig about the thickness of a matchstick. Starting about 4 inches (10 cm) from the end of your wire, wrap it around the matchstick three times tightly. Don't let your wire cross but keep the wraps close. When you have your wire wrapped, pinch the running and the standing end of your wire with your thumb and forefinger of one hand while pinching the matchstick or twig with the thumb and forefinger of your other hand. Twist the matchstick three times, creating three tight twists to hold your running and standing ends together. The next step requires breaking your twig or matchstick near the three wraps you made. After you break it, the wooden pieces should slip free from the wraps easily. This forms a very tight and uniform loop you can pass the standing end of your snare wire through to create a working snare. With the excess wire from your running end, you can make a small "hook" by bending the last ¼ inch (6 mm) into an acute angle. Positioned downward, the small hook can catch on the animal's fur and help pull the snare loop tighter.

Snare sizing is not universal. The same snare you set for a squirrel will not work on a rabbit and the snare you set for a rabbit will not work on a raccoon. Depending who you speak to, a squirrel snare might be described as 3 inches (7.5 cm) in diameter or three fingers wide. When sizing your snare, consider the animal you are trying to catch

large schools. You must secure the gaff hook firmly to your gaff pole. When fish are foul-hooked through the side, tail or gills, they fight differently than fish hooked conventionally in the lip. There is a chance your fish could wiggle free with the gaff pole and your hook still attached to its side. Whether you gaff a fish while fishing with hook, line and sinker or you snag a fish, make sure you throw it high on the bank near you.

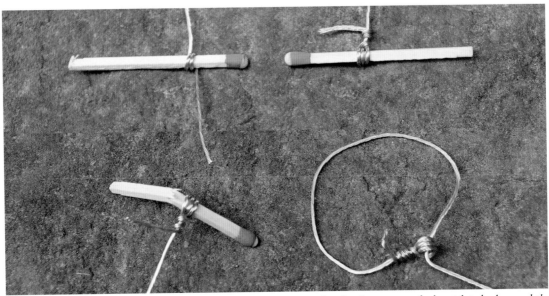

Snares are easily made by wrapping wire around small twigs or matchsticks. Once wrapped, the stick is broken and the standing end of the wire is pulled through the loops to make a snare.

and where their head is in relation to their height off the ground as they run. A squirrel snare might not pay off if the bottom of the snare is placed against the ground, but elevated two fingers high might give you better results.

Something else to consider is how you will force your prey into moving through your snare. Squirrel sticks are highly effective, as are runs across water features utilizing downed saplings as a makeshift bridge. Set up your squirrel stick or water run without any snares for a day or two, and let the animals learn it is safe to use the stick as a means to climb or cross. After the animals get accustomed to using the stick, add snares along its length. If you spot tracks, place your snare along this trail as animals tend to reuse the same paths over and over. Make sure you create fencing or some barrier that will funnel animals through your snare set. This is done by driving sticks and debris into the ground. Animals will

take the easy way and path of least resistance much like humans would.

As you'll discover, trapping and snaring is highly dependent on your understanding of animal behavior and habitat. Making the snares you'll need is easy. You can construct snares from wire salvaged from your vehicle, from paracord inner strands, from braided picture hanging wire or any other strong cordage. You'll have no trouble making snares if you ever need to. Placing snares will be your struggle. We used to say at the Wilderness Learning Center, "Making snares is 10 percent of the equation; 90 percent is placement." Take time to learn the behavior of those animals found in your area. Read up on trapping, and if you can buy a trapper a cup of coffee, pick his/her brain for local information. Trappers are, in my opinion, some of the most competent outdoorsmen around.

SKILL #98

FIGURE-FOUR TRAP TRIGGER

The figure-four trap trigger might be the most popular trap trigger covered in survival courses, found in the pages of manuals and attempted by those looking to improve their knife handling skills. Requiring no cordage, the figure-four trap trigger can be scaled up and scaled down to work with deadfalls of different sizes. Ideally made from seasoned hardwood for strength and durability, you can use green wood in the short term. The wood you use should be easy to carve with predictable straight grain and it should be free of knots, rot or any other feature that will prevent the trap from working as designed.

There are only three parts to the figure-four trap trigger you need to concern yourself with: the upright, the horizontal and the diagonal. If you are just learning to carve this trap trigger, don't select a piece of wood to work with that will require a lot of material removal. This means, don't select pieces as thick as your thumb when pieces as thick as your little finger will work. I tend to make my figure-four traps out of a single branch about as long as my arm from fingertip to armpit.

The figure-four trap requires knowledge of how to carve a chisel tip, 90-degree hooks, a 90-degree corner and beveled ends just for good measure. Starting with your vertical piece about 9 inches (23 cm) long end to end, you must create a chisel tip on one end and a beveled end opposite of it. On your chisel tip, you should create sharp cuts and leave a flat end to your chisel for strength. You don't need to work on

The three components of a figure-four trigger.

the vertical piece again until you are just about to assemble your figure four.

The next piece you will create is the diagonal piece that will measure about 5 inches (13 cm) long. One end of the diagonal piece will support the weight of your deadfall, and this end should be both the thicker end of the stick and beveled for strength. About 1 inch (2.5 cm) down from the beveled end, you need to carve a 90-degree ramped notch with the flat perpendicular portion of the 90-degree notch nearest the end. This notch will rest on top of the chisel tip of your vertical piece when you assemble your figure four. At the other end of your diagonal stick, you are going to carve another chisel tip. Make

A figure-four trigger in place under a deadfall.

sure when you carve this chisel tip at the end of your diagonal piece, you carve it in line with the 90-degree ramped notch. Many times, when students have trouble assembling their figure fours, it is because the notches and chisel tips are not in alignment with one another. Take your time carving your figure four and examine your trap trigger component sticks slowly and from all angles.

The final piece of your figure-four trap is your horizontal piece, sometimes referred to as your trigger stick. This piece can be about 1 foot (30.5 cm) long to work in this set. This piece requires two 90-degree ramps offset from each other and facing different directions. The first is carved at the thick end of your horizontal stick

about 1 inch (2.5 cm) from the end. Much like your diagonal stick, the 90-degree ramp should have the perpendicular piece nearest the end.

About now, you partially assemble your figure-four trap trigger flat on the ground and see how it is shaping up. You'll notice how the three pieces all pull on each other except the horizontal piece is not yet attached to the vertical and just rests on top of it. When shaped like the number four, with the diagonal piece at approximately 45 degrees, mark on the horizontal piece where the right outside edge of the vertical piece touches it. Take your horizontal piece and carve another 90-degree ramp facing in the opposite direction of your first and at a 90-degree offset to the first. This offset is critical. Remember how the second ramp you carve will pull back on the vertical piece, and it must be carved correctly. Your next step is taking your vertical piece and making a 90-degree corner on it. One flat side of your corner should be perfectly in line with the original chisel tip, and the other side should be carved on the same side where your horizontal stick touches it. With these cuts, your trap trigger should be functional.

To set your figure-four trap, hold the horizontal and diagonal pieces together with one hand while holding your deadfall weight (likely a log or a rock) up with your other hand. Do not drive your vertical stick into the ground but rest it on a solid surface like a rock instead. You can place your figure four upright underneath the weight as it will be thrown out of the way as the trap triggers. While holding the deadfall weight up with the diagonal piece, move your hand from the weight of the deadfall weight and grab your horizontal piece. By now, the full weight of the deadfall weight will be on your trap trigger. Place the 90-degree ramp of the horizontal piece on the chisel tip of the diagonal, and hook the other 90-degree ramp onto the 90-degree corner you made on your upright piece. Slowly remove your hand from holding the pieces together, and see if the weight of the deadfall will hold your three pieces together. During this process, it should go without saying not to get your fingers stuck underneath a falling rock if your trap trigger fires prematurely. I have more than a few friends who have earned blackened fingernails from that experience.

After you set your figure-four trap, you should test it and trigger it. If you want to make the trigger more sensitive, you can slightly round off the corner on the vertical piece. This will help the horizontal piece to slip off easier. When you are satisfied with how your trap fires, you can bait the horizontal piece with fish parts, berries, nuts or anything else you can find that might attract your prey. You can experiment with a horizontal piece that has multiple branches instead of a single straight stalk. Also, whenever you set a trap, make sure you drive sticks into the ground or place obstacles in the way to funnel your prey into your trap. It is highly unlikely for an animal to find its way into your trap unless you lead them to it.

Figure-four trap triggers work. You must carve at least a half dozen and set them properly to expect one trap to work effectively. In reality, 10 to 1 or 12 to 1 is a better ratio. I stated I can carve a trap in under 5 minutes, and that means for an hour of honest work, I can make all the traps I need to work with deadfall sets in rocky terrain. Learn to carve the figure-four trap trigger, and as long as you have a blade, you'll have the potential to make a game-getting tool that will work for you while you rest.

SKILL #99
FORKED SPEARS

The forked fishing spear does not operate the same way as the thrown, single-point Hollywood spear. A forked spear, whether it is two prong or four, is meant to pin the animal to the ground where it can be retrieved by hand. With either a two- or four-prong spear, you want to use a good sturdy hardwood, and it can be green when you carve it. You'll want to find a sapling about as thick as a broomstick and as tall as you are with your arm outstretched over your head. Ideally, your fishing spear should be straight and free of any forked branches that could interfere with the operation of your spear. When you decide which end of your spear shaft you want to make pointed, lead with the heavy end, and it will deliver with more force.

TWO-PRONG
The two-prong spear requires some knife handling skill and knowledge of one knot. If you have a Swiss Army knife, you can carve this spear and it doesn't require much removal of any significant amount of material. You can remove as little or as much outer bark from the spear as you want, but realize the wood found under the cambium layer can be very slick to hold on to. Sometimes having some bark left further back on the spear shaft will help you with gripping your hunting tool.

Before you split your prongs, about 1 foot (30.5 cm) down from the heavy end, you need to wrap the shaft of your spear with cordage using a whipping knot. This will prevent your forked spear from breaking off or splitting further than it should. Using the edge of your blade and small wooden baton, split the end of the spear in half to create the two prongs. If you are using a folding knife, you only need to get a small split in the wood and can use a wooden wedge to finish the job. There is no need for heavy pounding that will compromise the integrity of your folding knife. The prongs you make will be about 6 to 9 inches (15 to 23 cm) long—any longer and they could break more easily. When the prongs are split to the desired length, they can be held open with a twig pressed into the crotch of the fork.

This forked spearhead can work as is or you can use your knife to carve small barbs on the inside of each prong. Before you use it, make sure to bevel the edges on the ends of the prongs as they will make contact with the ground and can splinter. Beveling will increase the spear's durability. If you want to make the hawthorn barbed prongs, you'll need hawthorn needles or even sewing needles if you packed them in your kit. For either option, you must carve, burn or bore into the prongs at an angle. This can be done with the awl on our Swiss Army knife, a burning-hot piece of wire or by carefully splitting the prong between the tip and the whipping knot, although this last method is the weakest option. Don't drill all the way through the prong, but instead push the hawthorn thorn through the last $1/8$ inch (3 mm) of wood for a tight-pressure fit. If hawthorn needles aren't readily available, you can also lash a split section of blackberry bramble to the inside of the prongs. Use blackberry brambles, not raspberry, as the blackberry thorns are much sturdier.

One of the tricks to using a forked spear is subtlety. Walking barefoot in the water, you can simply wiggle your toes to stir up particulates in the water fish will come by to investigate. Small fish are curious and tend to be unafraid when the water is sloshed. Small sunfish will return to an area even if you disturb the water and seem to spook them. Be patient, move slowly until you need to move fast and be committed in your actions. Don't hesitate, and trust that your spear will thrust true. Assuming you make contact with a fish, work one hand down your spear shaft, and it will index you right down to the spearhead where you can grasp your fish behind the gills and retrieve it.

FOUR-PRONG

The barbed two-prong spear is popular, but you may lack the resources to create barbs from hawthorn thorns or another thorny plant. Another option for a pinning spear is the four-prong spear. The trade-off for practicality in the presence of few resources is decreased strength. Consider this: a single spear point has only so much strength. When it is split in half for a two-prong spear, its strength decreases, just as a four-prong spear has half the strength of the two-prong. What this means is you are likely to break off a prong if one makes contact with anything hard like a rock. Still, if you have the option of catching fish or a small critter at the cost of breaking a piece of wood, you could carve again and take the chance.

To create the four-prong spear, follow the same steps as the two-prong spear, including whipping the spear shaft 12 inches (30 cm) from the end of the heavier end. Split the spear tip down the center like the two prong, and insert a small wooden dowel down into the crotch of the fork. At this stage, turn your forked spear 90 degrees and split it down from the end to the wooden dowel you inserted into the first split. Place a second wooden

Four-prong spear

SKILL #100
ELASTIC-BAND HUNTING TOOLS

dowel into the second split. This should force your four prongs outward. Be careful not to split them too far apart as the further apart they sit from one another, the weaker they become. As a rule of thumb, I don't make my four-prong spears wider than twice the thickness of the spear shaft. At this point, you can either remove the dowels temporarily and sharpen the four prongs squeezed together as one (preferred) or you can keep the dowels in and sharpen the four points individually. The latter of the two options makes manipulating the blade inside the prongs awkward.

When you are done with your spearhead, you can fire harden it just like you would a digging stick, tent pegs or any other green wood project. Simply place the prongs underneath ashes where there is plenty of heat but no oxygen to burn the wood you just inserted. Make sure to remove your paracord whipping or any other cordage from the spear shaft, as the heat from the fire-hardening process could melt it.

One of my most prized possessions is a set of sketches my father made to help illustrate the tools he used while surviving in the jungle of the Philippines as a little boy. One game-changing detail was the elastic bands used to power them. My father told me about a dart shooter he constructed out of an old umbrella he called a "paray." As a child, I learned to see everyday items for their potential use in an emergency.

Elastic-band power gave my father and his family the upper hand to harvest small game and fish quietly and efficiently. Elastic bands, bike inner tubes, silicon tubing, SWAT-T tourniquets and any other strong elastic material can be used to power hunting tools you can make from off the land. Slingshot bands, especially those made from Theraband Gold, are the ultimate when it comes to power. If you have never tried dedicated slingshot bands before, they are extremely powerful and can propel lead/steel rounds over 100 mph (161 km/hour). Many casual slingshot users will be shocked when they compare the performance of real slingshot bands to the bands they've fashioned from your run-of-the-mill elastic material. For this reason, I suggest packing at least one slingshot band in your emergency kit, as this one item can be used to make three very capable game-getting tools. One word of warning before you attempt to build any of the following tools: wear eye protection. Slingshot bands can break, ricochets can hit you in the eye and eye injuries are a serious matter.

SLINGSHOT

When constructed with modern materials, slingshots are extremely capable of game getting, and plenty of grown men and women have used slingshots to dispatch garden pests, hunt small game and for outlandish acts of marksmanship found in online videos.

If you plan on building a slingshot in the great outdoors, look for a forked stick that fits your hand. The slingshot need not resemble a perfect *Y* and the grip can be offset from the slingshot arms. This may be more ergonomic for some shooters. What matters is the wood you select for your slingshot frame should ideally be strong and dried hardwood. While you can make a slingshot from green freshly cut wood, it runs the risk of cracking as it dries.

Before you attach your slingshot band to your frame, you should use your knife and smooth the grip and the place where the bands will touch the frame. This will make holding your slingshot more comfortable and prevent anything sharp on the frame from abrading or puncturing your slingshot band. To attach the slingshot band, tubular or flat, you must tie the band to the frame. Do not tie the slingshot band to itself unless you pass it through a hole you create in your slingshot frame. Otherwise the elasticized loop could slip off the arm of the slingshot as you draw it. You can use a whipping knot to secure the band securely with the bands either folding over the top of the slingshot arms or wrapping around them. I'm partial to the over-the-top style. If you wish to make an over-the-top model, make sure you don't leave a sharp corner the slingshot band will come in contact with. Rounding the top of the arms will give your slingshot more longevity.

The author using a pole spear.

Once again, it's good practice to use eye protection while you test your slingshot in case one of your knots slips or if a band breaks.

When using your slingshot, you can use lead ball, steel bearings or round stones. You'll find better accuracy using the right projectile weight and consistent shape given the type of band you are using. A very powerful slingshot band, for instance, would not be the best pairing with a very light .177 BB. Conversely, a light slingshot band would be ineffective with a .50 caliber lead shot. Experiment with your slingshot, store-bought or homemade, and you'll find a good combination that will give you the best performance and accuracy.

POLE SPEAR

The pole spear is an effective short-range game-getting tool. All that is required for a pole spear is a long pole shaft and an elastic band. The concept is simple: the elastic band is attached to one end of a pole shaft, forming a loop. This loop is placed around the palm of your hand with your thumb preventing it from sliding down your forearm. You stretch the elastic band as you reach for a point further down the pole shaft. You pinch the pole shaft with your thumb and fingers and release the pole shaft when you are ready to fire the pole spear. This sends the pole spear slipping through the palm of your hand and hopefully into your target.

If you have never tried using a standard spear to harvest small fish and game, you would not know how large of a motion your arm, shoulder and the rest of your body make as you thrust the spear forward. The pole spear lets you extend your arm toward your prey, and all that you need

to do to initiate the "attack" is loosen your grip in your shooting hand. Without any large motions, your prey will not realize the spear is a threat until it is too late. Also, since the pole is pointed at them, depth perception will be reduced or lost. Action beats reaction, and what you are hunting for will not be able to move out of the way of the rocketing elasticized pole spear as it finds its way to its target. Just make sure your aim is true.

To aim the pole spear, point the spear tip in the direction of your target. Since your pole spear is an extension of your hand, all you have to do is point your hand at your prey. At close range and out to a maximum range of about 5 feet (1.5 m), you will find the accuracy to be phenomenal. Make sure you smooth out the shaft of your pole spear if you harvest it from the land. This will prevent it from slowing down as it slips from your grip.

PARAY DART LAUNCHER

The paray is sometimes referred to as a Hawaiian sling. Think of it as a cross between a slingshot and a pole spear. Instead of a *Y* handle, you hold a tube with an elastic attached or gripped to the side of the tube body. You feed a thin diameter pole shaft down from the end of the tube, opposite of the end where the elasticized band is. With the tube held in one hand, the shaft of the spear is pinched in the other hand with the pouch of the slingshot band. Just like a slingshot, the band is stretched out, and when you release the band, the spear is launched.

I've used the paray on the shoreline while hunting for crab and have also used it in freshwater ponds for sunfish. Just like the pole spear, if you can point your hand at a target, you can likely hit it easily. You can also "charge" the paray, sneak up on your prey and launch a dart just by releasing the grip of your hand, avoiding any large motions that could scare off your prey. Depending on how large your prey is and how powerful your paray is, you can tether the dart and barb the tip to prevent losing your prey or your dart.

If you're wondering how you'll find a tube in the great outdoors, you can look at the gear you're carrying or take one off the land. Flashlight bodies make great paray tubes, as do the stiff screw-down openings of discarded plastic bottles. If you need a natural paray body, you can use bamboo like my father used or you can split a small log, carve out a channel and bind the pieces back together. If you need a paray dart, you can use tent poles, fire-straightened saplings or scavenged materials that are long, lightweight and strong.

SKILL #101
PROCESS FISH, FOWL AND SMALL GAME

When you catch an animal, you must quickly dispatch it. It is highly unlikely you'll reel in a dead fish, but there are some strange and rare scenarios when that could happen. Fish are humanely killed with a swift blow to the back of their head with a rock or the spine of your knife. Fowl can be dispatched by wringing their neck between your two hands. A neck break is also used on small game by grabbing them by their hind legs, bending the animal's head back using the web between your thumb and index finger against the back of its neck and stretching it until you hear the neck break.

Other methods you might stumble into out of trepidation or clumsiness is hitting the animal behind the head with a blunt object, stepping on its chest and crushing its lungs or thrusting it with a blade. While these methods aren't as clean or seemingly humane, they are effective when done correctly. What matters is that you put the animal down with no harm to yourself in the process. Remember, once that animal dies, the meat starts to go bad. You need to clean it, get it cool and keep it cool before you cook it. My friend Tony Nester suggests dunking mammals underwater for 30 minutes prior to cleaning them as it kills fleas and ticks living on the host animal. As a side benefit, the wet hair is less likely to fall off and get all over your cleaned animal meat.

CLEANING FISH

Depending on the type of fish you catch, you may or may not have to scale your fish. This is accomplished by running the spine of your knife against the direction of the scales on your fish. Some fish, like trout, will not have scales, and this step can be eliminated in the process. After this, you should gut your fish by running the tip of your knife up through the vent located on the underbelly up to the gills. Keep the tip of your blade shallow under the skin of the fish to avoid puncturing the bladder. When you reach the gills, you can cut them free with your knife and, using your fingers, pull the organs out.

At this point, you can examine the contents of the fish's stomach to see what it has been eating to try to mimic this on your next cast. You may even be able to reuse the contents if they are not fully digested. You don't have to remove the skin of the fish as it will keep the meat on the bone while it cooks. I prefer to cook my fish directly on the coals and know when it is done when the eyes turn white. There are many ways to cook your fish—just make sure to gut your fish first. The only time when cleaning isn't necessary is on small bait fish found in the ocean as they are commonly eaten whole. Also, keep in mind, any fish you catch in fresh water is safe to eat as none are poisonous.

CLEANING BIRDS

To clean an average-size bird, all you need to do is the following: Snap the lower part of the bird's legs off where there is no meat. Just work the joint backwards against the direction it wants to hinge, and it will snap off. Do the same for the wings where you feel the first joint of the

Be careful cleaning fish, as their bodies may be slick and your knife can slip.

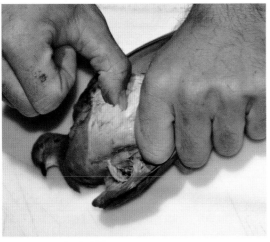

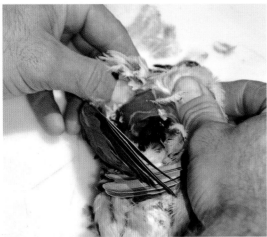

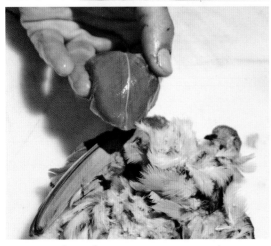

Breasting, shown here, is one way to access the majority of meat on a bird. Photo credit: Price Brothers Outdoors.

wing from the tip. Remove the head by twisting it off or cutting it. Start removing feathers and skin from the breast, back, wing and leg areas to expose the skin. This will let you get a firm grasp on the bird with your hands. When you get down toward the tail, you can remove it by snapping it off, or if you have a small blade, cut it free from the body. Insert your index finger at the bottom of the breastbone and reach into the bird's chest cavity until you feel the internal organs on your index and middle fingers. Pull them back, and you'll find that the gizzard, guts and other organs will follow. Through this process, you'll find out why birds are referred to as "fowl." At this point, you can pull the guts free and clean up the rest of the bird by removing the skin and feathers. I prefer to butterfly large breast meat and grill it on a hot rock. You can also boil the entire bird in a stew pot and waste no nutrition it offers you.

GUTTING/SKINNING SMALL GAME

Think about the animals that can be found in your backyard. You're more likely to see small game than large game. The fantasy of taking down a large buck in a survival situation and having endless supplies of meat is truly that, a fantasy. Unless you are equipped with modern hunting implements or have phenomenal trapping skills, large game don't make sense as survival food. You should seek out more plentiful and more easily caught small game. In reality, even rodents are on the menu.

Assuming you have a squirrel or similar small mammal to process, gutting and cleaning it requires very few steps. A sharp knife will help you make clean cuts and remove the stubborn parts of the animal that don't break off easily. The instructions that follow can be applied to chipmunks, rabbits and other small game of similar size and shape.

Take your knife and make a small cut in the skin about halfway down the animal's back. This incision should just expose the muscles and not cut them. If you are near a water source, wet your squirrel, rabbit or other small mammal in water to mat the fur down. Insert the index fingers or index and middle fingers of both hands into the incision you just made, and hook the skin so the knuckles of your fists touch. Pull the skin free from the animal's body. When you get to the head, feet and tail, you can cut them free. This will leave you with a skinned but not gutted animal. To gut your squirrel, just make a very small incision just below the breastbone to expose the entrails. Pull them free with your fingers, and your animal is ready to be rinsed and cooked up.

If you have managed to harvest enough game beyond the amount you can eat in one sitting, you should strongly consider preserving it. Meat, left to sit out on its own in warm temperatures, will spoil. You won't have a refrigerator or vacuum sealer and must resort to the time-tested ways of those that came before us. This primarily means drying, smoking and salting. Drying is simple enough: Meat is sliced very thin, around ⅛ inch (3 mm), and left to dry out in the air and sunlight. If you are familiar with beef jerky, this is how it was done prior to modern dehydrators. The key to drying is to be mindful of moisture buildup and also fat content. Fats can turn rancid, and lean meat dries better. Ideally, you want good air circulation during this drying process.

If you are in an area with a lot of flies, you may want to dry out and preserve your meat

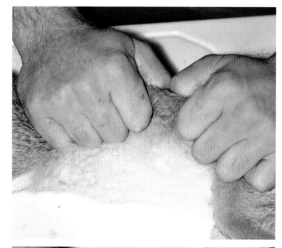

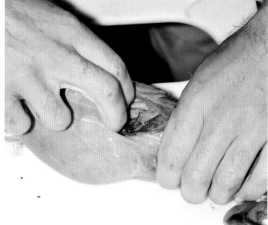

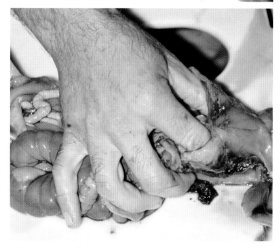

Cleaning small game requires both skinning and gutting. Photo credit: Price Brothers Outdoors.

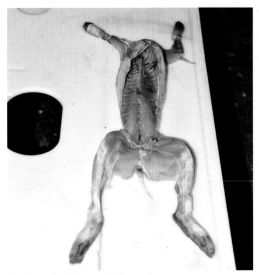

A cleaned rabbit ready for cooking.

by smoking. The smoke will prevent insects from landing and laying eggs. Smoking is done over a period of hours at extremely low heat. A makeshift smoker can be made with a tripod, a tarp, a few pieces of cord to string meat on and a small smoky fire. Low and slow is what properly smoked meat requires.

If you are near the coastline, you can likely find salt deposits on shoreline rocks where the seawater has pooled and evaporated. Salting is a proven way of storing fish, pork and other meats by removing their moisture content and creating an environment where bacteria and fungus don't like to live. Some of the finest meats in the world are cured with salt. Assuming you have the resources, take your knife and cut a criss-cross pattern in the meat you wish to preserve with salt. Apply liberal amounts of salt and rub it in between each criss-cross cut. Set the meat aside in a way that moisture is left to run off of it.

NEXT LEVEL TRAINING

At the start of this chapter, I mentioned how true survivor skills are plant-recognition skills. firmly believe you can study a lifetime and neve learn them all. The average person can get by easily in your normal 72-hour emergency with out food. I like being ready in case the emergency I experience is anything but average. I want t be ready to take the sport out of fishing and hunting. I want to eat.

In previous chapters, I've provided ways t modify your training to make these skills mor complex and challenging. The "next level" advic this time around is to become a better predato through acquiring modern hunter/gatherer gear thinking long-term food needs and learning from true professionals from the hunting, fish ing, trapping and plant-gathering fields.

At some point, you should learn to be pro ficient with a .22 rifle. Pound for pound, th .22 is the best cartridge on the planet for drop ping critters of all sizes with proper shot place ment. Modern target pistols are capable of rifl accuracy, but rifles are easier to shoot all around What that means is a rifle has a longer sight radi us, has multiple points of contact in your shoot ing stance and delivers higher velocities out o longer barrels. Handguns require more training Firearms are a game changer, and a true predato knows their value. Interesting fact: a Mossber; .22 rifle helped put food on the table for m father's family during their time in the jungle. I worked there, and it will work for you too.

There are some incredible options a predator can choose that will eliminate much chance of failure. Certain plants (black walnut, mullein, soapwort) contain chemicals in their structure that can be crushed and introduced into slow-moving/low-volume water to suffocate fish temporarily. The chemicals won't hurt you when you consume the fish, and eventually they wash away as new water enters the small pools. This practice is illegal in most places under any circumstance other than an emergency. You can use mechanical fishermen, essentially a spring-powered yo-yo, that automatically sets the hook when a fish takes the bait. Again, these devices may be illegal to use, but they might be legal to own. Know the laws where you live and operate within them.

Another skill set you should consider is how to keep animals alive until you need to butcher one. Historical fish pens allowed water to flow through rock in coastal areas and rivers but fish could not escape. Cages and pens can be constructed for birds and small animals, but they must be monitored as they can escape. The skill of long-term food management and procurement will have you question what you should carry with you into the wild. Is a container of cooking oil better than a pound (454 g) of rice? What spices will you crave, and which can be used for multiple purposes—like cayenne pepper having coagulating properties on cuts or being placed on your food for heat and flavor? When do you appreciate the natural flavor of food without those spices and learn to acquire the taste of eating animal bits and pieces you normally would discard like fish cheeks and organ meat?

The modern predator is constantly feeding, constantly seeking out the next meal, constantly acquiring better gear or learning how to be more proficient with what they have. The modern predator is constantly improving his or her situation. It's a lot to ask, and some people are not ready for it. This will separate the survivors from those who perish. Eat to live or die.

A .22 rifle is the best firearm for small game hunting and is easier to shoot than a pistol.

CONTINUATION

This section of most books is usually called the conclusion. You finished reading a book, but you haven't finished your training. Just like I hate using the word "weak," I don't want to call this a "conclusion," because nothing is over. Your training and education doesn't end simply because you purchased this book or accomplished a skill you have been working toward. You can revisit any of the skills in this book at any point and see it from a different set of eyes. You can also use this book as a teaching tool to help someone else learn how to reach your level of outdoor skill proficiency. If anything, this section is not a conclusion but a continuation. It is a charge to never stop learning and always seek out additional training. It is a challenge to be the feeder and adopt the skills that will make you stronger.

As you read this book, perhaps you created a list of gear you intend to purchase to supplement your training. I believe having quality gear is important, but resist the temptation to be too gear dependent. Remember, focus on being resourceful and not carrying many excessive resources. I believe in having a solid set of skills to fall back on, and this is usually what you need when your gear fails. Some of the skills in this book are perishable if you let them perish. Keep practicing skills, installing software to use when your hardware fails, and you'll never be without a solution to the problems you face. Rather than investing all of your money in gear, invest more of your time in learning to do more with less. If you need the incentive to keep up on your skills, become the teacher to someone, and the pressure will be there to be an example. Just like the seasons change, you can change from

student to teacher and student again. Remember what you do in your younger years is not the same in your older years. What you once found difficult may now be easy, and what you once found easy may now be difficult. We are always changing; your ability to perform the skills in this book will also change with time.

Survival skills are incredible confidence builders, but don't let that confidence go to your head. You may be more skilled after reading this book, but you must still apply good judgment when calculating the risks you take. Survival is about risk mitigation, and with a better understanding of what it takes to survive and readiness training, you will likely never find yourself in a situation where you need to apply these life-saving skills. Just because you have the skills, don't seek out the opportunity to use them. Negligent behavior isn't respectable. Instead, be the person others recognize as solid, capable and reliable with a level head who carries him/herself humbly.

One of the greatest skills is realizing the training never ends. Injuries slow you down but they don't stop you. Sprain an ankle, practice whittling from a chair. Hurt your hand, watch videos about skills or read a book. Never stop learning; be a student for life. That's advice that comes directly from my father to me and now to you. Even when you learn a skill, you'll approach it differently the next time you try it and see it with a new set of eyes. I can't make you ready for everything out there, but I can give you a set of skills and a way of thinking that will give you a better chance than before.

Kevin Estela
June 2018

ACKNOWLEDGMENTS

To Mom, Dad, Wendy and Sherri, thank you for putting up with me as a rambunctious kid, teenager and young professional with an adventurous spirit. While some of my fondest youthful memories are from the outdoors, the ones I hold dearest to my heart are found at home. We've been through a lot, and no matter where we are, we're always going to be close. You are my greatest supporters, and I appreciate you more than you know.

Thank you to my niece Lauren for participating in this book with her incredible illustrations. You are a rising star, kid! You make me a proud uncle!

Thanks to Marty and Aggie for making Chateaugay, New York, and the Wilderness Learning Center (WLC) a second home. From the first time we met in 2006 at Terrill's in North Carolina to all the times at the WLC and on our trips, I've always appreciated your company and friendship. You two are family to me.

Thanks to the Sayoc Tribe, including all the Tuhons, instructors, apprentices and practitioners, and the Atienza Tribe for welcoming me into the brotherhood. To Mangog Rich and Mangog Sue Smith at RiSu Martial Arts for jump-starting my interest in martial arts. To all my martial-arts training partners, including my longest-running training partner, Todd Jensen of IPD in Tolland, Connecticut. You've all made me stronger with each training session.

To my Brazilian Jiu Jitsu instructor SiFu Chris Smith for inspiring me to be equal parts philosopher and fighter, as well as the entire IMBCT crew for keeping it real. Friday night open mats and the IMBCT annual campouts are times that will always make me smile, whether we're choking each other or sharing food by a fire.

Thank you to my cadre, Lt. Mike Lychock, "Big" John Brown, Benjamin "Sweet Bologna" Legrande, Dwayne Unger and Mike Travis. You gentlemen have been incredible, never hesitating to help me on the courses I've run. Here is to many more years of success, training and camaraderie.

To all of the Estela Wilderness Education associates and former students since 2011: You keep me going, inspire me, and your interest in what I do fuels my desire to teach. A teacher is best judged by his/her students, and you all make me proud.

To Craig Caudill, thanks for making the recommendation and connection with Page Street. I appreciate your ongoing guidance and all your answers to my questions.

Thank you to Sarah Monroe at Page Street Publishing, along with my editor Karen Levy for making this book a reality.

To Jack Casey for giving me my first outdoor education teaching position at Mainstream Canoe and Kayak Corporation.

My many thanks go to Sayoc brother Dave Kalstein for inspiring me to write more and being my creative filter for many projects. SFY!

And to my Eastern Mountain Sports family from West Hartford and Fairfield. We had some great times and lots of laughs.

To Mike McCourt, Ryan Lee Price, Nino Bosaz, Patrick Vuong, John Schwartz, Patrick McCarthy, Iain Harrison, Garrett Lucas and Jim Cobb for being great editors and sounding boards for my ideas.

For David Morrel, the "Father of Rambo," and Sylvester Stallone, who brought a character to life that encouraged me to get outdoors and become skilled in survival. Every kid needs a larger-than-life hero, and Rambo was mine.

To all the companies who have sponsored me over the years, including Prometheus Design Werx, Bark River Knives, Gossman Knives, Fiddleback Forge, Martin Knives, Mountain Khakis, EXOTAC, Center Line Systems and others. I appreciate you trusting me with the reputation of your company's products and having faith in what I do.

To my coworkers at Bristol Central High School, and especially my fellow social studies teachers, for being a true work family. "C" lunch has been my daily break from the realities of teaching. To School Resource Officer George Franek of the Bristol Police Department for being a true friend. My former "team" teachers and the folks who really deserve a serious hand: the custodians, paraprofessionals, nurses, cafeteria workers and office staff. To all my students past and present too. We are BC!

And to Kifaru, International for equipping me with the best gear to unlock the backcountry. I've carried your equipment ever since I started teaching at the Wilderness Learning Center up to the present day, and it has never failed me.

Thanks to the boys at Jojo's Gunworks for always arming me with the best firearms around and keeping my pistols, rifles and shotguns running.

To Amanda, for taking so many of my photos and putting up with my hectic schedule. I know it is frustrating to hear "just one more photo" while out in the wild. Here is to many more great experiences abroad.

For the Environmental Learning Center of Connecticut at Indian Rock and Barnes Nature Center. The first time I hiked was on your trails, and it was a pleasure to serve as a trustee and guest instructor for the summer camp programs.

And to my friends at Jack Mountain Bushcraft School and the Maine Primitive Skills School. You helped me in my quest to formalize the outdoor survival education my father taught me. You are welcome by the fire any day.

To my Fairfield University roommates from Town House 156 junior year: Mike, Matt, Strohmaier, Kleps and Darts. And to the "Kool House": Jared, Scott and Petersen. I won't mention any particulars, but you are my brothers. What happens at Fairfield stays at Fairfield! Fear the deer!

Thanks to my former teachers from St. Joseph Middle School, Bristol Central High School, Fairfield University, Trinity College and the University of Bridgeport, especially Mrs. Mary Carrucci, Mrs. Gale Dickau, Dr. John Orman and Dr. Robert Gerace. Ms. Foo Field for being my guidance counselor and always caring about me as a student, graduate, coworker and friend. Your help has never been forgotten. Respect and appreciation to Joe Morgan, Bob Christino, Sal Coppola and Nancy Nevins for serving as my cooperating teachers at Wolcott High School, too.

For all those not included here who have been supportive over the years and to the friends of Estela Wilderness Education, thank you.

And lastly to God above: I don't wear my religion on my sleeve but not a day goes by that I don't thank you for giving me this life to make a difference with. My faith is deeply personal and will always be a part of who I am and what I do.

ABOUT THE AUTHOR

KEVIN ESTELA was born and raised in Connecticut. He first became interested in bushcraft and survival as a child when he heard stories of his father's survival during the Japanese occupation of the Philippines during WWII. His father taught him many skills as a boy and spurred his love for the outdoors. As a young man, Kevin could also be found hiking, fishing, mountain biking and canoeing/kayaking with his friends.

In college and part of graduate school, Kevin worked for Eastern Mountain Sports as well as Mainstream Canoe and Kayak Corporation. He worked seasonally for the Wilderness Learning Center as Lead Survival Instructor from 2007 to 2012, where he met his mentor, Marty Simon, and wife, Aggie. In 2011, Kevin started Estela Wilderness Education, LLC and began teaching bushcraft and survival skills, speaking at seminars, providing technical advice and product designs to many companies and writing articles for magazines. In 2012, Kevin created the Estela Wilderness Education Fund, a permanent endowment fund to provide financial assistance for underprivileged youth to attend camp programs at the Environmental Learning Center of Connecticut at Indian Rock.

Kevin has taught many individuals from all walks of life and around the country. He regularly travels to share his skill set in private and semiprivate classes. He has worked with the History Channel and has been a featured guest on many podcasts and broadcasts. Kevin is a highly sought after freelance writer with well over a hundred articles in seventeen different magazines, including *RECOIL, Survivor's Edge, American Frontiersman* and *Knives Illustrated*. He is also a regular provider of online web content for various companies who sponsor him.

Kevin is an associate-level instructor in Sayoc Kali, a black belt at RiSu Martial Arts in Bristol, Connecticut, and a purple belt in Brazilian Jiu-Jitsu under Sifu Chris Smith of IMBCT in Waterbury, Connecticut. Kevin is an avid marksman and has attended many courses with top pistol, carbine, shotgun and precision-scoped rifle instructors.

Kevin received a BA in American Studies from Fairfield University, an MA in American Studies from Trinity College and his CAS and teaching certification from the University of Bridgeport. He has been a full-time high school history teacher since 2006.

When not working, Kevin is an avid world traveler and thrill seeker. He enjoys downhill skiing, SCUBA diving and trekking. He also can be found at his home in Farmington, Connecticut, cooking, enjoying a good movie and planning his next adventure. His website can be found at www.kevinestela.com and social media presence @estelawilded.

INDEX